Birdwatching in Vermont

Birdwatching
in Vermont

Ted Murin and Bryan Pfeiffer

University Press of New England

Hanover and London

University Press of New England, One Court St., Lebanon, NH 03766

Printed in the United States of America

5 4 3 2 1

Library of Congress Cataloging-in-Publication Data

Murin, Ted.
   Birdwatching in Vermont / Ted Murin and Bryan Pfeiffer.
      p.   cm.
   ISBN 1–58465–188–1 (pbk. : alk. paper)
   1. Bird watching—Vermont—Guidebooks. 2. Vermont—Guidebooks.
I. Pfeiffer, Bryan. II. Title.
   QL684.V5 M87 2002
   598'.07'234743—dc21   2002007391

Front cover photographs: Belted Kingfisher by Steven D. Faccio; Black-legged Kittiwake
by Richard Lavallee; Black-capped Chickadee, Northern Hawk Owl, and Northern
Cardinal by Ted Murin; Moose Bog by Bryan Pfeiffer; Wood Duck by Roy Pilcher.
Back cover photograph: Barred Owl by Steven D. Faccio.
These and all other photographs in this book were taken in Vermont.

Northern Cardinal and Magnolia Warbler drawings from *New England Wildlife:
Habitat, Natural History, and Distribution* by Richard M. DeGraaf and Mariko Yamasaki,
published by University Press of New England. Used with permission of Richard M. DeGraaf.

FOR

Ruby and Gale

Joe and Betty

CONTENTS

ACKNOWLEDGMENTS

Birdwatching is a collaborative outdoor pursuit. So many people toting binoculars have expanded our knowledge of Vermont's birds that it would be impossible to name them all here. Yet we owe thanks to certain people whose insights, expertise, and efforts contributed to the creation of this book. Our sincere apologies to anyone we've inadvertently left off the list.

Our gratitude goes first to birdwatchers themselves, especially the contributors and editors of *Records of Vermont Birds*, the quarterly chronicle of sightings from around Vermont. The Vermont Institute of Natural Science under the leadership of Sarah B. Laughlin had the vision to publish *Records of Vermont Birds*, the *Atlas of Breeding Birds of Vermont*, and the forerunner to this book, *A Guide to Bird Finding in Vermont*, by Walter G. Ellison and Nancy L. Martin. Another trailblazer, Robert N. Spear Jr., compiled valuable data on bird abundance and historical records for the book *Birds of Vermont*, published nearly three decades ago by Green Mountain Audubon Society. All of these people and the hundreds of others behind these publications laid the foundation for our own birding education and exploits in Vermont.

As we researched and wrote this book, the following astute Vermonters offered tips on where and when to find birds in areas we don't visit nearly as much as we would like: Don Clark, Chip Darmstadt, Mary Droege, Bonnie Dundas, Elizabeth F. Gilbert, Steven LaBombard, Kent McFarland, Julie Nicholson, William Norse, G. Frank Oatman, Jim Osborn, Roy Pilcher, Michael T. Quinn, Mark Rosenthal, Ana Ruesink, Wayne Scott, Bill Shepard, Ruth Stewart, and Sue Wetmore. Richard "Dick" Lavallee has our gratitude for sharing his knowledge gained during pioneering explorations of Lake Champlain.

Steve Faccio, Dave Hoag, David Jenne, Dick Lavallee, Christopher McBride, Mitch Moraski, and Roy Pilcher have our appreciation for sharing their excellent photographs of Vermont birds. Thanks to Paul Kissell for assistance with directions, Steve Parren for insights on endangered species, and Bill Crenshaw and Cedric Alexander for advice on wildlife management areas. And thanks to these eagle-eyed folks who reviewed drafts of portions of this book: Don Clark, Elizabeth F. Gilbert, Scott Morrical, Dick Park, Judy Peterson, Chris Pratt, Craig Provost, Peter Riley, and Allan Strong.

Our special thanks and recognition go to Frederick "Pat" Pratt, who reviewed most of our manuscript and offered invaluable suggestions, to Julie

Nicholson for important assistance with accidental records, and to Dave Hoag, who loaned us his photographs, scrutinized portions of our manuscript, and spent countless hours creating the maps for this book.

Thanks to everyone at University Press of New England for putting these pages into print. And finally, Helen Whybrow, our editor, has our gratitude and admiration for introducing us to University Press of New England and for her wise advice and thoughtful improvements to this project.

Ted Murin is thankful for the patience of family and friends as he virtually disappeared to work on this project; for his mother and grandfather, who instilled a love of nature; and for birds, without which this book would be much, much thinner.

Bryan Pfeiffer is grateful for many people who inspired, taught or simply walked with him along life's long, green path: Ross and Joyce Bell, Paul Brunelle, Chip Darmstadt, Nona Estrin, Steve Faccio, Jerry Jenkins, Charles Johnson, Kent McFarland, Don Miller, Hugh McGuinness, G. Frank Oatman, Peter Polshek, Annie Reed, Chris Rimmer, Susan Sawyer, Alcott Smith, Sue Swindell, Tom Will, and, for their youthful exuberance, the teenaged members of the Twin-State Tanagers, repeat champions at New Jersey's World Series of Birding. Bryan's parents, Joe and Betty, extended love and encouragement to pursue anything in life. And immeasurable love and respect go to Bryan's partner and favorite walking companion, Lori Barg, who knows more than anyone how to enjoy being outside.

INTRODUCTION

At the first hint of dawn on Mt. Mansfield, Vermont's highest peak, where a forest of twisted fir clings to life near the summit, a Bicknell's Thrush launches skyward and unleashes a nasal, flutey song certain to arouse females waiting nearby.

Meanwhile at Berlin Pond, only a few miles from the capital city of Montpelier and the gritty granite sheds of Barre, a Common Loon howls his eerie yodel, a trademark of the north, and slips quietly beneath the surface.

Across the state at Red Rocks Park in South Burlington on the shores of Lake Champlain, flocks of glittering warblers, tired from a full night of migration, drop from the sky to the trees as eager birdwatchers there welcome the fallout.

And in backyards and family dairy farms across the state, American Robins, among the most familiar and reliable of songbirds, push earthworms into the gaping beaks of young in the nest.

Another morning dawns in Vermont, where in bogs and backyards, marshes and meadows, forests and fens, birds brighten the landscape in one of nature's most captivating displays. This book is a ticket to the show. It is for anyone curious about the birds of Vermont: the expert wondering when and where to find Ross's Goose or Boreal Chickadee; the casual birdwatcher wanting to learn more or simply find a new hotspot for warblers; and especially the novice looking beyond the backyard feeder to discover fully the pure pleasure of watching feathered life on earth.

There is more to birdwatching than simply watching birds. Even in Vermont, renowned for a connection between people and the land, life can move faster than a speeding computer. Far too often this pace propels us away from the natural world. But birdwatching is an ode to slowing down. It reconnects us to nature, stirring our senses with sights and sounds. More than 350 bird species have nested in, migrated through, or accidentally visited Vermont during the last hundred years or so. Nearly 300 of those species inhabit or visit on a regular basis, and about 190 of those find the terrain appealing enough to build a home and raise a family. Their stories, conveyed in a remarkable synthesis of color, song, and flight, are unveiled in the pages of this book. So grab the binoculars and get outside. The birds will take it from there.

Common Loons, endangered in Vermont, return in April to inland ponds from wintering areas on the Atlantic Ocean.
Photo: Mitch Moraski

🖋 How to Use This Book

This is first and foremost a guide to the discovery and enjoyment of birdwatching, not a tool for bird identification. It is designed as a companion to, rather than a substitute for, a field guide and binoculars. Like a standard birdfinding guide, this book describes the seasonal status and distribution of birds in Vermont as well as places to find them. But unlike similar guides, this book includes a comprehensive chapter on the art and practice of birdwatching.

The first chapter, "The Landscape and Seasons," is a general introduction to the lay of the land and the seasonal nature of birds in Vermont. It provides an overview of where birds live in Vermont and when to find them. Habitat and timing are critical to birds, so learning the common habitats of Vermont, which bird species occupy them, and when they are there is a helpful prerequisite to watching and enjoying birds.

Chapter 2, "Watching and Enjoying Birds," covers the art and skill of birdwatching. Describing everything from optics to ethics, this chapter offers essential advice to beginners, including what's necessary to start from scratch. It offers guidance on how to locate, approach, watch, and enjoy birds. But birdwatchers at any level will also find advice on building their skills and enhancing their understanding and enjoyment of birds, including advanced activities such as migration watching. Chapter 3, "Conservation," discusses threats to birds everywhere and suggests how anyone who enjoys birds can easily become a conservationist by taking some simple steps, including activities that put birdwatching skills to use.

Chapters 4 and 5 are pathways to the birds of Vermont. Together they describe where to go, when to go, and what to expect. While most anyone can experience wonderful birds close to home, chapter 4, "Birdwatching Areas," includes directions to and descriptions of more than 120 birdwatching spots around Vermont. Chapter 5, "Species Accounts," includes the most up-to-date look at the status of the nearly 300 bird species that occur regularly in Vermont and a roster of irregular visitors as well. These two chapters can be used separately or in tandem. Someone who wants to visit a nice place for warblers or waterfowl, for example, should consult "Birdwatching Areas" for a destination close to home or across the state. A birdwatcher who wants to find a given species or group of species should first consult the "Species Accounts." Each account describes the species' preferred habitat and includes a seasonal graph illustrating when it is present in Vermont. Some accounts also include the species' distribution across the state, and suggested locations in the "Birdwatching Areas" chapter for finding it. The book's index also points to suggested locations for certain species.

Finally, "Resources" offers a wealth of information on birding and conservation organizations and written and electronic sources of information about birds.

Birdwatching in Vermont

CHAPTER 1

The Landscape and Seasons

✒ *The Lay of the Land*

The place now known as Vermont has been a work in progress for at least the last billion years. The shifting and colliding of the earth's continental plates left Vermont as a mountainous zone in a temperate region of the continent. All four seasons happen here. While varying with altitude, the climate is wetter and colder than most of the continental United States. Glaciers put the finishing touches on the region. And while the Wisconsin ice shield completed its most recent retreat about 13,000 years ago, it left behind sands, silts, soils, and other deposits that shape the distribution of habitats and of the birds of Vermont.

That's not to discount the human influence on the landscape, which has been and continues to be substantial. In the mid-1700s settlers began clearing old growth forests on a massive scale for crop and grazing land and a timber industry. So relentless was the force of the axe and saw that nearly three-quarters of Vermont was cleared of its forests by the mid-1800s. What returned in the ensuing 150 years was a landscape, now 75 percent woodlands, of varied forest communities—from boreal woods in the northeastern corner of Vermont to stands of oak and hickory in the southwestern portion.

The landscape of Vermont is often divided into six or more large regions, each with distinguishing geology, climate, topography and soils. These biophysical regions help shape not only the distribution of habitats in Vermont, including the birds they support, but even to some extent human culture:

- **Champlain Valley:** With the lowest elevation in Vermont, the Champlain Valley is comparatively dry and warm. Its dominant feature is Lake Champlain, which

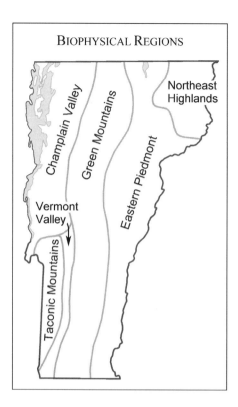

BIOPHYSICAL REGIONS

Champlain Valley

Green Mountains

Northeast Highlands

Eastern Piedmont

Vermont Valley

Taconic Mountains

after the Great Lakes is the largest lake in the country. Also notable in this region are extensive wetlands, agricultural lands, and interspersed (mostly deciduous) woodlands. Owing to the habitat diversity here and the influence of Lake Champlain as a migratory corridor, nearly 95 percent of all bird species recorded in Vermont have been encountered in the Champlain Valley at one time or another.

- **Taconic Mountains:** This highly variable terrain in Vermont's southwest corner produces equally variable elevations, weather, rainfall, vegetation, and birdlife. Most of the region's bedrock consists of metamorphosed mudstones originating between 540 and 443 million years ago. Varying elevations in this region offer forest habitats ranging from high-elevation spruce and fir to lower-elevation oak and hickory.

- **Vermont Valley:** The narrow valley between the Taconic Mountains to the west and the Green Mountains to the east is a compact mixture of wetlands and agricultural lands. Forests are few in this region. Originating in the valley's midsection is Vermont's longest river, Otter Creek, which flows north toward Lake Champlain.

- **Green Mountains:** Running the length of the state, the Green Mountains, a section of the Appalachian chain, tower over much of the Vermont landscape. These high places have higher rainfall and cooler temperatures, as well as upland spruce-fir forests and their hearty avian inhabitants. Below, on the slopes of the mountains, are deciduous and mixed forests.

- **Eastern Piedmont:** The lower, eastern slopes of the Green Mountains are for the most part hilly deciduous woods dissected by rivers and streams. The climate is cooler and moister than the Champlain Valley and warmer but drier than the mountains to the west. Interspersed in the low, forested hills in this region are patchworks of open land, mostly dairy farms, as well as lakes and wetlands. The warmest, lowest portion of this region, at its eastern edge, is the Connecticut River Valley.

- **Northeastern Highlands:** With lower temperatures and a comparatively northern latitude, the northeast corner of Vermont lies at the southern edge of the boreal forest zone. Spruce-fir woods and wetlands are common, particularly in lowland areas. Deciduous forests are also widespread throughout. This region is known to Vermonters as the Northeast Kingdom for its remote, frontier nature.

✒ Habitats and Their Birds

While birds can show up anywhere, particularly during migration, distinctive habitat types harbor characteristic, predictable species. Boreal woods are welcome habitat for Black-backed Woodpecker, Gray Jay, and Boreal Chickadee. Northern hardwoods are often home to Red-eyed Vireo, Black-throated Blue Warbler, and Rose-breasted Grosbeak. Wetlands can host American Bittern, Northern Waterthrush, and Swamp Sparrow. Of course, some bird species can occupy more than one habitat type (these animals do have wings, after all). But generally birds are quite consistent in their habitat preferences. As members of ecosystems, they have evolved to find food, water, and shelter in familiar places. Recognizing this is no different than, say, knowing that an arctic ice floe is a suitable habitat for a polar bear but a poor choice for a bamboo-loving giant panda.

This guide will often refer to birds and the habitats they prefer. It is a traditional and convenient way of thinking about how birds fit into the landscape (and where to find them). But in some ways it is an incomplete view. In any given place, birds are actually among the more conspicuous members of a much larger community of living things—trees and plants, to be sure, but also insects, reptiles, amphibians, mammals, lichens, fungi, bacteria, and other microorganisms. These communities exist much like a single entity composed of many parts, each interacting with, and interdependent upon, many others. Familiar phrases like "food chain" and "web of life" reflect these interactions. Remove, alter, or add something to the mix, and the consequences—sometimes adverse—ripple through the entire community.

Throughout nature, certain plants and animals have a tendency to occur

A Great Egret hunts among cattails at a marsh in Shoreham. These lanky waders regularly wander to Vermont after the breeding season.
Photo: Roy Pilcher

together. They form recognizable communities of living things, sometimes called ecosystems or "natural communities." In Vermont, for example, lowland coniferous woods often host not only Yellow-rumped Warbler and Red-breasted Nuthatch but also red squirrel and fisher, black fly and mosquito, bluebead lily and Schreber's moss, as well as many other organisms. They convene in the landscape under the right environmental conditions, including soil, climate, and water. (See "Resources" at the back of this book for a reference to *Wetland, Woodland, Wildland: A Guide to the Natural Communities of Vermont* by Elizabeth H. Thompson and Eric R. Sorenson, an excellent work on Vermont's landscape.)

Vermont has scores of distinctive natural communities. But a few general varieties, routinely called habitats, are common and easily recognized by their plant composition. Deciduous Woods are often dominated by maple species, American beech, and yellow birch. Understory plants can vary according to the amount of calcium and other nutrients in the soils. Coniferous Woods are dominated by balsam fir and spruce species (mostly red spruce). Understory vegetation diversity is limited. Mixed Woods, comprising a good portion of Vermont, consist of varying combinations of deciduous and coniferous trees and understory vegetation. Wetlands come in many varieties. Bogs are often acidic peatlands that get most of their water from rain. Swamps tend to be wet or flooded forests. Marshes are dominated by cattails and other herbaceous vegetation. Grasslands, most often "artificial" in Vermont, are found where there is agricultural land, an airport, or other

Table 1.
Habitats and Their Birds

Deciduous Woods ("Hardwoods")
Broad-winged Hawk
Ruffed Grouse
Wild Turkey
Downy Woodpecker
Hairy Woodpecker
Eastern Wood-Pewee
Red-eyed Vireo
Black-capped Chickadee
White-breasted Nuthatch
Veery
Wood Thrush
Black-throated Blue
   Warbler
American Redstart
Ovenbird
Scarlet Tanager
Rose-breasted Grosbeak

Coniferous Woods ("Softwoods")
Barred Owl
Red-breasted Nuthatch
Hermit Thrush
Golden-crowned Kinglet
Winter Wren
Yellow-rumped Warbler
Blackburnian Warbler
Blackpoll Warbler (high
   elevation)
Dark-eyed Junco
White-throated Sparrow
Purple Finch

Mixed Woods*
Sharp-shinned Hawk
Blue-headed Vireo
Common Raven
Brown Creeper
Black-throated Green
   Warbler

Wetlands
American Bittern
Great Blue Heron
Green Heron
Canada Goose
Wood Duck
American Black Duck
Mallard
Virginia Rail
Spotted Sandpiper
Common Snipe
Warbling Vireo
Belted Kingfisher
Tree Swallow
Marsh Wren
Yellow Warbler
Northern Waterthrush
Common Yellowthroat
Swamp Sparrow
Red-winged Blackbird
Common Grackle
Baltimore Oriole

Grasslands and Agricultural Lands
Turkey Vulture
Red-tailed Hawk
Rough-legged
   Hawk (winter)
American Kestrel
Killdeer
Ring-billed Gull
Eastern Kingbird
Barn Swallow
American Crow
Eastern Bluebird
European Starling
Savannah Sparrow
Song Sparrow
Snow Bunting (winter)
Bobolink
Eastern Meadowlark
Brown-headed Cowbird
American Goldfinch

Residential
Mourning Dove
Ruby-throated
   Hummingbird
Downy Woodpecker
Hairy Woodpecker
Eastern Phoebe
Blue Jay
American Crow
Black-capped Chickadee
House Wren
American Robin
Gray Catbird
European Starling
Cedar Waxwing
Chipping Sparrow
Song Sparrow
Northern Cardinal
House Finch
American Goldfinch
House Sparrow

Urban
Rock Dove
American Crow
Chimney Swift
European Starling
House Finch
House Sparrow

*In addition to those listed here, Mixed Woods often include many species found in both Deciduous Woods and Coniferous Woods.

large openings. RESIDENTIAL habitat is a mix of trees, shrubs, and openings that varies widely from home to home. Lawns are relatively devoid of wildlife, but a mixture of native trees, shrubs, and other vegetation in the backyard can attract a diversity of species. URBAN areas are largely lacking in bird diversity, with the exception of a few street-smart warriors. This book will sometimes refer to terms such as "deciduous species," "coniferous residents," or "wetland specialists." These are general terms for characteristic birds of those habitats.

Table 1 is an abridged list of typical Vermont habitats and some of the more common birds that they harbor during the breeding season (or as otherwise noted). These habitats and their birds are hardly as distinct and segregated as they might seem. Nature often blurs borders. Mixed woods, for example, can include a combination of species commonly found in deciduous woods and coniferous woods. There are no guarantees that birds will be in each of these habitats, or that a birdwatcher will find them there. A habitat damaged or depleted in some way—by human or natural disturbance, pesticides, invasive plant species, or even pets, for example—can be lacking in its typical bird diversity. But on balance some, most, or all of the listed species can be expected to occur in a given habitat.

✎ The Seasons of Vermont Birds

The diversity and sheer number of birds in Vermont are rhythmic, surging during spring and fall migrations and waning during winter. The graph below illustrates how species diversity varies widely during the course of a year. The peaks of spring and fall migrations are evident in the graph, but diversity and numbers are in flux throughout the year. Understanding seasonal cycles and the birds' calendar of events can be nearly as important as

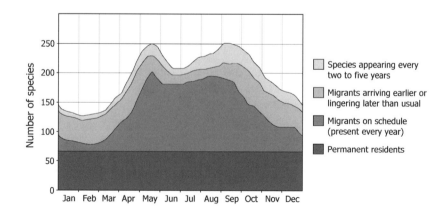

knowing which end of the binoculars to look through. A Vermont calendar of bird activity follows.

January. With the last of the southbound stragglers either leaving Vermont or arriving from the north, fall migration ends and the birds of winter settle in. Snow Bunting, Horned Lark, Lapland Longspur, and Red-tailed and Rough-legged Hawks work the fields, wintering ducks and gulls ply open water, and periodic finch and owl invaders mix with permanent residents.

February. In the ebb and flow of bird biomass, this is Vermont's low tide. Wintering birds are tested by dwindling food and temperature. By late in the month, however, ducks begin to press the northern edges of open water and the first Red-winged Blackbirds arrive. Spring migration begins.

March. Waterfowl, gulls, and blackbirds arrive en masse, peaking late in the month. Killdeer arriving in Vermont lead the early northbound shorebirds, and winter visitors begin their exodus. Bald Eagle migration peaks as other raptor movement begins.

April. Hawk and sparrow migration peaks, and the first of the warblers and other neotropical songbirds arrive. Waterfowl movement begins to taper by the middle of the month.

May. This is the height of bird biodiversity in spring. Shorebird and songbird migration peaks as flycatchers, vireos, warblers, and other passerines (perching birds) ride the wave of emerging leaves and insects north.

June. With the last of the northbound stragglers, spring migration ends. Nesting activity peaks for most species.

July. More and more parents set fledglings free, and some postbreeding birds begin to wander. With barely time to pirouette, the first of the shorebirds head south from the Arctic. Fall migration begins.

August. Shorebird movement peaks on available habitat. Early warblers and hawks shuffle southward.

September. This is the most diverse month of fall migration, led by conspicuous waves of warblers and hawks. Shorebird movement tapers mid-month.

October. Waterfowl migration shifts into high gear. Snow Goose, sparrow, and kinglet movement peaks.

November. Loon and grebe migration peaks, and winter waterfowl numbers swell. The woods quiet until, in some years, Purple Finch, Evening Grosbeak, and other winter finches rise in number.

December. Loon and grebe activity wanes. With the arrival of Herring and Great Black-backed Gulls, male Common Merganser, and the last of the hawks, owls, and geese, fall migration draws to a close.

Once driven to extinction in Vermont, Wild Turkey has repopulated much of the state since its reintroduction in 1969.
Photo: Dave Hoag

✒ *Vacationing in Vermont*

Vermont cannot offer the out-of-state birdwatcher the diversity of Pt. Pelee, Cape May, or other famous migrant traps. Yet birdwatchers from "down-country" do make Vermont a destination now and then for boreal species, Bicknell's Thrush, northern breeding warblers, wintering owls, and the gathering of Snow Geese (along with a few Ross's Geese), just to name a few of the avian attractions.

Deciding when to come depends, of course, on what birds are on the agenda. The boreal specialties (Spruce Grouse, Black-backed Woodpecker, Gray Jay, and Boreal Chickadee) are year-round residents. Most northern warblers arrive in mid- to late May and depart in early September. Look for Bicknell's Thrush after June 1 (when the mountains still can have snow). The goose spectacle happens throughout October, peaking around the second week of the month; it coincides nicely with the fall foliage season. Consult chapter 5, "Species Accounts," page 121 for details on when these and other birds are most common.

Weather happens in Vermont—serious weather, especially in the mountains and on Lake Champlain. Vermont winters can be harsh and winter driving hazardous, so plan accordingly. Consult a forecast before setting out. For help on accommodations, climate, events, festivals, and other travel information contact the Vermont Department of Tourism and Marketing at 1-800-Vermont or at its web site, <www.1-800-Vermont.com>. And have a nice visit.

CHAPTER 2

Watching and Enjoying Birds

🪶 *Getting Started: Tips for Beginners*

Watching birds is almost too good to be true. After all, it is a relatively inexpensive pursuit. All it takes is a decent pair of binoculars, a field guide, a place to go (even a backyard will do), and some desire. Beginners who discover birds are often amazed at how they had managed to walk though life overlooking creatures that sing *and* fly. Every morning walk can bring excitement, discovery, tranquility, and a better understanding of the natural world.

Tools of the Trade

Binoculars

Binoculars come with a set of two numbers, 7×35 or 8×40, for example. The first is simply the magnification power. A 7× pair of binoculars makes an object appear seven times closer than the view with the naked eye. The second number is the size of the larger lens (the objective lens) in millimeters. Binoculars with larger objective lenses tend to have better light-gathering ability, which is good. But they also tend to weigh more.

Bigger is not necessarily better. Beginners should consider 7× or 8× binoculars, which tend to have a wider field of view than 10× binoculars. That means the birdwatcher sees more territory through the binoculars, which makes it easier to locate birds. Binoculars labeled "wide angle" generally have an extra-wide field of view that can help beginners struggling to find birds in their binoculars. Avoid compact models; they are lightweight but their quality and light-gathering powers suffer accordingly (although there are a few exceptions). Stay away from zoom-lens binoculars, and steer clear of models with 50mm objective lenses or larger, which can be heavy and bulky.

Eyeglass wearers should fold down the rubber eyecups that are standard on most binoculars. This brings the binocular lenses closer to the eyeglass lenses, which widens the field of view and makes it easier to locate birds. The bespectacled should also select a model with good "eye relief," which provides a full field of view when the user's eyes, because of the glasses, are farther from the lenses. Some manufacturers use adjustable turn-and-lock eyecups, which keep the binoculars the proper distance from the eyes; the designs are wonderful in some models and poor in others.

Butterfly and dragonfly watchers take note: many binoculars on the market today cannot focus on objects closer than fifteen feet or so. Many birders later discover the joy of butterfly and dragonfly watching through binoculars only to back up grudgingly to get them in focus. Birders who plan on enjoying other BFOs (Beautiful Flying Objects) should consider buying binoculars that focus as close as five to eight feet.

Finally, don't skimp on quality. Lousy binoculars can produce lousy views of birds. For backyard, casual, or intermediate birders, some fine optics are available in the $100 to $150 range. Those who suspect birds will become a major part of the rest of their lives might consider spending more. Before buying, try to take the binoculars for a test drive for optical quality and ease of use.

Spotting Scopes

Some birds—notably ducks, shorebirds, and hawks—can be too distant for even the best binoculars. This is the occasion for high-powered optics—the spotting scope, a small telescope mounted on a tripod. A scope can be the difference between finding that rare Harlequin Duck among the flock of scoters on Lake Champlain and passing off the entire bunch as nothing more than a uniform flock of distant ducks. In fact, many Lake Champlain birding experiences are incomplete without a scope. A spotting scope is typically added to the gear after binoculars and once it is clear that birds will be a big part of a birder's life.

Spotting scopes vary in price from about $200 to $1,500. Again, stay away from zoom lenses on lower-end optics. New generations of scopes are giving birders amazing views. These larger scopes have superior optics that particularly excel in low-light conditions. They're bigger, better, and carry heartstopping prices. Zoom eyepieces on most of the higher-end scopes (typically 20×–60×) are standard equipment and perform well. The scope market is ever changing. Read current reviews, ask around, and if at all possible test different models (birders with scopes will often oblige) before making a purchase.

The world's best spotting scope is worthless on a shaky tripod. Since scopes tend to be put into play in wide open spaces—shorelines, wetlands, and mountaintops, for example—wind can rattle the view. A bombproof tripod is worth the investment (which could run in the neighborhood of $200). Make sure the head of the tripod, which allows the scope to be panned horizontally across the landscape, moves smoothly without vibration. Big scopes and solid tripods can be heavy to lug around in the field. Backpack-like gear specifically designed for scopes distributes the load but makes it tough to set up the scope quickly. Foam padding on the tripod legs is a simple solution and can ease the pain of hauling the scope and tripod over the shoulder.

Field Guides

Love your field guide. Study it often. It will forever offer new insights into birds. Here are a few guides to consider:

A Field Guide to the Birds of Eastern and Central North America by Roger Tory Peterson. Beginners have done well for decades with the guide that started popular birdwatching. Peterson's system includes drawings with arrows on them pointing out the key differences between similar species. The latest edition places range maps, which show a species' distribution in North America, alongside the illustrations. It remains a great guide for beginners.

National Geographic Field Guide to the Birds of North America. Many birders graduate from Peterson's guide to this guide. It includes more species and more information than most other field guides. Covering all of North America, it is one of the best all-around field guides for most birders.

The Sibley Guide to Birds by David Sibley. This guide is nothing short of a masterpiece. It is the most comprehensive field guide to North American birds, with almost every species shown flying and at rest. Juvenile, immature, and adult plumages are included. And the guide is loaded with short essays on solving some of the classic bird identification problems. In addition, separate eastern and western editions will be available in spring 2003. But the beginner should use this guide as a secondary reference. Sibley's comprehensive treatment of each species (with lots of renditions to look through) can make the guide a bit daunting to the novice.

Beginners will notice that most field guides don't organize birds by color or habitat. Instead, they are arranged in phylogenetic order, which places birds in a kind of ancestral lineage. North American field guides begin with loons, the most primitive of our birds, and end with finches, the most recently evolved. (Birds listed in this book follow this order, as described in the seventh edition of the American Ornithologists' Union's *Check-list of North American Birds.*)

Learning the phylogenetic order of birds helps a birder become aware of the critical differences among families of birds. It also makes for a more efficient use of time in the field. A birdwatcher lost in the pages of a field guide will certainly miss seeing real birds in real life. Beginners who find themselves wasting valuable time turning to the guide's index instead of flipping to the correct page have two options: on the inside cover, tape or glue a cheat sheet with the page numbers of common bird families—ducks, hawks, woodpeckers, flycatchers, warblers, etc.—or attach binder tabs with labels to quickly open the guide to the correct bird family.

Finally, a note on one of the more weighty choices of our time—nope, not paper or plastic but drawings or photos. While field guides with photographs of birds are nice to look at, these snapshots don't always capture the bird in a way that represents its typical appearance. Good drawings collapse the basic nature of a bird into a single image. Select a field guide with drawings.

Technique

The Rewards of Patience

With more than 800 bird species in North America and nearly 250 appearing every year in Vermont, the beginner is easily overwhelmed. It pays to start small, perhaps in the backyard. Learn the common birds first. After all, it will be nearly impossible to find that one rare Bohemian Waxwing without first recognizing field marks on the numerous Cedar Waxwings in its company.

From wintertime through the first week in May isn't a bad time to start birdwatching. The bird diversity then is at a manageable level, and the view isn't yet blocked by foliage. Wetlands or ponds, where birds are low in shrubs or otherwise relatively visible, can make for pleasant introductory birdwatching from spring through fall. Every so often, stop walking, find a nice spot, and relax and sit still for five minutes. After the initial disturbance, birds will settle in and begin to go about their business. It is also much easier to detect a bird's movement when not in motion yourself.

Learn the distinctive features shared among members of major families of birds. For example, ducks share a similar shape and habitat preference; so do owls. Ducks and owls are easily recognized as members of two different bird families. But differences between the various families of *songbirds* are much harder to discern. To the beginner, flycatchers, vireos, thrushes, warblers, sparrows, and other songbird families can appear to be quite similar. So the novice should first learn the differences between, for example, the flycatcher family and the similar vireo family (shape, plumage, bill, feeding habits,

What's That Bird at My Feeder?

An easy introduction to birdwatching awaits in the backyard. A diversity of trees, shrubs, and other vegetation around the home offers food and cover for common birds. The variety of species in the yard depends on the quality and diversity of the habitat.

Backyard feeders introduce many people to birds. Feeders can be training grounds for birdwatchers who later enjoy birds in their natural habitats. But feeding comes with responsibility. In some cases, bird feeding can actually harm birds. (See "Responsible Birdwatching," page 18.)

For those who watch birds through the window, it helps to know what to expect. Here is the cast of characters that sometimes visit Vermont feeders: Rock Dove, Mourning Dove, Ruby-throated Hummingbird, Downy Woodpecker, Hairy Woodpecker, Blue Jay, Black-capped Chickadee, Tufted Titmouse, Red-breasted Nuthatch, White-breasted Nuthatch,

A Black-capped Chickadee discovers a surprise guest, a Pileated Woodpecker, which exceeds the design specifications of a feeder in Grand Isle. Photo: Dave Hoag

European Starling, American Tree Sparrow, Song Sparrow, Fox Sparrow, White-throated Sparrow, White-crowned Sparrow, Dark-eyed Junco, Northern Cardinal, Rose-breasted Grosbeak, Indigo Bunting, Red-winged Blackbird, Common Grackle, Brown-headed Cowbird, Purple Finch, House Finch, Common Redpoll, Pine Siskin, American Goldfinch, Evening Grosbeak, and House Sparrow. Sharp-shinned Hawk, Cooper's Hawk, and Northern Shrike occasionally lurk at feeders, not for seed but rather an easy songbird meal.

vocalizations) before trying to learn the minute differences between Alder Flycatcher and Willow Flycatcher. The family distinctions may appear subtle at first, but with time and study, the differences between flycatchers and vireos and all other songbird families will be as clear as the differences between ducks and owls.

Finding and actually seeing birds through binoculars takes some practice. Too many beginners who see a bird flitting in the trees rush closer for another look, raise the binoculars—and end up seeing nothing but leaves. Nothing more effectively scares away birds than sudden movement. Even raising binoculars from chest to eyes can startle a nearby songbird and send it off into the woods. The skilled birdwatcher moves slowly but deliberately, speaks in a low voice, and keeps a respectful distance. A great look at a bird is the reward for being alert yet *patient*.

A warbler pops into view on the branch of a sugar maple. The beginning birder, getting a clear look at the gray head, sunny yellow undersides, and olive-colored back, turns confidently to the field guide. But there's a problem: was this bird a Nashville Warbler or a Mourning Warbler? The birder stashes the field guide and turns for another look. The warbler is long gone.

A crucial skill in birdwatching is learning to take long, meticulous looks at birds. A Great Blue Heron wading in a pond is easy. But a tiny songbird flitting among the foliage won't always be as cooperative. So the birdwatcher must make the best use of every glimpse and every bit of information gathered to record a complete mental image *before* turning to the field guide.

First note overall shape. Is the bird plump like a thrush or slender like a cuckoo? How about its posture and behavior? It is bent forward and on the move among the foliage like a warbler? Or is it perched upright and still like a flycatcher? Size can help but is surprisingly hard to measure. The skilled birdwatcher rarely uses size in identification without an accompanying reference, such as a known species nearby.

Try to note bill shape and length. An American Pipit might look like a streaky sparrow, but its slender bill exposes it as a sparrow imposter. Tail length sometimes helps. The Song Sparrow has a relatively long tail that flops around a bit when the bird is in flight. The Savannah Sparrow has a short tail.

When noting color and other marks, be specific about extent and location. Sure, most everyone knows an American Robin has a red breast. But how extensive is the red plumage? Does it continue up the throat and under the tail? These fine details in plumage are "field marks." Take note of them. They are vital evidence of a bird's identity. Because birds have similar assemblages of feathers, they tend to share field marks, such as one or two white bars across the wing (wing bars), a distinct ring around the eye (eye ring), or colored inner wing feathers on ducks (the speculum). (Most field guides include an introduction to the plumage structure of birds. It is vital reading, even for advanced birdwatchers.) Some vireos have wing bars; others don't. Most North American owl species have yellow eyes, but four species have black eyes. Some sparrows are streaked below; others are clean. Least Sandpiper has yellow legs; its close relatives have black legs. Observing these kinds of subtleties in a bird can clinch its identity. After all, if that confusing warbler in the maple had a prominent white eye ring and yellow throat, a novice birder could have identified it as a Nashville Warbler instead of Mourning Warbler.

By the way, locating a bird and its field marks through binoculars takes some practice. Most binoculars should first be adjusted for an individual's eyes. Consult the owner's manual for the diopter setting. Then, when out watching, first pinpoint the bird's location with the naked eye and note conspicuous landmarks or vegetation to help orient the binoculars. Raise the

A male Yellow-rumped Warbler greets dawn from a willow perch in Strafford.
Photo: Steven D. Faccio

binoculars, and if the bird is not in view, don't scan the landscape through the binoculars. Instead, lower the binoculars and search again for movement with the naked eye. This is the best way to relocate a bird that has changed its position.

Be aware of the sun's location. Try to stand between the sun (at your back) and the bird. A bird viewed against a sunny sky will often appear as little more than a silhouette. Walking to a different spot so that the background becomes a tree or hillside can bring a backlit bird into sharper view. Never point optics directly at the sun. Also, be aware that lighting conditions can alter the perception of a bird's color. Early morning or late evening sunlight can sometimes make plumage appear more yellow, orange, even red. Shadow, backlighting, and the light of dull, overcast days can sometimes appear to drain the color from a bird's plumage or make pale feathers look dark.

The Dawn Chorus

Bird*watching* is a misnomer. The birder who only watches will certainly miss seeing many birds. Any expert knows it is often easier to hear songbirds than to see them. Take the Scarlet Tanager, for example. This drop-dead beautiful songbird, which tends to nest in deciduous or mixed woods, is often hidden behind the leaves. As a result most birdwatchers hear them before seeing them. (The males sound like an American Robin with a sore throat.) Once the tanager sings and reveals his presence among the trees, the search can begin.

During May and June, when songbirds are quite vocal, birders with trained ears hear most of the birds they encounter before actually looking at them. So don't wait to learn bird songs. Start by learning the songs of common birds. A good reference is the *Birding by Ear* series (cassette tapes or compact disc) in the Peterson's field guide series. In any event, while out birdwatching zero in on new or unfamiliar songs and then track down what birds are making them.

Timing Is Everything

Weather, seasons, and time of day are all factors in successful birdfinding. Early morning (even just before dawn) is the best time to find birds in spring; time of day is less important in winter. Beginners should understand how Vermont's bird diversity changes with the changing seasons. (See "Seasons of Vermont Birds," page 6.) Checklists of local birds, available in some locations, often show when a species is present and whether it breeds there. The "Species Accounts" chapter of this book offers this information in detail for Vermont. Each account includes a graph showing when a species is most abundant in Vermont. While field marks and vocalizations have the final say in determining the identity of a bird, the graphs can help a birdwatcher prepare for what species are likely to be expected—or ruled out—during an outing. As a result, they can help a beginner struggling to identify an unknown bird. When watching an unknown gull, for example, a birdwatcher can use the abundance graphs to narrow the list of gull species likely to occur in Vermont at that time. Then the birder can check for the identifying field marks of these likely candidates first, a much simpler task than checking for the field marks of all the gulls in a field guide. Finally, birdwatching is hardly a fair-weather pursuit. Overcast and drizzly days can be quite good for finding birds, particularly those driven out of migration (and into view) by foul weather.

Sharing Knowledge

The next best thing to a good field guide is a good guide in the field. Experienced birdwatchers or professional guides have much to offer the beginner. When a novice is stumped, an expert can explain why the mystery bird is a House Finch and not a Purple Finch. Beginners should by all means enjoy the rewards of discovering birds on their own. But birds are also a joy to share, and most experts are happy to share their expertise. So don't be bashful about asking.

Organized birdwatching outings are a fine way for beginners to get started. Local Audubon chapters, conservation organizations, clubs, and private nature touring companies regularly offer guided bird walks ideal for novices. (See "Resources" at the back of this book.)

✒ Building Skills and Understanding Birds

Watching birds is easy. But *knowing* them is another matter. It is one thing to glance at a bird, mark it off on a checklist, and move on to the next species. It is another to look beyond plumage, even beyond the bird itself, to discover more and more about these creatures and their habitats. The observer who looks long at birds, recognizing subtle details and behaviors, will consequently become skilled at bird identification. While there is nothing at all wrong with remaining a beginner, the advancing birdwatcher will find birds an infinite source of insight into the workings of nature. Below are tips for becoming a better birder:

- **Get outside.** Nothing can substitute for time spent observing birds "in the field" (or even the backyard).

- **Slow down.** A hunting Red-throated Loon spends more time underwater and out of view than on the surface. Patience is a virtue in birding. So are long looks.

- **Spend quality time with the field guide.** Regular perusal of field guides at home prepares a birdwatcher for the field. It is important to know in advance what to look for and what other species to consider when an unusual bird pops into view.

- **Watch birds with experienced birdwatchers.** Don't be bashful about asking lots of questions. Most experts enjoy sharing their knowledge. A beginner or intermediate birdwatcher can learn a lot by spending time with experts or joining an organized outing with a skilled guide.

- **Scrutinize the flock.** All those common species might not be so common after all. Painstaking inspection, bird by bird, through flocks of waterfowl, shorebirds, gulls, or songbirds can reveal a lone rare relative lurking among the masses.

- **Notice chips, whits, peeps and other odd sounds.** Most songbirds make diagnostic call notes or other strange noises. A student of these sounds can identify a darting warbler simply by the quality of its *chip* or can name a distant woodpecker based solely on the cadence of its drumming.

- **Let some go (unidentified).** Rather than guess at or assume the identity of a confusing bird, spend more time with it. Take notes on plumage, behavior, song. Make a sketch in the field or take photographs. But realize that some birds escape unidentified—even from experts.

- **Consult advanced references.** The market is full of textbook-style references specializing in in-depth accounts of individual bird families: waterfowl, gulls, shorebirds, and warblers, for example.

- **Learn habitat preferences.** Knowing which birds prefer certain habitats gives a birdwatcher a head start, a sense of what to expect. Habitat preference can also be a tool in identification, a fact excluded from most field guides.

- **Watch bird behavior.** Birds do more than just look good—their actions tell a story. A White-breasted Nuthatch dusts the opening to its nest cavity with a bill-full of dead insects or leaves. Seeing birds copulate or carry nesting materials confirms that a species is nesting in the area. American Robins survive a snowstorm by eating wild fruit. Many species fake an injury to distract predators from the nest. Recognizing and understanding behavior offers insight into how birds live in and interact with their surroundings.

- **Consider distribution and population.** Birds have a great advantage over many forms of life: they can fly to greener pastures—if they exist. The presence or absence of birds is perhaps their most telling message about the state of an ecosystem. When a species suddenly expands or contracts its range or numbers, some change in the environment is the likely cause, either natural or by humans. An awareness of changes in the status of birds leads the birder to a deeper understanding of the interdependencies inherent in nature.

- **Get involved.** A community awaits. Join conservation groups, participate in Christmas Bird Counts and breeding bird surveys, report bird sightings. These activities not only improve skills and the understanding of birds but are great ways to give something back to the birds.

✒ *Responsible Birdwatching*

In their pursuit of birds, birdwatchers must always respect wildlife and its dwelling places. The American Birding Association (ABA) puts it well in its "Principles of Birding Ethics": "In any conflict of interest between birds and birders, the welfare of the birds and their environment comes first." Yet it is surprising how easily a birdwatcher, caught up in the thrill of the chase, can threaten birds and harm the environment. Below is an informal code of ethical birding behavior:

Respect birds. Keep at a respectful distance, particularly from nests or critical feeding areas. Watch a bird's behavior to determine how close is too close. If the bird spends as much time watching the observer as vice-versa, it is a signal to back off. Refrain from extensive "spishing"—repeating a *pisshh-pisshh-pisshh* sound to attract birds—or other disturbances when birds are raising young. (As an aspiring naturalist once said, "Don't come knockin' if the nest's a rockin'.") Never use recordings to attract rare, threatened, or endangered species. The repeated broadcast of a song, which after all is a territorial message, may cause a bird to unnecessarily vacate its territory. It is against the law to shine a spotlight on almost any wildlife in Vermont.

When they invade Vermont from the north in winter, Pine Grosbeaks often seek the fruits of ornamental trees. This male dines at a shopping center in Waterbury.
Photo: Mitch Moraski

Respect private property and public safety. Do not enter private land without the owner's permission. Avoid parking on roadways or otherwise creating traffic hazards.

Promote a positive image of birdwatching and birdwatchers. Be courteous to birders and nonbirders alike. Pack out your trash. Follow rules and regulations on public lands.

Feed birds responsibly. Avoid window strikes by placing feeders at a safe distance. Do not expose birds at a feeder to predation by domestic cats or dogs. Don't feed squirrels and chipmunks; they prey on songbirds in their nests. Feeders can spread avian diseases, so regularly clean away seed hulls and disinfect feeders with a weak bleach solution.

To obtain the ABA's "Principles of Birding Ethics," write to the organization at P.O. Box 6599, Colorado Springs, CO 80934 or visit its web site at <www.americanbirding.org>.

✒ Christmas Bird Count

The Audubon Christmas Bird Count is an annual, early-winter bird census, touted as the largest and longest-running bird survey ever conducted. The first count was held on Christmas Day 1900 by twenty-seven participants in the United States and Canada, and a century later it has grown to involve more than 50,000 volunteers throughout the Western Hemisphere. The methodology is pseudoscientific, yet by its sheer magnitude many insights about birds, especially long-term population trends, can be gleaned from Christmas Count data.

The actual counting takes place in "count circles," each of which is fifteen miles in diameter. More than 1,800 such circles are scattered about, with the majority in North America and eighteen in Vermont. Each count takes place on a single day, chosen in advance, from December 14 through January 5. (Few counts take place on Christmas Day anymore.) The intent is to identify and count as many birds as possible within the circle. Participants head out in cars, on foot, or even on cross-country skis, in small groups traditionally called "parties." Most circles hold a "countdown" dinner at the end of the day, during which participants gather to compare notes and review results.

Table 2.
The Christmas Bird Count in Vermont

Count circle location	Year began	Average per year		
		Species	*Birds*	*Participants*
Barnet	1996	39	9,700	18
Bennington	1911	47	7,400	14
Brattleboro	1963	46	3,800	17
Burlington	1948	61	10,700	36
Champlain Islands	1983	66	18,600	23
Craftsbury/Greensboro	1974	33	2,900	11
Ferrisburgh	1961	78	15,800	37
Hanover/Norwich	1960	49	7,500	23
Hinesburg	1990	40	3,100	9
Island Pond	1974	28	1,700	10
Middlebury	1989	66	13,400	40
Mt. Abraham/Bristol	1998	41	1,700	11
Plainfield	1960	47	3,500	21
Rutland	1974	49	7,400	25
Saxtons River	1956	54	6,900	11
Springfield	1978	48	8,400	16
Winhall	1967	30	1,400	10
Woodstock	1975	40	4,500	17

Averages are calculated from 1990 through 1999 for species and individual birds, and from 1996 through 1999 for participants (except Brattleboro through 1998 and Barnet and Mt. Abraham beginning with their first year). Total birds are rounded to the nearest 100. "Year began" is the year the circle began a largely uninterrupted history of counts. Source: Published Vermont Christmas Bird Count results.

The cost to participate in a count is $5, which is used to defray the cost of maintaining the count. All the bird numbers eventually find their way into a central database, which can currently be viewed via the internet at Cornell University's website <birdsource.cornell.edu>.

To participate, contact Audubon Vermont or a local Audubon chapter in November (see "Resources" at the back of this book). For scheduling simplicity, most counts look for a full day's commitment. Beginners are welcome and will often be teamed with one or more experienced birdwatchers. Christmas Counts are held rain or shine, snow or blizzard. Accordingly, the most important advice to any Christmas counter is to bring tons of warm clothing. Snacks and a warm drink also help. Be keenly aware of fingers and toes and exposed skin. Reattaching body parts is much trickier than keeping them connected in the first place.

🖋 Migration Watching

The appeal of birds is almost certainly rooted in their gift of flight, which is best portrayed in the miracle of migration. But there is more to migration watching than enjoying the spectacle of flight. All these individual birds have pulled up stakes and embarked on a timeless procession, moving with singular purpose to an ancient rhythm. Migration watchers witness an annual pilgrimage that has taken place for eons. And with diligent respect for birds and stewardship of their habitats it will continue for eons to come.

While spring is a most welcome time for migration in Vermont, it offers limited opportunities for actually *seeing* birds flying north en masse. But in fall, when the air becomes crisp and the north wind signals a change in season, the skies fill with southbound birds.

Hawkwatching

A hawk soars overhead, a curious blend of power and grace, floating in such casual defiance of gravity. Sensing an updraft, the bird circles. It is joined by a second, then a third, a fourth, and soon fifty hawks are wrapped together in a swirling stack that defines the thermal, the rising column of warm air that suspends them. A "kettle" of hawks is born. They circle and rise, reach the column's crest and boil over the top, peeling out southbound again, gliding toward the next thermal elevator.

This is the migration technique of the Broad-winged Hawk, which has every intention of traveling to Central and South America with nary a flap. This parade of raptors takes place every year like clockwork. The only trick is to look up when it's underway.

Vermont's hawkwatch season extends from late August through early December. All Vermont's hawk, eagle, and falcon species pass through, but Sharp-shinned Hawk, Broad-winged Hawk, Red-tailed Hawk, and American Kestrel comprise the majority of migrants. Broad-winged Hawks, which travel alone or in groups of up to 100 birds (sometimes more), represent more than half the hawks seen passing through. Their big show peaks during the second and third weeks of September. On a good day, more than 1,000 hawks can pass by a hawkwatch site. Most other birds' movements are less condensed, and the raptor mix on a given day can vary dramatically by date. The species accounts and graphs later in this book present a good overview of the abundance and passage of different species.

Weather is as important to hawkwatching as is the calendar, and serious migration watching often leads to serious weather watching. The best weather condition is the arrival of a high pressure system on the heels of a passing low. In the northern hemisphere, high pressure systems rotate clockwise and lows counterclockwise, and in North America weather systems generally pass from west to east. So the transition from a low to a high pressure system produces a shift to a north or northwest wind. (Weather forecasters often refer to this border of shifting wind as a "cold front," since the leading edge of a north wind is usually accompanied by cooler air.) The farther this system extends to the north, the better, since that's where the birds are coming from. Many southbound birds find the onset of this tailwind irresistible. Although things aren't always so black and white, a sample week from Mt. Philo in Charlotte, a popular hawkwatch site, demonstrates the point.

Table 3.
A Week of Hawks at Mt. Philo

Date	Sept. 6	Sept. 7	Sept. 8	Sept. 9	Sept. 10	Sept. 11	Sept. 12
Average wind direction	South	South	North	South	South	South	South
Wind speed (miles per hour)	20	5	10	5	10	15	15
Hawk numbers	0	8	1,893	239	48	15	18

Hawks can be seen flying all day, but the busiest time is usually from around 11 A.M. to 2 P.M., particularly for the thermal-loving Broad-winged Hawks. Sunny days can make birds a bit harder to spot, due to less contrast between bird and blue sky. Midday birds, with high-rising thermals and no low cloud ceiling to contain them, can sometimes fly up and out of sight. A sky generously filled with cumulous clouds is ideal. Any seasoned hawk-

Ted Murin and Steve Antell counting hawks on Mt. Philo, September 16, 1993. The final tally for the day: 3,688 southbound raptors. The photograph is by Mark Wilson, who remarked at the end of the day that the migration was "like counting mosquitoes in a swamp." Photo: Mark Wilson

watcher will admit that there is plenty of quiet time spent waiting for those busy moments—time to watch the weather, appreciate the view, and catch up on thoughts. Even time to let one's mind wander and contemplate weighty things such as crop circles, and if there actually is a parallel universe do they find extra socks in their laundry.

Hawks have been seen migrating over most every corner of Vermont. These migrants probably vary their course to take advantage of, or avoid, local weather conditions. Owing to their north-south orientation, the Champlain and Connecticut River Valleys seem to attract more birds, but in the right season and weather most any place in Vermont with a wide view can make a viable hawkwatch site. (One veteran of Vermont hawkwatching successfully uses large parking lots due to their unobstructed views.) Sites with some altitude are helpful to get a little closer to the action. But while any such spot might do, and many have proven good, two sites consistently record the largest numbers of migrating raptors in Vermont. Ironically, both these sites have restricted northern views—but that doesn't seem to bother the birds.

Mt. Philo in Charlotte, in the windy Champlain Valley, epitomizes the feast or famine nature of hawkwatching. This site holds the record for the largest number of migrating hawks seen in Vermont in a day (3,688). Another time nearly 1,200 raptors passed by in an hour, or roughly one hawk every three seconds. A west wind here, however, can shut down the show. Resident raptors and Common Raven occasionally entertain when the migrant stream runs dry. A state park entrance fee is charged, and a bathroom made available, through mid-October. See chapter 4, "Birdwatching Areas," page 58 for more about Mt. Philo.

Putney Mountain seems to receive a bit more consistent and diverse raptor traffic than Mt. Philo. The Broad-winged Hawk show here is quite good, and the Sharp-shinned Hawk movement far exceeds that of the Champlain

Valley. An indication of the dependability of its hawks and hawkwatchers is that this site has recorded the most raptors seen in a season in Vermont (7,783). On the rarer end of these superlatives, more Golden Eagles have been seen here than at any other place in Vermont. See chapter 4, "Birdwatching Areas," page 90 for more about Putney Mountain.

Anyone hawkwatching for the first time should be aware that most migrating hawks are observed only at a considerable distance, at first appearing more like gnats than raptors. (Every now and then, however, birds can pass nearby.) If possible, try taking that maiden hawkwatch voyage with someone who has some experience. Join an organized hawkwatch or visit a mountain that has a hawkwatch in progress. Mt. Philo during the second and third weeks in September and Putney Mountain during September and October are usually tended by hawkwatchers (in decent weather). By the way, there *is* an answer to that age-old question, "How do you know you're not seeing the same birds over and over?" Migrating birds appear from the north, have a directed southbound flight, disappear to the south, and don't waste a fraction of a calorie on anything that doesn't support that effort. Resident birds tend to wander about. So hike up a mountain and watch the sky. And if not a single bird flies by, the views are still well worth the effort.

Lakewatching on Lake Champlain

Brant are rarely seen parked anywhere in Vermont, including on Lake Champlain. But several encounters with southbound flocks in 1997 spurred a notion that perhaps Brant, and many other birds, were regularly using Lake Champlain as a migration highway without ever stopping to visit. Four seasons of lakewatching later, this premise appears to be correct.

The Lake Champlain flyway has been found to host unusually large numbers of migrating loons, geese, ducks, and gulls, and a sprinkling of various rarities including the rare and raucous jaegers. Other birds take advantage of this large navigational aid as well, including raptors, shorebirds, and passerines. Many of these birds are representative of what can ordinarily be found lingering on and around Lake Champlain. But some, such as the Brant and the jaegers, seem to treat the lake like an interstate with no exits, making a lakewatch the best opportunity to encounter them in Vermont.

Some highlights of only four seasons of sporadic watches along the lake include 425 loons in a day (46 Red-throated Loon and 379 Common Loon), more than 1,200 Brant in a two-morning flight, more than 1,400 scoters in a morning (10 Surf Scoter, 488 White-winged Scoter, 940 Black Scoter), nearly 300 Long-tailed Ducks in a morning, and 17 species of duck in a morning. Also parading by was a who's who of species rarely seen in Vermont, includ-

Rarely landing in Vermont, Brant is among the arctic breeders that often use the Champlain Valley as a migratory flyway. This juvenile pauses at Lake Bomoseen in Castleton. Photo: Roy Pilcher

ing Leach's Storm-Petrel, Northern Gannet, Black Guillemot, Northern Fulmar, Barnacle Goose, Eurasian Wigeon, Common Eider, Black-headed Gull, Sabine's Gull, Ivory Gull, Black-legged Kittiwake, and all three jaeger species.

Timing and weather are as important to lakewatching as they are to hawkwatching. Southbound birds can be seen from August through December, with the bulk of them cruising by in October and November. The same weather pattern that is best for hawkwatching is best for lakewatching—the onset of a north or northwest wind, known as a cold front, that occurs when a passing low pressure system begins relinquishing control to an ensuing high. (Jaegers have been seen on several occasions virtually surfing this initial wave of north wind and have rarely been seen bucking a south wind.) The farther north the weather system extends, the better, particularly if it reaches as far north as James Bay (the southern lobe of Hudson Bay, Canada). Unlike hawkwatching, lakewatching is an early-morning adventure. The first two to three hours of light are usually the best, with the second hour often representing the peak time. A strong north wind can extend this period. However, whenever the wind direction changes from south to north, regardless of the time of day, there is the potential for birds.

Lakewatching may not be ideal for beginners. Many of these birds, distant and moving fast, can be hard to identify. A spotting scope is nearly mandatory. And the prime weather conditions are, in a word, nasty-cold.

Considerations for choosing a lakewatch spot include elevation (higher is better), field of view (wider is better), distance across the lake (shorter is better), and of course accessibility. Lakewatches have been tried at a number of public and private locations (with permission). A few of the best public sites found so far are below. All sites hold the possibility for viewing the standard migratory fair of loons, geese, ducks, and gulls.

Charlotte Town Beach provides a gorgeous, unrestricted view of the lake.

Leach's Storm-Petrel, Northern Gannet, Common Eider, Black-headed Gull, Sabine's Gull, Black-legged Kittiwake, numerous jaegers (including an adult Long-tailed Jaeger), and hundreds of Brant have been seen passing here. An added feature is a small stretch of good shorebird habitat, available for weary travelers. The downside here is that most migrant traffic is distant, and some birds can elude identification even with a scope. Flocks of migrant passerines, however, can fly nearby, including swallows, American Robin, American Pipit, Yellow-rumped Warbler, and blackbirds. See chapter 4, "Birdwatching Areas," page 55 for information about the beach.

DAR State Park offers a relatively short distance across the lake (1.6 miles), pretty scenery, and a reasonable field of view. Good numbers of loons, Brant, and scoters have been seen here, occasionally flying close by. In fact, this site often imparts a sense of being within the migration, as birds periodically fly overhead, along the water's surface below, and at eye level. From the park entrance, continue straight in toward the lake. The best vantage is from a grassy slope facing the lake, next to the stone pavilion. See "Birdwatching Areas," page 69 for information about the park.

The Grand Isle Ferry Landing affords a similar distance to the opposite shore as DAR State Park, a fairly open view, and the convenient comforts of a restaurant and bathroom. Southbound jaegers and large numbers of scoters, Brant, and other geese have been seen passing a private lakewatch nearby. A Snowy Owl was seen migrating by here once. Cars and development dilute the wilderness experience, but a ferry ride is close at hand when things get slow. See chapter 4, "Birdwatching Areas," page 38 for information about the ferry landing.

One of the most exciting aspects of lakewatching is that it is a new frontier in Vermont and many more discoveries are almost certainly in store.

Night Flight

While hawks and waterfowl migrate south in broad daylight, most songbirds wait for darkness. Theories vary as to why and point to the cooler temperatures (to lessen the chance of the bird overheating) and calmer air, the visibility of stars for navigation, and the absence of bird-eating hawks, who are sleeping. But whatever their reasons, about an hour after dark these tiny balls of energy rise up and take their turn flying well into the night. This flight can be encountered just about anywhere in Vermont from August through October, with its peak in September.

There are two ways to witness this spectacle. The first is to point binoculars or a scope at a full or nearly full moon. (WARNING: Doing this for too long may damage your eyes.) When birds are flying, their silhouettes will periodically pass by. A second technique allows identification now and then and with much experience: find a fairly quiet place, preferably away from traffic and city noise, and simply listen. The flight calls of many species are audible and recognizable. The flow of feathered biomass on some nights can be surprising.

🖋 Safety

More Americans are hospitalized for unfortunate encounters with boats or barbecues than with, say, Bobolinks. Nevertheless, the birdwatcher in the wilds of Vermont does face some hazards.

Perhaps the greatest threat, hardly a wild one, is the automobile. Some fine birdwatching areas are along highways, and it is easy to forget traffic when a Black Tern or an Osprey comes into view. Getting run over can ruin a birdwatching trip (not to mention binoculars). Never watch birds from the middle of the road, and look both ways before crossing to look at birds. Finally, don't bird and drive. Never watch birds from behind the wheel of a moving vehicle.

Many Vermonters love to hunt. The turkey season coincides with the best part of the spring migration—the month of May. The fall waterfowl hunting season can pose a risk to people who get too close to hunters; for safety and out of courtesy, give duck blinds a wide berth. Bear and small game hunting seasons begin in September. Hunters fill the woods during the November rifle season for white-tailed deer, and as a result many birdwatchers catch up on their reading during deer season. It is a good idea in the fall to wear blaze orange (and never white, as in white-tailed deer) in the woods and to avoid known hunting locations altogether. Check with the Vermont Fish and Wildlife Department for hunting season dates, or pick up a pocket-sized copy of the department's annual *Vermont Guide: Hunting, Fishing and Trapping Laws*. It lists times and dates for all hunting seasons.

Vermont hosts a panoply of biting insects. Black flies can be a nuisance from Mother's Day to Father's Day. These miniature pests (only the females bite) go for blood near the body's surface, often behind the ears or on the forehead. Citronella or similar natural repellents work well on them. Mosquitoes begin flying in force as the black flies subside, usually early to mid-June (mid-May in warmer, wetter locations). Long sleeves and long pants can be preferable to the toxic bug dope necessary to keep them at bay. Deer flies and their relatives, which can inflict a painful bite, join the fray in late June and early July. A swift, direct blow with a sledge hammer slows them down a bit. It is perhaps best to know that all these insects are most active on still, humid, overcast days. (It is also good to know that without birds, insects would probably eat the world.) Cool temperatures and low humidity are often the best repellent. Finally, Lyme disease is a risk, although its rates in Vermont hardly approach those of southern New England. The Vermont Health Department reported twelve indigenous cases of Lyme disease in year 2000 (and another twenty-eight cases presumed to be imported). The best prevention includes wearing light-colored clothing, including long pants tucked into socks; conducting a full-body inspection after birding for the tiny tick that can carry the disease; and noticing the telltale bull's-eye rash that spreads after infection. Early treatment is critical.

Black bears want nothing to do with birders. Give them a wide berth anyway. Rarely encountered, bears do everything they can to elude humans. A threatening or charging bear will most often retreat when faced with a shouting, arm-waving birder. Rabies occurs occasionally among some Vermont mammals, so a wild animal acting not so wild is best avoided (or even reported to the Rabies Hotline at (800)472-2437). And isolated populations of timber rattlesnakes inhabit the towns of West Haven and Fair Haven. This book includes advice for birdwatching in their neighborhood.

Plants pose a minor threat. Poison ivy is most likely to occur in the Champlain and Connecticut River Valleys. It is sparsely scattered elsewhere in the lowlands of central portions of the state. It can creep up a tree, grow as a shrub or sprout ankle-high. A set of three terminal, shiny leaves (often with wavy edges) is the giveaway. Poison sumac, which can also cause an itchy allergic reaction, has a sumac-like leaf and tends to be limited to wet areas of southern Vermont and the Champlain and Connecticut River Valleys. Finally, a brush with wild parsnip can cause a similar itchy rash. A member of the parsley family, it grows (often along roadsides) up to five feet tall and has a thick stem, divided leaves, and yellow flowers in flat-topped, umbrellalike clusters (known as umbels) up to six inches across. A vigorous soapy scrub at the end of the day and laundering clothes can ease the result of exposure to these plants.

Common sense is always a good companion, even on a leisurely birdwalk. Be prepared for unexpected weather, particularly rain and cold. Pack rain gear, even if it's sunny before the trip, and extra layers of warm clothing in winter. Bring gloves or mittens and a warm winter hat no matter what the weather. Sturdy, waterproof boots and warm socks are better than sneakers. Bring along water and fruit or snacks.

When boating for birds, be aware that the waters of Vermont, particularly Lake Champlain, remain cold much of the year. A capsized boater is often not far from hypothermia. Vermont law requires that all boats carry one life jacket per person.

✐ Road Maps

A good road map is a useful companion to this birdfinding guide. Many Vermonters (including the authors) have adopted the *Delorme Atlas and Gazetteer* to help navigate back roads, shorelines, and perhaps even a few logging roads. The atlas is widely available in Vermont. Note that a few of the road names in the Delorme atlas may differ from more up-to-date names used in this guide.

The Vermont Department of Forests, Parks and Recreation and the Vermont Fish and Wildlife Department publish and distribute guides and maps to state parks, forests, wildlife management areas, and other public properties suitable for birdwatching. Both departments have headquarters at 103 South Main Street, Waterbury, Vermont 05671, (802)244-3600 or visit the Agency of Natural Resources web site at <http://www.anr.state.vt.us/>.

CHAPTER 3

Conservation

Anyone who's witnessed the raw force of a Peregrine Falcon, heard the lively serenade of a Ruby-crowned Kinglet, or gawked at the glow of an Indigo Bunting would have to agree with Roger Tory Peterson, who once called birds "the most vivid expression of life." These wild creatures, in their own expression of life, unwittingly enrich human life as well. They give so much and ask so little in return. Yet birds most certainly do need a great deal from human beings. Anyone who enjoys their gifts has many opportunities to contribute to the wellbeing of birds. A birder of conscience is a believer in conservation. One person's efforts *can* make a difference.

Our respect for the environment is decidedly mixed. In 1962 Rachel Carson, revealing the devastation of pesticides, wrote in *Silent Spring*: "It was a spring without voices. On the mornings that had once throbbed with the dawn chorus of robins, catbirds, doves, jays, wrens, and scores of other bird voices there was now no sound; only silence lay over the fields and woods and marsh."

At that time, Peregrine Falcons were on their way to extinction in the eastern United States. The last few Bachman's Warblers were singing in vain for mates in depleted bottomland habitats of the American Southeast. The Ivory-billed Woodpecker was well on its way to being logged into oblivion. Carson's seminal work helped to spawn a new wave of conservation. Since then the conservation movement has claimed victories and suffered defeats. Peregrine Falcons are back, but Bachman's Warblers are gone for good.

Today the diversity of life on earth is vanishing at an astounding pace. Rainforests are falling at a reported rate of about one acre per second. Harvard zoologist E. O. Wilson's conservative estimate is that the planet loses

A Peregrine Falcon surveys its cliffside territory from a snag in Fairlee. Endangered in Vermont, this raptor is making a steady comeback with human help.
Photo: Steven D. Faccio

27,000 species each year—that's seventy-four a day. "If we continue at the current rate of deforestation and destruction of major ecosystems like rainforests and coral reefs, where most of the biodiversity is concentrated, we will surely lose more than half of all the species of plants and animals on earth by the end of the 21st century," Wilson once said. Plants and animals are becoming extinct at a rate faster than the planet's last major extinction event, the demise of dinosaurs sixty-five million years ago. The tropics is home to a lot of the action—and the biodiversity. Evidence has been mounting for years that neotropical migrant birds—those that winter in the tropics and come north to breed—are declining at a rapid rate. These victims include some of our most stunning and musical songbirds—thrushes, warblers, and tanagers, for example.

So what's causing the current extinction event? It turns out that the rise of the human being (six billion and counting) is an earth-shaking force. We appropriate—and often waste—a disproportionate share of the planet's natural resources. We clear rainforests, kill coral reefs, and damage precious wetland, grassland, and shoreline habitats. Even our morning cup of coffee can harm the birds we love.

But we have alternatives, even for coffee drinkers. The planet is not lost. Anyone can tread more lightly within the natural world. The rainforest gets most of the press, but habitat destruction, or preservation, begins at home. Here are a few suggestions:

Conserve Habitat and Birds Close to Home

- Create wildlife habitat in the backyard. This includes native food supplies (seeds, fruits, and insects) and vegetation for shelter. Set free existing habitat—mow smaller lawns, preserve the forest understory, or simply let more land grow wild. It's amazing how fast birds and other wildlife will respond. Avoid introducing invasive, exotic plant species, which crowd out native plants that are important to native wildlife.

- Minimize or eliminate pesticide and herbicide use. Bugs are bird food. Use organic pest controls in the garden. Lawns need not be perfect—homeowners should embrace their inner dandelion.

- Keep cats indoors. Cats are known to kill millions of songbirds every year in North America. (It's not their fault—they're predators.) Cats stalk and pounce, so bells on their collars make little or no difference. Owners of outdoor cats should avoid feeding birds. Always spay or neuter the cat.

- Stall sprawl. Join land conservation efforts and promote housing and commercial development that maximizes wildlife habitat in the community.

Conserve Habitat and Birds Far Away

- Drink shade-grown coffee. Coffee drinkers can choose coffee grown traditionally in dappled sunlight beneath the tropical forest canopy. While not as diverse as unspoiled forest, this canopy provides much better habitat for birds than coffee grown in the sun on large plantations dependent on pesticides. It is a safe bet that coffee labeled as organically grown is shade-grown coffee.

- Avoid purchasing tropical hardwoods. Rainforests fall in the harvesting of a few mahogany trees. Seek out "certified" wood that has been harvested responsibly.

- Leave wild birds in the wild. Don't purchase pets caught in the wild, including tropical birds and birds of prey captured for the medieval practice of falconry. True respect for a wild bird includes respect for its freedom.

- Reduce, recycle, reuse. Trees (bird homes) are cut down to make paper. Choose recycled paper. Avoid products with excessive packaging. Buy in bulk. Recycle all paper and anything else when possible. Stop junk mail by subscribing to the Direct Marketing Association's Mail Preference Service (P.O. Box 9008, Farmingdale, New York 11735-9008 or <www.the-dma.org>). Also use any junk mail's enclosed postage-paid envelope to return your mailing label along with a request to be removed from the mailing list.

- Curb fossil fuel consumption. Energy use contributes to global climate change and habitat destruction. Hang clothes on a line rather than burning fuel to dry them. Turn lights and appliances off when not in use. Carpool or bicycle to work or birdwatching areas. Consider gas mileage before purchasing a vehicle.

Keep Track of Birds

- Survey bird populations. Birds are conspicuous and excellent indicators of environmental health. Christmas Bird Counts, breeding bird surveys and atlases, and other population studies monitor trends and can call attention to environmental problems. Volunteer survey opportunities are mentioned in "Resources" at the back of this book, and the Christmas Bird Count is described on page 19.

- Report encounters with rare or banded birds. Statewide birding organizations or committees keep track of rare bird sightings. ("Rare" birds are those that have a limited population or occur outside, or on the periphery of, their ranges.) In Vermont rare birds can be documented and reported to the Vermont Bird Records Committee, c/o the Vermont Institute of Natural Science in Woodstock (see "Resources"). Birds marked with identifying leg or neck bands can be reported to the United States Geological Survey's Bird Banding Laboratory (see "Resources"). Researchers, and conservation efforts, can benefit from reports of rare or banded birds.

Get Involved

- Support conservation organizations with time and money. They protect and preserve habitats, represent many voices (including those of birds), and offer ample opportunities for volunteers. These organizations can even include hunting groups or clubs, whose members know well the value of habitat preservation. After all, there can be no ducks to hunt without the habitat to support them. Several active conservation organizations are listed in "Resources."

- Speak out for conservation: options include letters to the editor or lawmakers, lobbying for conservation laws (such as the state and federal endangered species acts), or simply talking to friends and family about the importance of wildlife in wild places.

Can one person make a difference? Consider this example: An eleven-year-old boy and his friend came upon a lump of feathers in the woods. They assumed the bird was dead. When the boys took a closer look and began petting its feathers, the bird, a Northern Flicker, burst to life and flew away. It startled one of the boys, but that chance encounter also sparked a fascination with birds that lasted his lifetime. That boy was Roger Tory Peterson, who by sharing his love for birds and the wild places they inhabit became one of the twentieth century's most important conservationists. All lovers of birds have an opportunity to make a contribution of their own.

BIRDWATCHING AREAS

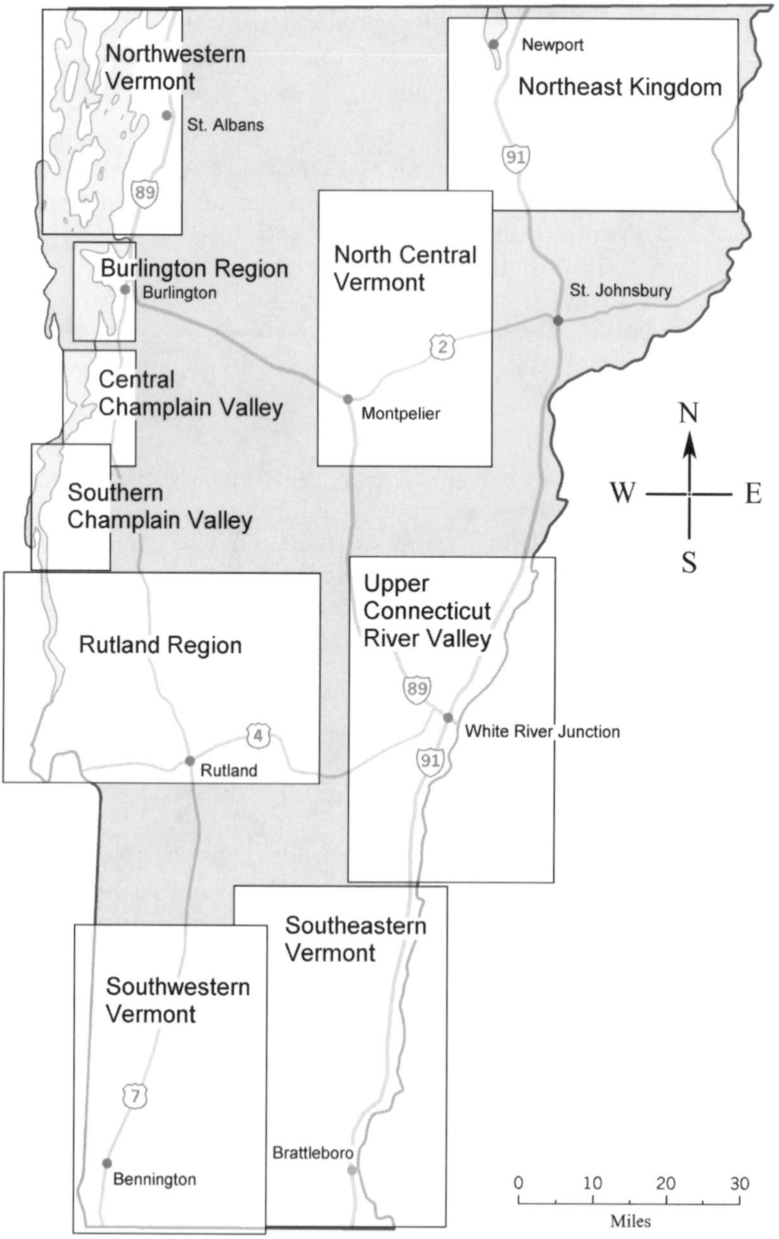

Northwestern Vermont
St. Albans
89

Newport
Northeast Kingdom
91
St. Johnsbury

Burlington Region
Burlington

North Central Vermont
2
Montpelier

Central Champlain Valley

Southern Champlain Valley

N
W — E
S

Rutland Region

Upper Connecticut River Valley
89
91
White River Junction

4
Rutland

Southwestern Vermont
7
Bennington

Southeastern Vermont

Brattleboro

0   10   20   30
Miles

CHAPTER 4

Birdwatching Areas

Beyond the feeder in the front yard or the woods out back lies a landscape rich with the color and chorus of birds. Here are the paths to those birds. They are for the most part well-worn roads, trails, and waterways notable for their convenience, public access, and diversity of birds. They are the pleasant dwelling places of birds and nice locations in their own right.

But they are hardly the only places to find birds in Vermont. Birds can turn up virtually anywhere, and no guide can account for or predict all the inclinations of creatures that fly. Some birdwatchers will be justly disappointed to find their favorite sites missing. Yet the limitations inherent in this book only underscore one of birdwatching's true delights—that birds are surprises with wings. Birdwatchers who follow paths not described here will no doubt find rewards of their own, feathered and otherwise.

In this guide, Vermont is divided into ten regions. They are included in a counterclockwise sweep of the state, beginning in northwestern Vermont and ending in the Northeast Kingdom. Each is not a distinct biophysical region. To the contrary, many span more than one biophysical zone and include many habitats. Instead, the ten regions, each containing a cluster of bird-watching sites, were chosen for their fairly even distribution across Vermont.

Within each region are many places to visit for birds. Each birdwatching area description includes directions from major roadways. The species listed for each location represent only a sampling of those that occur. They are either representatives of a location's habitats (see "Habitats and Their Birds," page 3), noteworthy specialties for a given site, or rarities worth mentioning.

Not one of these regions can be thoroughly covered in a single morning or even a full day. To the contrary, rather than rushing from place to place hoping for better birds to come, birdwatchers are encouraged to linger in these

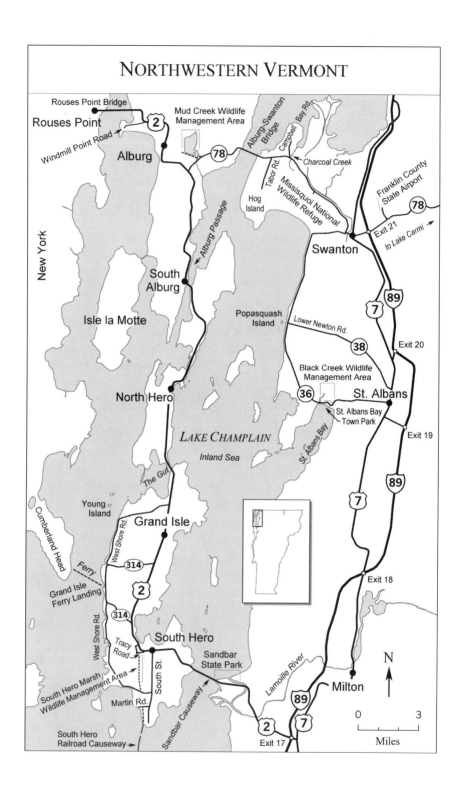

NORTHWESTERN VERMONT

Rouses Point Bridge

Rouses Point

Mud Creek Wildlife
Management Area

Windmill Point Road

Alburg

2

78

Alburg-Swanton
Bridge

Campbell Bay Rd.

Tabor Rd.

Charcoal Creek

Franklin County
State Airport

Mississquoi National
Wildlife Refuge

78

Hog
Island

Exit 21

to Lake Carmi

Swanton

New York

Alburg Passage

South
Alburg

Popasquash
Island

Lower Newton Rd.

7

89

Isle la Motte

38

Exit 20

Black Creek Wildlife
Management Area

36

St. Albans

North Hero

St. Albans Bay
Town Park

LAKE CHAMPLAIN

Exit 19

Inland Sea

St. Albans Bay

The Gut

89

Young
Island

7

Cumberland Head

West Shore Rd.

Grand Isle

Ferry

314

Exit 18

Grand Isle
Ferry Landing

2

314

West Shore Rd.

South Hero

Tracy
Road

Sandbar
State Park

N

South St.

Larmoille River

South Hero Marsh
Wildlife Management Area

Martin Rd.

Milton

0   3

Sandbar Causeway

89

South Hero
Railroad Causeway

2

7

Miles

Exit 17

Snowy Owls regularly invade Vermont from the north in early winter. Some, like this individual in Charlotte, remain until early spring.
Photo: Ted Murin

places—to park the car, escape the computer-paced rush of life, and gaze long at birds and their surroundings. After all, these are the special places birds occupy—both in the habitats of Vermont and in the hearts of its bird-watchers.

Northwestern Vermont

The Northwest is Vermont's island paradise. Lake Champlain, its odd-shaped islands, and its expansive wetlands attract waterfowl, shorebirds, gulls, terns, and marsh species. East of the lake, dairy farms carve wide openings in the northern hardwood forests, creating good habitat for songbird diversity. But what makes northwestern Vermont most appealing to bird and birdwatcher alike is the lure of Lake Champlain. Its north-south orientation offers an irresistible route for migrants. And its scenery is some of New England's finest.

The Champlain Islands

A trip to "the islands" often evokes images of palm trees and sandy beaches. Vermont's islands offer their own charm without a single coconut. This is one of the best places in Vermont to see waterfowl in spring as birds follow the receding ice northward. (For a sense of the waterfowl species here, see "The Bridges of Grand Isle County," page 41.)

Begin an island tour at the mile-long **Sandbar Causeway**, which connects South Hero to Milton at the southern end of the Inland Sea. (The Inland Sea is the portion of Lake Champlain east of the Champlain Islands and north of the Sandbar Causeway.) Parking lots are available along the causeway toward the eastern end and at a fishing access at the eastern end opposite the state park entrance (watch the traffic). Osprey nest here. Waterfowl, including Ring-necked Duck, infiltrate the area near the fishing access in April. And in October and November migrating waterfowl intermittently include scoters and Long-tailed Duck. From Interstate 89, take Exit 17 to Route 2 west for 5 miles to the causeway. **Sandbar State Park**, at the eastern end of the causeway, can be good for small numbers of migrating passerines and shorebirds, but birds don't typically linger.

An island highlight is the old **South Hero Railroad Causeway** connecting South Hero to Colchester. Birding from the causeway is like standing in the middle of Lake Champlain, with the Green Mountains rising to the east and the Adirondacks to the west. Strong lake currents moving through cuts in the causeway slow the formation of ice in winter and hasten its retreat in spring, creating a refuge for waterfowl. Visit from November through April, provided there is open water (late March and early April are best). With few exceptions, most of the ducks seen on Lake Champlain can be found here, along with Common Loon, grebes, and gulls. Less frequent visitors include Red-throated Loon, Redhead, and Canvasback (usually in spring), Bald Eagle, Gyrfalcon (rare), and Iceland and Glaucous Gulls. This is the best place in the islands to enjoy waterfowl without the vehicle traffic.

To reach the causeway from Route 2 in the village of South Hero, drive south on South Street for 2.5 miles and turn right on Martin Road. The old railroad bed, appearing as a single-lane dirt road, is about 0.4 mile ahead on the left. Park along the shoulder of Martin Road. Walk 0.8 mile to the start of the causeway and another 0.5 mile to the cut (there is no bridge). Spring rains and snowmelt can turn the railroad bed into a streambed. The walk can range from a moderate challenge to a Navy Seal training course. Brush and poison ivy can also complicate circumnavigation of the puddles. But the ducks and the view make it worth the walk. With heavy snow this is a pleasant cross-country ski outing. An alternative approach is to walk the causeway from the south (see "Colchester Railroad Causeway," page 47).

Although the Champlain Islands are famous for ducks, an excellent spot for viewing landbirds from spring through fall is **South Hero Marsh Wildlife Management Area**. From the sharp bend on Route 2 at the western end of South Hero village, turn south on Tracy Road. After 0.2 mile cross the wetland and enter the parking lot on the left. Walk an old railroad bed south through a swamp of silver maple, green ash, and American elm that opens into a cattail marsh in less than a mile. The open areas are particularly popular with migrating sparrows in October. Yellow-rumped Warbler flocks move through from late September into early October, occasionally harboring Palm Warbler and, rarely, Orange-crowned Warbler.

The **Grand Isle Ferry Landing,** depicted on many maps as "Gordon Land-

Birds spend a fair amount of time at rest. This female Mallard remains wary while conserving calories on the Lake Champlain shoreline in Grand Isle. Photo: Ted Murin

ing," can be another good waterfowl spot from November through April—best in years when the bulk of the lake freezes over and the ferry keeps the channel open. This can also be a good location to witness the spectacle of migration on Lake Champlain. (For more about migration watching and the Grand Isle Ferry Landing, see "Lakewatching on Lake Champlain, page 24.) A small restaurant with restrooms (which closes mid-afternoon in wintertime) is located at the ferry landing. To reach the ferry continue north from South Hero on Route 2, take Route 314 west, and follow the signs. Park at a small state-owned lot just north of the ferry access on the lake side of Route 314. (From the ferry landing, enterprising duck fans can also travel south, checking the coves along **West Shore Road** for migratory and wintering waterfowl.)

From the ferry landing continue north on Route 314 for about 1 mile. Turn north at a sharp bend onto West Shore Road and look for the boat launch 1.3 miles ahead on the left. Either launch a boat or point a spotting scope toward two islands to the north. **Young Island** and nearby Bixby Island comprise the Sister Islands. Young, also known as South Sister, harbors the largest "seabird" nesting colonies in Vermont, mostly Ring-billed Gull and Double-crested Cormorant as well as Herring Gull and a few Great Black-backed Gulls. This maritime scene, unique in Vermont (except on the Discovery channel), is best observed by boat. Beware the shallow reefs around each island, not to mention the eye-opening aroma on the lee side of Young. (Note that Young Island is posted and Bixby is private, preventing a landing on either one.) The islands are also popular with shorebirds in migration, especially in late summer. WARNING: Approach boating the "Broad Lake" with due respect as boats here are exposed to the full beauty, fickleness, and fury of Lake Champlain.

Continue north on Route 2 to a drawbridge between the islands of North

The Bridges of Grand Isle County

One sure way to find waterfowl on Lake Champlain in early spring is to locate the interface of water and ice. As the ice mass breaks up and recedes northward, ducks in migration can be found pressing the water's edge. The same narrows that appeal to bridge builders cause strong, waterfowl-friendly currents that resist ice buildup and promote thawing. Even though birders must share space with vehicles, these bridges and adjacent causeways (and even a ferry landing) are convenient for watching the wild world of webbed feet. Described elsewhere in this chapter, these vantages include Sandbar Causeway, South Hero Railroad Causeway, Grand Isle Ferry Landing, The Gut, Alburg Passage, Rouses Point Bridge, and the Alburg-Swanton Bridge.

WARNING: Spotting scopes in this territory are mandatory and a birdwatcher here need only consider three thoughts: traffic, ducks, and traffic. Never set up on the roadway. Park at designated spots and always remember to look both ways (for vehicles, not ducks) *before* crossing.

The best times to see birds at these bridges are in March and April as ducks gather in open pockets of water, and to a lesser degree from October through December as ducks head south and gulls stage in the Inland Sea.

The spring pile of ducks found at these bridges and throughout Lake Champlain begins with a substrate of Common Goldeneye and Common Merganser and a liberal layer of American Black Duck, Mallard, Ring-necked Duck, Greater Scaup, Lesser Scaup, and Bufflehead. Added to these are (fairly common) Wood Duck, Gadwall, American Wigeon, Northern Pintail, Green-winged Teal, Hooded Merganser, Red-breasted Merganser; and (uncommon to rare) Eurasian Wigeon, Blue-winged Teal, Northern Shoveler, Canvasback, Redhead, all three scoter species, Barrow's Goldeneye, and Ruddy Duck. As fields and wetlands thaw, the dabblers of this crew gradually desert the lake for those calmer accommodations.

Hero and Grand Isle. The water to the west of the bridge, named (not quite poetically) for its shape, is called "**The Gut.**" Pull-offs are on the east side of Route 2 beyond either end of the bridge. The viewing here is best in morning to avoid the sun's glare. While The Gut offers some of the islands' most reliable waterfowl watching (see "The Bridges of Grand Isle County" above), birds are often far out on the lake.

The Champlain Islands tour ends with a stop at the Route 2 bridge over **Alburg Passage**, the waterway between South Alburg and the island of North Hero. Park at a small pull-off on the south side of the road west of the bridge. The narrow passage is a pseudo-refuge for waterfowl because boats can't get through until the ice at each end melts. Typically, when the ice plugs go, so go the ducks. The dirt road south of the parking area along the western side of the passage can be very good for viewing ducks, though muddy during spring. This is one of the favorite gathering places on the lake of Ring-necked Duck in spring.

Rouses Point Bridge

The Rouses Point Bridge spans Lake Champlain between Alburg, Vermont, and Rouses Point, New York. Driving west on the causeway along Route 2, approaching the bridge, park in a lot on the right and scope there for ducks. In May and early June Cliff Swallows gobble mud from the parking lot and carry it to use in the construction of their gourdlike nests on the sides of the bridge. About 1 mile east of the bridge, at a big bend in Route 2, turn onto **Windmill Point Road** and follow it a short way to a wetland. This spot hosts migrant songbirds, resident Common Snipe, and perhaps the densest population of nesting Yellow Warblers in the solar system.

Mud Creek Wildlife Management Area

One of Vermont's largest cattail marshes, Mud Creek Wildlife Management Area is also one of the most accessible. An abandoned railroad bed through the marsh is the pathway to a wet and wild wetland experience. Best visited from April through October, the marsh is on full display in May. It is an excellent place for a long, slow visit. (The railroad bed is closed in the morning during portions of the duck hunting season in fall.)

Mud Creek is located on Route 78 about 2 miles west of the Alburg-Swanton Bridge or 0.8 miles east of the intersection of Route 2 and Route 78. The entrance is at a curve in the road a few tenths of a mile east of the official state fishing access. There is usually room to park a few cars if the gate is closed. The railroad bed, rechristened the Alburg Recreation Path, can be found at the left end of the parking lot (watch for poison ivy here).

The maple-ash swamps, cattail marsh, and open water attract a diversity of waterfowl, marsh birds, and landbirds, including Pied-billed Grebe and Wood Duck, Ring-necked Duck (during migrations), Green Heron, Least Bittern (rare), Northern Harrier, American Bittern, Virginia Rail, Sora, Black Tern, and Rusty Blackbird (best found in the swamp south of the railroad bed during migration in April and October). Mud Creek is also one of Vermont's most dependable spots for Common Moorhen, particularly at the southwest corner of the marsh. During springtime swallows and Purple Martins swoop and swirl above as Baltimore Orioles and Yellow Warblers glow and fill the refuge with vibrant song. Watch also for Red-shouldered Hawk, Bald Eagle (uncommon), and resident Great Horned Owl.

Missisquoi National Wildlife Refuge and Hog Island

Encompassing nearly 6,000 acres at the mouth of the Missisquoi River, **Missisquoi National Wildlife Refuge**, Vermont's first national wildlife refuge, is a wetland wonderland. It hosts Vermont's largest Great Blue Heron rookery and Black Tern colony, as well as a healthy population of Pied-billed Grebe. And no other place in Vermont is as welcoming to migrating and nesting waterfowl. Spring and fall are the best times to visit, fall in particular for waterfowl. A boat affords the full Missisquoi experience, particularly for shorebirds. Hunting is permitted seasonally in the refuge.

To reach the refuge from Interstate 89, take Exit 21 in Swanton to Route 78 west and drive 3.4 miles to the refuge headquarters on the left. (Along the way, at the Swanton village green, turn right, cross the bridge over the Missisquoi River, and bear right again to stay on Route 78.)

Huge sections of the refuge are closed to visitors (it is a refuge, after all), and much of the Missisquoi delta is accessible by boat only. Birders on foot do have options, however. A kiosk at the rear of the headquarters parking lot contains refuge information and maps. A 1.5-mile nature trail, open the entire year from dawn to dusk, leaves the parking lot and passes through a floodplain. From April through May a walk along this trail can be soggy but delightful—the possibilities range from woodcock to warblers to Wood Duck.

To reach another spot on solid ground continue west on Route 78 for 2.4 miles. The bridge over **Charcoal Creek** crosses to Hog Island, which is the westernmost area of Swanton. Turn right just past the bridge onto Campbell Bay Road and park immediately on the left. WARNING: The raging current of cars and trucks on Route 78 here can be hazardous to a birdwatcher's health. However, this is probably the best place in Vermont to see Black Tern, which nests on the marsh on the north side of the road. Osprey also nests here, and waterfowl can be abundant during migration in April, October, and November.

From Campbell Bay Road continue west on Route 78 for 0.9 mile and turn left on **Tabor Road**. Cross the railroad tracks and locate a tiny pull-off for parking on the left. From late March through April, the field to the west, if flooded, can attract an excellent diversity of dabbling ducks, particularly Mallard, American Black Duck, Gadwall, Northern Pintail, Green-winged Teal, American Wigeon, and Eurasian Wigeon (rare). Look for Wood Duck toward the back among the trees. With sufficient floodwater, diving ducks here can include Ring-necked Duck, Common Goldeneye, and Bufflehead.

Birding Missisquoi by Boat

Refuge visitors with a boat can either dabble or adventure. The adventurous will enjoy one of Vermont's finest birding experiences along a 10-mile canoe loop. In June and July it passes the state's largest Great Blue Heron rookery and signature wetland species, including Osprey, Virginia Rail, Belted Kingfisher (abundant), Marsh Wren, Northern Waterthrush, and Swamp Sparrow. Breeding ducks along the loop include Green-winged Teal (uncommon), Blue-winged Teal, Wood Duck, Common Goldeneye, and Hooded Merganser (uncommon). In late summer through fall the same canoe route can be a shorebird extravaganza, particularly in a dry year when the lake level drops to expose mud flats. Some of the best shorebirding in Vermont is at the mouths of Dead Creek and the Missisquoi River. Most any shorebird found in the state can occur here.

To begin the canoe loop from the refuge headquarters, drive west on Route 78 for 1.3 miles to a boat launch into the Missisquoi River on the right. The route heads out the river toward the heron rookery on Metcalfe and Shad Islands, and then into Missisquoi Bay and returns via Dead Creek (at the eastern edge of the refuge) and back on the Missisquoi River to the boat launch. WARNING: This is a substantial amount of paddling in a sea kayak and a full day in a canoe. Don't go without a map. And don't bother going during hunting season, which varies from year to year—check dates with headquarters in advance of your trip. By the way, this canoe route is prime habitat for the endangered spiny softshell turtle, which suns itself on logs near the shoreline. View the turtles from a distance so as not so scare them from their basking logs.

The less adventurous can explore the wetlands in more relaxed fashion by putting in at Charcoal Creek, which is 2.4 miles west of the refuge headquarters on Route 78 at the intersection of Campbell Bay Road. (Access to the river, down a steep bank without a ramp, is for hand-carried boats only.) The channel through the marsh to the north leads to the open lake and to Shad and Metcalfe Islands, in case high adventure beckons. This is one of the few places the declining Black Tern nests in Vermont, so please give them plenty of elbow room by remaining in the channel. Access to Charcoal Creek south of Route 78 is prohibited. Easy access to Missisquoi Bay itself and the mouth of Dead Creek is also available at the state boat launch north of Highgate Springs on Route 7 at the mouth of the Rock River.

Canada Goose and American Bittern will sometimes prowl the field as a Northern Harrier hunts from above.

Return to Route 78 and proceed west for about 0.5 mile to the **Alburg-Swanton Bridge**. Before crossing, park at a boat launch on the right. From March through April, as the lake ice breaks and melts, this can be a decent

Green Herons, which lurk and hunt at water's edge, depend on healthy aquatic ecosystems for food. Photo: Roy Pilcher

spot to see scaup and the occasional Snow Goose megaflock off in the distance. In the fall, Common Tern and Bonaparte's Gull will sometimes roost on the railroad trestle south of the bridge between feeding sorties on the lake. Little Gull occasionally cruises by.

St. Albans Bay and Popasquash Island

The quiet **St. Albans Bay** offers two rarities for Lake Champlain, a long, sandy beach and a nesting colony of Common Terns. From mid-August through October this is also one of the best locations on land in Vermont for watching Bonaparte's Gulls and any attendant Little Gulls. A nearby marsh and swamp make St. Albans Bay a worthy place for birds during summer and fall.

To reach the bay from Interstate 89, take Exit 19 in St. Albans. Proceed straight 0.9 mile and turn right on Route 7/South Main Street. Drive 0.7 mile and turn left on Route 36 at a traffic light. Go 2.9 miles to St. Albans Bay. The fishing dock is straight ahead.

The dock is a good place to look over St. Albans Bay. Gulls and terns often congregate on and around the dock and trawl behind feeding flocks of Double-crested Cormorant. Vermont's first Forster's Tern was seen here. The large island in the distance obscures Rock Island, the much tinier home of the Common Terns.

From the dock, continue west on Route 36 for 0.5 mile to the entrance (on the left) to **St. Albans Bay Town Park**. (When the entrance gate is closed, there is ample room to park well off the road.) When the lake level and human activity are low (particularly in late summer or fall), gulls and shorebirds jockey for position on the beach. Hundreds of Bonaparte's Gulls and Ring-billed Gulls often rest and preen on the sandbars. Notable rarities seen here in years past include Black-headed Gull and Western Sandpiper. The cedars at the parking area can attract warbler flocks during fall migration. Another migrant draw is the swampy margin of the marsh, across Route 36, part of **Black Creek Wildlife Management Area**, where Rusty Blackbirds squeak their presence in October.

Return to Route 36 and continue west for 0.3 mile to a small pull-off on the right. This is an excellent location for observing Wood Ducks and other waterfowl in the wetland's open water and a fine vantage point for action over the marsh and bay.

For a closer look (relatively speaking) at a tern nesting island, continue 4.1 miles northwest on Route 36 to its intersection with Route 38/Lower Newton Road. The island on the left is **Popasquash Island**, one of the few Common Tern nesting islands in Lake Champlain. Use a spotting scope to get a decent look. The island is posted to protect the terns (so don't try swimming out for a better view). Caspian Tern has been seen here on several occasions and perhaps nested on the island in 2000.

Franklin County State Airport

The grasslands at this state airport can harbor flying objects of two varieties: stiff-winged and feathered-winged. Grassland specialists here include Horned Lark, Vesper Sparrow, Savannah Sparrow, and the Vermont-threatened Grasshopper Sparrow. "Taping" (the use of recorded bird song) to attract rare species can be construed as harassment and as such is illegal in Vermont. But no instigation is necessary—a leisurely walk along the entrance road from late spring through early summer will usually reveal the Grasshopper Sparrow's insectlike buzzing. From Interstate 89 take Exit 21 in Swanton and go east on Route 78 for 1.1 miles to the airport entrance road on the left.

Lake Carmi State Park

Named for local Civil War veteran Carmi L. Marsh, Lake Carmi (pronounced *Car-my*) alone makes this park attractive to birds. But the bonus here is a 140-acre black spruce-tamarack bog, an interesting exception to the landscape in northwestern Vermont. The best times to visit are during spring and fall migrations.

From the intersection of Route 105 and Route 236 (about 3 miles west of Enosburg Falls and 7 miles south of the Canadian border), head north on Route 236 for 2.9 miles to find the park entrance on the left (not shown on map). Expect to pay an entrance fee from mid-May to Labor Day.

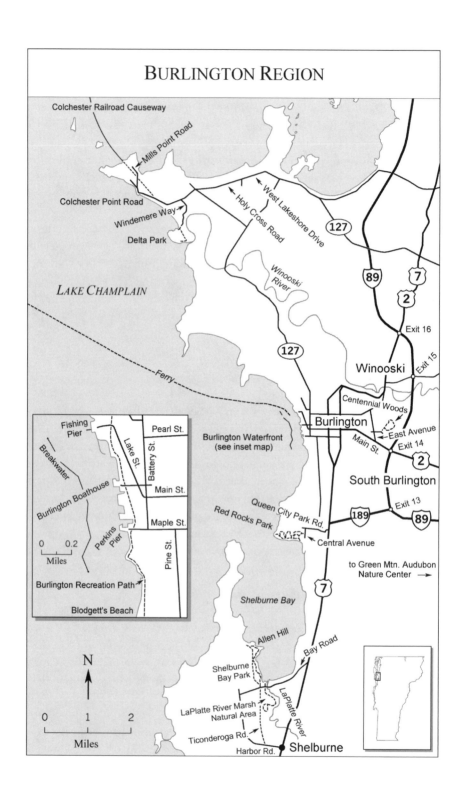

BURLINGTON REGION

Colchester Railroad Causeway

Mills Point Road

West Lakeshore Drive

Colchester Point Road

Holy Cross Road

127

89

7

2

Windemere Way

Delta Park

Winooski River

LAKE CHAMPLAIN

Exit 16

127

Ferry

Winooski

Exit 15

Centennial Woods

Burlington

East Avenue

Main St.

Exit 14

2

Fishing Pier

Pearl St.

Lake St.

Battery St.

Burlington Waterfront
(see inset map)

South Burlington

Breakwater

Main St.

Exit 13

Burlington Boathouse

Maple St.

Queen City Park Rd.

Red Rocks Park

189

89

Perkins Pier

Central Avenue

0   0.2
Miles

Pine St.

to Green Mtn. Audubon
Nature Center →

Burlington Recreation Path

Blodgett's Beach

Shelburne Bay

7

Allen Hill

Bay Road

N

Shelburne
Bay Park

LaPlatte River

LaPlatte River Marsh
Natural Area

0   1   2
Miles

Ticonderoga Rd.

Harbor Rd.

Shelburne

The varied habitats in this state park have hosted a dazzling diversity of birds over the years, including Black Scoter, Least Bittern, Northern Saw-whet Owl, Three-toed Woodpecker, Blue-gray Gnatcatcher, and Eastern Towhee. Most bird activity is at the southern end of the park, along the campsite access road near the bog—a popular spot for migrant warblers and wetland species. Vehicle access to the road, however, is generally limited to campers only. But ask at the entrance booth for permission to drive toward the camping area and bog. To get there turn left onto the campsite road just beyond the entrance station. Otherwise continue on the main park road, park at the boat launch ahead, and walk back to the campsite road and bog. (Birdwatching is allowed past the "campers only" sign.)

In April and October migrant waterfowl stop on the lake. Later in spring thrushes and other songbirds frequent the camping area along the lake's southern edge. A nature trail toward the mouth of Marsh Brook leaves from the day use area north of the boat launch.

Campsites are available in the park. Other amenities include swimming, boating, fishing, and restrooms (in season).

🖊 *Burlington Region*

From Colchester Point to Shelburne Bay, Vermont's most developed and populous region offers excellent birdwatching. The Lake Champlain flyway certainly contributes to this apparent contradiction, and Burlington itself probably plays a part as well. Its urban landscape squeezes landbirds into the oases of city parks. And its tame waterfront birds advertise safe harbor to others moving through. Also part of this region is one of Vermont's great rivers, the Winooski, which empties into Lake Champlain and forms a delta north of Burlington. In spite of its traffic and sprawl, the Burlington region is an exceptional year-round birding destination for warbler fallouts in spring, wandering herons in summer, shorebirds in fall, waterfowl and gulls in winter, and rarities at any time.

Colchester Railroad Causeway

The Colchester Railroad Causeway is an excellent way to venture out onto Lake Champlain with neither a boat nor the ability to walk on water. With the tracks removed, the causeway is now a public recreation path. And from November through April, depending entirely on ice conditions, it becomes a three-mile-long, front-row seat to one of the best duck shows in Vermont. The causeway is a wonderful place for a walk. Pack a lunch, spend the day, and enjoy the show.

From Interstate 89 take Exit 16 and go north on Route 2/Route 7 for 1.7 miles to Route 127. Turn left on Route 127. After 3.7 miles, where Route 127 turns left, continue straight on West Lakeshore Drive (which soon changes its name to Holy Cross Road) for 1.9 miles to a four-way stop. Continue straight through yet another name change onto Colchester Point Road and go 1.5 miles to Mills Point Road, forking to the right. Drive 0.2 mile on Mills Point Road to a parking lot on the right. Mills Point Road crosses the railroad bed just beyond the parking lot.

The railroad bed to the right can lead to an earful of Northern Water-thrush in May. The main attraction, however, is the railroad bed to the left, which leads to the southern end of the causeway. The southern cut in the causeway, about 1.2 miles from the parking lot, has a bridge; the northern cut, about 1.6 miles beyond that, does not. (See "South Hero Railroad Causeway," page 38, for access to the other end.)

From early winter to early spring—as long as the water remains open—most species of waterfowl found on Lake Champlain can be found here. Patience and persistence may reveal a Barrow's Goldeneye among the large numbers of Common Goldeneye lingering in deeper waters. Male golden-eyes, their hormones ablaze, perform whiplash-threatening courtship dis-plays all winter. Common Merganser also overwinters here, along with a shifting mix of American Black Duck, Mallard, Ring-necked Duck, Greater Scaup, Lesser Scaup (to a lesser extent), and Bufflehead.

From late March to early April the feathered activity heats up with warmer weather and melting ice. Often centered around the causeway cuts, where strong currents accelerate melting, the birds swell in number, particularly Ring-necked Duck and both scaup species. This is also one of the best places in Vermont to see Canvasback and Redhead in spring. And if the ice on Lake Champlain had been extensive, a good variety of dabbling ducks join the fray. The causeway is also a fine place to view the spring waterfowl migration in action, with tremendous lines of northbound Snow Geese and Canada Geese arrayed overhead. (One of the authors of this book had the great honor of being bombed at this very spot with fresh, green Snow Goose manure—a certain sign of spring.) Killdeer, Snow Bunting, and blackbirds often pass by on their way north as well.

Closer to shore, where the lake is shallow, mud flats exposed in dry years will attract waders and shorebirds from August through October. This weedy area is also popular with dabbling ducks—and duck hunters—in the fall.

Binoculars will work here, but spotting scopes were designed for places like this. Snowshoes or cross-country skis can be helpful in winter. If the wind is blowing anywhere in the known universe, it will be blowing more than that here. So if it is very windy, consider saving this place for another day.

Delta Park

The public park at the mouth of the Winooski River offers birds and birders a variety of habitats: a delta, a marsh, woods, and a sandy beach. Warblers and other landbirds move through the woods during migrations in May, September, and October. Shorebirds can visit the mud flats in late May and from July through September. Waterfowl gather out on the lake in late fall and, from late March through April, tend to congregate at the mouth of the river.

To reach the park, see the directions to the Colchester Railroad Causeway above. From the four-way stop where Holy Cross Road changes to Colchester Point Road, drive 0.4 mile on Colchester Point Road to Windemere Way. Turn left onto Windemere Way and drive 0.6 mile to a state boat launch parking lot on the left. The entrance to the park and a small parking area are just beyond that on the left. (Note that because the land use at Delta Park is undergoing changes, access to birding here is subject to change.)

From the park entrance, walk a short path west to the lake (in spring look for songbirds on the way). In spring and fall scan the lake for shorebirds and investigate the shrubs for Yellow-rumped Warbler, Palm Warbler (uncommon), and sparrows. A variety of waterfowl gather here in fall, from Wood Duck to scaup. Rarer appearances on the fall guest list have included sharp-tailed sparrow species in the marsh, a Connecticut Warbler skulking the undergrowth, Forster's Tern hunting the shallows, Tundra Swan grazing the lake-bottom, and Ruddy Turnstone, Red Knot, Stilt Sandpiper, Buff-breasted Sandpiper, and Lapland Longspur walking the water's edge.

Follow the trail south toward the mouth of the Winooski River. Along the way, in spring and fall, look for kinglets, vireos, warblers, sparrows, and other migrants. At the mouth of the river, watch for waterfowl in early spring and shorebirds on any exposed mud during late summer and fall. Be advised that park visitors can inadvertently scatter the shorebirds, so arrive before they do. Note that this park can be dense with mosquitoes in spring (hey, birds and frogs need to eat too). And seeing that this is a river delta, be aware that the park can be flooded in wet springs.

Burlington Waterfront

Vermont's largest city offers some of the state's best birdwatching from October through April. A beach, open water, and limited opportunities for duck hunting combine to attract shorebirds, gulls, and waterfowl. Burlington's highly developed shoreline—its boathouse, recreation path, ferry landing, and pier—offers full access to the lake. The birds here tend to be habituated to people, and comfortable birds seem to entice even more birds to drop in for a visit. The waterfront is a perfect place for beginners to get acquainted with less bashful birds and for the experienced to study the endless variation of gull plumages and the occasional, but regular, rarity. The waterfront is best explored on foot.

To reach the waterfront from Interstate 89 take Exit 14W onto Route 2 West. Drive on Route 2 (Main Street) about 1.8 miles to its end at Battery Street. Parking can be found (or filled up) throughout the Battery Street area, but one of the best places is Perkins Pier. Turn left on Battery Street, drive 0.3 mile, and turn right on Maple Street to the pier parking lot. If this lot is full, from the Main Street and Battery Street intersection go west (toward the lake). The road immediately bends north and the Burlington Boathouse appears 0.1 mile ahead on the left. Parking might be found here, or by continuing north along Lake Street 0.4 mile to the Fishing Pier. Expect to pay a fee to park during the warmer months.

The Burlington Recreation Path (locally called the "bike path") connects the waterfront's several vantages (watch for bicyclists and in-line skaters). **Blodgett's Beach** to the south provides the only shorebird habitat and can brim with waterfowl and gulls. **Perkins Pier**, about one-half mile north of Blodgett's, offers a good view of the long breakwater's southern half and panhandling ducks and gulls among the docks. The **Burlington Boathouse**, 0.4 miles farther north, provides a feel of the sea as it sways on its barge foundation. The boathouse's second floor is a fine spot to set up out of the wind and scope gulls on or past the breakwater. And the **Fishing Pier**, another 0.4 mile farther north (between public works buildings just north of the Coast Guard station), provides a more intimate look at the northern end of the breakwater. North of the Fishing Pier the Recreation Path passes through wooded habitat with a nice mix of landbirds during spring and fall migrations.

During the shorebird migration from late July through October Blodgett's Beach provides some of Vermont's more reliable habitat. The beach property in front of the Blodgett Oven Company is private but can be viewed through the lens of a spotting scope from the recreation path. The sand and muddy margins here are popular with Vermont's more common shorebirds and some less common species—such as Ruddy Turnstone and Sanderling— that use small Champlain islands during migration. Shorebirds can also blend into the small rock breakwaters extending from and lying just off the beach—one of the few places in Vermont to see Purple Sandpiper (rare) from shore.

From October through April, as long as the water remains open, the waterfront is one of the best places in Vermont to view gulls. A considerable turnover of migrating Herring Gull and Great Black-backed Gull peaks on or

American Black Duck and Mallard occasionally hybridize. This hybrid female watches over her precocious young.
Photo: Dave Hoag

around the first week of December, coinciding with occasional visits by Iceland Gull and Glaucous Gull. Ring-billed Gull is common here year-round. In October Bonaparte's Gull and an occasional Little Gull feed in the broad lake beyond the breakwater. Lesser Black-backed Gull and Thayer's Gull (usually among Herring and Great Black-backed) and Black-legged Kittiwake (usually with Bonaparte's) are rare.

From October through April, again while the water remains liquid, the waterfront is also a major waterfowl hangout. The biggest congregation of birds usually feeds off Blodgett's Beach northward to the sewage treatment plant, although ducks can be seen, as if strewn about, most anywhere. Regular visitors include Mallard and American Black Duck, which have recently taken to diving for zebra mussels, with smaller numbers of Common Loon (farther offshore), Common Goldeneye, Bufflehead, and Common Merganser. They are occasionally joined by Red-necked Grebe, Canada Goose, Gadwall, Northern Pintail, American Wigeon, both scaup species, Barrow's Goldeneye, Long-tailed Duck, all three scoter species, Red-breasted Merganser, and American Coot.

Finally, with its bustling birdlife the waterfront inevitably attracts birds hungry for other birds, such as Peregrine Falcon, Merlin, Bald Eagle, and, rarely, Gyrfalcon. This is one of the best places in Vermont to see Snowy Owl, usually pausing on the breakwater in November or December as it drifts south. Occasionally a Snowy Owl, finding the waterfront a nice alternative to tundra life, will settle in for a while.

Red Rocks Park

This park of mixed woods at the northern end of Shelburne Bay is named for the reddish Monkton quartzite forming cliffs along the Lake Champlain shoreline here. The property's former owner cleared carriage roads so that his ill daughter could enjoy the woods and views of the lake by pony-drawn carriage. Nowadays birdwatchers stroll those paths looking for warblers and other songbirds. Red Rocks Park is one of the Champlain Valley's hot spots for the spring songbird migration. During a fallout in May between fifteen and twenty warbler species can show up in a single morning. (Spring fallouts tend to happen here after overnight rains.) In total, nearly 150 species have been recorded in this small park in recent years. Red Rocks is a popular dog-walking park, so birdwatchers are advised to watch their step as they watch the birds.

From Route 7 (Shelburne Road) just south of its intersection with Interstate 189, take Queen City Park Road west. After 0.1 mile turn right to remain on Queen City Park Road. Continue for another 0.4 mile, turn left on Central Avenue, and watch for the park entrance 0.1 mile ahead on the right. From June through September enter the park and pay a fee. During the off season park on Central Avenue.

Most of the warblers found in Vermont pass through Red Rocks in May, including Golden-winged (rare), Tennessee, Orange-crowned (rare), Nashville, Northern Parula, Yellow, Chestnut-sided, Magnolia, Cape May (uncommon), Black-throated Blue, Yellow-rumped, Black-throated Green, Blackburnian, Pine, Palm (uncommon), Bay-breasted (uncommon), Blackpoll, Cerulean (rare), Black-and-white, American Redstart, Ovenbird, Northern Waterthrush (around the shallow pond northwest of the entrance), Mourning (uncommon), Common Yellowthroat (uncommon), Wilson's (rare), and Canada. The park is also vigorous with vireos in migration, including Yellow-throated (rare), Blue-headed, Warbling, Philadelphia (uncommon), and Red-eyed. Thrushes, including Veery, Gray-cheeked (rare), Swainson's (uncommon), Hermit, Wood, and American Robin, also visit. Pine Warbler, uncommon in northwestern Vermont, nests here. Fish Crow tried to nest in the park in 1998 and 2001.

The best birding here is usually along Central Avenue from Queen City Park Road to the park entrance and, inside the park, along the road and parking lanes from the entrance to the pumphouse. Enter the park and bear left onto the downhill road. The parking lanes branch to the right off this road, and the pumphouse is at the road's end about a quarter mile from the entrance. Migrant flocks tend to wander, and the park is rich with trails and wildflowers, so investigation beyond the pumphouse is also worthwhile. In particular, the western end of the park and the hilltop on the northern side of

These Short-billed Dowitchers, uncommon in Vermont, rest and refuel at Shelburne Bay on the way to their boreal breeding grounds.
Photo: Ted Murin

the park are often popular with birds. From the cliff-top lookouts on the southern edge of the park, affording excellent views of Shelburne Bay, look for occasional Common Loon and ducks during spring and fall.

Shelburne Bay Area

Within walking distance of **Shelburne Bay** is tremendous bird diversity. More than 200 species have been encountered here in recent years. Waterfowl, waders, shorebirds, and swallows attend the bay itself. A nearby river marsh is heron heaven. And a bayside park can harbor songbirds from spring through fall. The best evidence of the bay area's diversity is its list of rarities: Northern Gannet, American White Pelican, Yellow-crowned Night-Heron, Tufted Duck, Common Eider, Black-headed Gull, Red Phalarope, Forster's Tern, and Orange-crowned Warbler.

From the intersection of Interstate 189 and Route 7 (Shelburne Road), reach the bay by driving south on Route 7 for 2.7 miles to Bay Road. (Approaching from the south on Route 7, Bay Road is 1.4 miles north of the bridge over the LaPlatte River.) Drive 0.8 mile west on Bay Road. Immediately after crossing a bridge over the mouth of the LaPlatte, park at a Vermont Fish and Wildlife Department boat launch on the right.

The rock outcropping at shoreline near the boat launch offers a fine view of the bay. In April and from October through December waterfowl and gulls can be abundant. During migration from the last week of April through early May the boat launch is an excellent place to study all varieties of swallows (and Purple Martin) gobbling insects on the wing. This is also a nice spot to see Great Egret (mostly in August) and, rarely, Snowy Egret, Cattle Egret, and

Glossy Ibis feeding in the shallow waters. Black-crowned Night-Heron is a regular visitor, shuttling in late afternoon between feeding areas in the marsh (and farther inland) and nesting sites on New York's Four Brothers Islands to the west. Arrive early because boat traffic here can scatter birds in warmer months. So can duck hunters in fall (usually at dawn). Uncommon ducks visiting the bay in fall include scoters, scaup, Long-tailed Duck, and Ruddy Duck (rare).

Directly across Bay Road from the boat launch parking lot is The Nature Conservancy's **LaPlatte River Marsh Natural Area**. Stop at the kiosk for information and a trail map. The self-guided trail in spring and summer offers views of the river and its residents, including Great Blue Heron, Green Heron, and Black-crowned Night-Heron. (In wet springs the trail will be muddy and can be partially flooded.) The trail ends at a flooded silver maple swamp and cattail marsh. Watch for Wood Duck and woodpeckers such as Red-bellied (rare), Downy, Hairy, Northern Flicker, and Pileated among the swamp's dead maples, and Great Horned Owl in surrounding white pines.

Shelburne Bay's next major attraction is **Shelburne Bay Park**, only 0.1 mile west of the boat launch on Bay Road. The trail leaving the first parking lot winds about a mile to the lake. (A park map is posted at the second lot.) Watch for landbirds in spring and fall and, with an abundant local fruit crop, American Robins and Cedar Waxwings in winter. The **Allen Hill** trail (branching from the main trail) is a short, steep hike to a nice overlook of the bay, sometimes offering closer looks at loons, ducks, and gulls.

Finally, more off the beaten path, locate the trail directly across Bay Road from the Shelburne Bay Park. This is the old **Ticonderoga Road**, a temporary railroad bed built to move the paddle-wheeler *Ticonderoga* from Shelburne Bay to its home at the Shelburne Museum. This trail, along the western edge of the LaPlatte River Marsh Natural Area, connects to Harbor Road about a mile south. It can be overrun with birds from where it abuts the wetland southward, especially sparrows and late warblers in September and October. From late March to early April the start of this trail is a nice place to enjoy at dusk the acrobatic flight display of American Woodcock. Late in May, Willow and Alder Flycatchers can be found along the way.

Centennial Woods

This patch of woods in Burlington west of Interstate 89 can be busy with thrushes, warblers, and other songbirds during spring and fall migrations. Convenient for University of Vermont students, the parking is limited for others. From Interstate 89 take Exit 14W (Burlington), drive about 0.3 mile on Route 2 West (Main Street), and turn right on East Avenue. Drive 0.2 mile, turn right at a light on an unmarked street, and look for one of the precious few parking spaces at the end of the last parking area on the right. (As parking in Burlington is ever-changing, this situation may vary.) The trailhead (and a map) is across the road from the parking lot.

Green Mountain Audubon Nature Center

The Green Mountain Audubon Nature Center in Huntington lies about 17 miles southeast of Burlington. The 255-acre property, run by Audubon Vermont, features a small nature center and a nice network of trails exploring beaver ponds, fields, and upland forest. This diversity of habitats induces a diversity of nesting birds, including Wood Duck, Barred Owl, Pileated Woodpecker, Blackburnian Warbler, Northern Waterthrush, and a forest full of thrushes—namely Veery, Hermit Thrush, and Wood Thrush. The nature center is open year-round, and its bird activity peaks in May. The center's focus is environmental education, offering a variety of programs for adults, children, and the family.

From Route 2 in the center of Richmond, go south on Bridge Street. After crossing the Winooski River turn right at the end of Bridge Street onto Huntington Road. In 4.6 miles turn right onto Sherman Hollow Road. Go about 0.2 mile up the hill to a parking lot on the left beyond a barn (not shown on map). The nature center headquarters (open 8 A.M. to 4 P.M. weekdays) is in the adjacent farmhouse. Call ahead for more information at (802)434-3068 or stop by for a visit.

Central Champlain Valley

Four major rivers course toward Lake Champlain in this small region of Vermont, and a sinuous shoreline forms a complex of small bays and peninsulas. The resulting landscape invites waterfowl and eagles to linger. Here, where Lake Champlain begins to narrow, southbound waterfowl, gulls, and wayward seabirds funnel into view from shore. Mt. Philo offers yet another perspective on the migration as one of Vermont's best spots for watching southbound hawks. The marshes of Little Otter Creek only enhance the scenery and bird diversity. This varied terrain means birds will be flying or swimming here at any time of year.

Charlotte Town Beach

With a stunning view of Lake Champlain and the Adirondacks, a parking lot, lakeside benches, and even a covered bridge, Charlotte Town Beach is

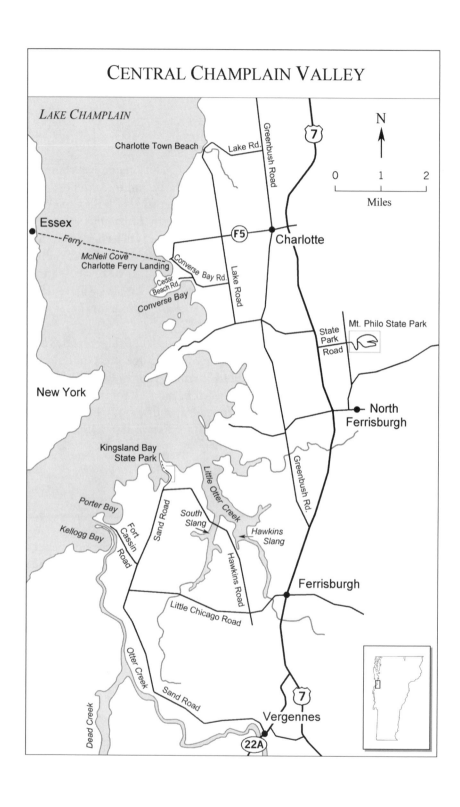

CENTRAL CHAMPLAIN VALLEY

LAKE CHAMPLAIN

Charlotte Town Beach

Lake Rd.

Greenbush Road

7

N

0   1   2

Miles

Essex

Ferry

F5

Charlotte

McNeil Cove
Charlotte Ferry Landing

Converse Bay Rd.

Cedar Beach Rd.

Lake Road

Converse Bay

State Park Road

Mt. Philo State Park

New York

North Ferrisburgh

Kingsland Bay State Park

Little Otter Creek

Porter Bay

Sand Road

South Slang

Hawkins Slang

Greenbush Rd.

Kellogg Bay

Fort Cassin Road

Hawkins Road

Ferrisburgh

Little Chicago Road

Otter Creek

Sand Road

Dead Creek

7

Vergennes

22A

Rarely found in the East, Sabine's Gulls probably visit Lake Champlain in small numbers each fall before wintering at sea. Most visitors, including this bird, are juveniles. Photo: Richard Lavallee

shoreline birdwatching at its finest. The main attractions here are loons, grebes, waterfowl, an occasional shorebird, a window on the fall seabird migration, and some of the nicest sunsets on the planet. The average loon is about one mile from shore here, grebes and ducks about a half mile. While these positions do vary, of course, a spotting scope is always helpful for enjoying the show.

From Route 7 in Charlotte go west on F-5 (toward the ferry dock) for 1.4 miles and turn right on Lake Road. Drive 1.8 miles to a parking lot just beyond a covered bridge. Pay a small fee from about Memorial Day to Labor Day (depending on weather). Restrooms are open during the summer season.

In April assorted waterfowl gather in modest flocks. This is one of the best opportunities in Vermont to see Bufflehead and Red-breasted Mergansers performing courtship displays and Horned Grebe dressed to breed.

From late July through October shorebirds occasionally feed in small numbers on the gravel bar close to shore. Semipalmated Plover, Killdeer, Greater and Lesser Yellowlegs, Semipalmated, Least, and Spotted Sandpiper, and Dunlin are most likely. But also look for Black-bellied Plover, Sanderling, and White-rumped, Baird's, and Pectoral Sandpiper. This same stretch of gravel is popular with American Pipit in September and October. (Note that dogs and people playing close to shore can scatter birds.)

Charlotte Town Beach is also a prime lakewatch spot (late August through November is best) for observing the mass movement of southbound seabirds (loons, gulls, scoters, and other waterfowl in good numbers) as well as jaegers, which are always rare in Vermont. (For more about Charlotte Town Beach and its rare migrants, see "Lakewatching on Lake Champlain," page 24.)

In late fall and winter the open water off the beach oozes with activity (although a little wind and some waves can hide the evidence). This is one of the best sites in Vermont to see Common Loon and Horned Grebe, often joined by Red-necked Grebe, hunting. Waterfowl regulars here include American Black Duck, Mallard, Bufflehead, Common Goldeneye (sometimes in large numbers), and Common Merganser. Joining them periodically are Canada Goose, Barrow's Goldeneye, Red-breasted Merganser, and Hooded Merganser. Small numbers of scaup and scoters are fairly regular as well, and Harlequin Duck has stopped here on several occasions.

The small woods adjoining the parking lot, thick with cedar, can be good for migrant songbirds in spring and fall, particularly both kinglet species and Yellow-rumped Warbler.

McNeil Cove (Charlotte Ferry Landing) and Converse Bay

During much of the winter the ferry crossing Lake Champlain between Charlotte and Essex, New York, is an icebreaker keeping **McNeil Cove** in open water. This cozy and secluded spot is popular with waterfowl, gulls, and an occasional Bald Eagle.

From Route 7 in Charlotte, drive west on F-5 for 2.7 miles (F-5 makes a sharp left at 2.4 miles) to the ferry parking lots and landing. Parking in the lots is for ferry traffic only, but ask at the booth for permission. (The twenty-minute ferry trip across the lake is well worth the price, offering a pelagic fix along with pleasant views of Lake Champlain and a chance to explore the small village of Essex.)

The cove in winter is often bustling with Bufflehead. Look also for Common Loon (uncommon), American Black Duck, Mallard, Ring-necked Duck (spring and fall), both scaup, Common Goldeneye, Common Merganser, Hooded Merganser (hunting crayfish), and Red-breasted Merganser (uncommon). Canvasback, Redhead, Common Eider, and American Coot have put in cameo appearances.

At the ferry parking lot turn southeast onto Converse Bay Road, drive 0.7 mile, and turn right on Cedar Beach Road. A Vermont Fish and Wildlife Department boat launch is 0.3 mile ahead on the left. This is the northern lobe of **Converse Bay**. From late fall through spring, provided there is open water, the aforementioned waterfowl will linger in the bay. Dabblers may be more common here close to the shoreline. Boating and hunter traffic here can empty the bay of its birds.

Mt. Philo State Park

The summit of Mt. Philo, in Vermont's first state park, offers a grand view of the Champlain Valley below and the Adirondacks rising in the distance. That view has changed over the millennia. After the most recent glacial retreat from Vermont about 13,000 years ago, Mt. Philo was an island in an inland sea. Marine sands and fossils can still be found at its base. Today Mt. Philo is not only a stopover for migrant songbirds, it is one of Vermont's premier hawkwatching spots.

From Route 7 about 2.5 miles south of Route F-5 in Charlotte, drive east on State Park Road for 0.6 mile straight into the park entrance. Either park at the bottom and climb a little more than a mile to the top or drive the steep road. Because this is a popular leafpeeping spot, the fee season extends into October (driving or walking). The road is open to vehicles mid-May to mid-October, 10 A.M. to sunset.

In spring consider hiking the road or the trail to the top; the trail begins just uphill from the lower parking lot. Along the way look for scattered flocks of migrants. Mt. Philo used to be a hot spot for migrating warblers and thrushes, but the ice storm of 1998 devastated the forest canopy. Roughly half the trees were damaged and others were clearcut. Where trees once stood, shrubby overgrown areas (particularly on the northeast side) are now more hospitable to Mourning Warblers, Eastern Towhee, and Indigo Bunting. Other migrants linger near the summit and along the summit ridge, which affords nice views of the treetops lower on the mountain. As the forest here regenerates, the throngs of warblers and thrushes are gradually returning, making Mt. Philo a living classroom in forest succession.

From September through November Mt. Philo is hawk heaven, notable for the mass movement of Broad-winged Hawks, mostly from September 7 to September 20. The largest flight of broadwings ever recorded in Vermont happened here on September 16, 1993, when more than 3,500 were counted in a single day. But any eastern hawk species might fly by here, including Golden Eagle (rare), Northern Goshawk (uncommon), and Peregrine Falcon. Mt. Philo is also a great spot to see migrating Bald Eagle and Osprey. Generally in fall most hawks move past the mountain when winds blow from the north. Watch the show from the rock outcropping with a metal railing on the southwest corner of the summit area. (For more about Mt. Philo and hawkwatching in Vermont, see "Hawkwatching," page 21.)

Kingsland Bay Region

Big, slow bends in the Little Otter Creek and several nearby bays in Lake Champlain make this corner of the Champlain lowlands a playground for waterfowl and wetland species. Begin a tour of the region in the center of Ferrisburgh. From Route 7 drive west on Little Chicago Road for 0.9 miles, turn right on Hawkins Road, and drive 1.5 miles to **Hawkins Slang** on the right.

Often eluding the eyes of predators, prey, and birdwatchers, American Bitterns rely on their mastery of camouflage as they hunt in fields and marshes.
Photo: Dave Hoag

Access here is limited, but pull carefully off the road and respect private property. Here at a wide lobe of the Little Otter Creek (and the edge of Little Otter Creek Wildlife Management Area) are typical marsh species, Pied-billed Grebe (uncommon), American Bittern, Virginia Rail, Sora, and Marsh Wren. Wood Duck and Blue-winged Teal nest here, as does Osprey. Hayfields in the neighborhood brim with Bobolinks. And this is where long-time Vermont birdwatcher Bea Guyett, at the age of 90, surprised herself and won the hearts of legions of birdwatchers in June of 2000 when she discovered a Fork-tailed Flycatcher, a visitor from South America.

From Hawkins Slang continue another 0.5 mile to **South Slang**, which has a state boat launch and parking lot just beyond the causeway on the right. Look and listen for many of the same species. (Watch also for abundant pedestrian traffic on the causeway.)

From here continue another 1.4 miles on Hawkins Road to the entrance to **Kingsland Bay State Park** on the right. Drive the half-mile-long entrance road (walk it in winter) into the park. A trail leaves the open area beyond the park buildings and runs 0.4 mile along limestone ledges to a nice view of the lake, with Mt. Philo and the Green Mountains beyond. In March watch for Bald Eagles sitting on the ice in Hawkins Bay or farther north toward Long Point. From fall through spring waterfowl gather in the bay, provided it has open water.

Continue south on Sand Road (Hawkins Road changes names) for another 1.6 miles, turn right on Fort Cassin Road, and continue 0.6 mile to the state parking lot on the right. Spring seems to come early here, with silver maples flowering and northern leopard frogs hopping on warm days in April. Up ahead 0.1 mile is a boat launch into Otter Creek (yes, river otters live there). The causeway beyond leads to a private community (please respect its privacy) at the former site of Fort Cassin. Fort Cassin was built during the War of 1812 to protect ironworks up Otter Creek in Vergennes. In early spring look for Wood Duck, Hooded Merganser, and more common waterfowl toward the mouth of the river and in swampy areas. Later in May resident Blue-gray Gnatcatcher and invading Blackpoll Warbler, Northern Waterthrush, and other migrants lay siege to the silver maple and green ash from the parking lot westward. In winter Bald Eagles sometimes loiter in trees across **Porter Bay** to the north of the causeway or on the ice in **Kellogg Bay** (Fields Bay on some maps) to the south of the causeway and river.

🖋 *Southern Champlain Valley*

No discussion of birdlife in Vermont can understate the value of the bays, waters, wetlands, grasslands, scattered woodlands, and mountaintops of Addison County. Here, near the shores of Lake Champlain, the soils are richer and the climate milder. Dairy farms and their pastures and hay fields offer habitat for grassland bird species. The Dead Creek drifts through this region, nurturing its wetland diversity of waders, shorebirds, and marshbirds. Hawks frequent the open spaces and waterfowl linger on Lake Champlain. This proliferation of birds includes one of Vermont's greatest avian events—the gathering of Snow Geese from October through November. As a result, it is no wonder that more than 80 percent of all bird species recorded in Vermont have appeared in this region at one time or another. For that reason alone, this is one of Vermont's most prolific year-round birdwatching destinations.

Restrooms, gasoline, and food are scarce in this region, with the notable exception of the West Addison General Store (on Route 17 between Dead Creek and the Champlain Bridge), which over the years has been a welcoming stop for birders and hunters alike.

Button Bay

With the high peaks of the Adirondacks rising behind a broad view of Lake Champlain, the panorama at Button Bay is one of the finest in Vermont from sunrise to sunset. Button Bay can be extraordinary for waterfowl. Owls and hawks visit or migrate past. And nearby Button Bay State Park is a stopover for migrating songbirds. In short, the birdwatching here is great any time of year (with July being a possible exception).

From the bridge over Otter Creek on Route 22A in Vergennes, drive south 0.2 mile and turn west (right) onto Panton Road. Proceed 1.4 miles and turn right on Basin Harbor Road. Continue 4.4 miles, turn left here to stay on Basin Harbor Road, and go another 0.8 mile to the Button Bay State Park entrance. Another 0.4 mile ahead is an entrance road to a state boat launch and bay overlook on the right.

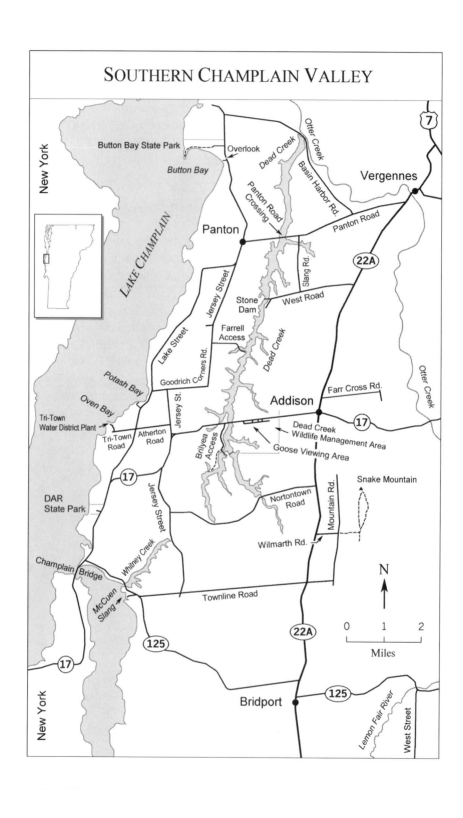

SOUTHERN CHAMPLAIN VALLEY

New York

Button Bay State Park

Overlook

Button Bay

Dead Creek

Otter Creek

Basin Harbor Rd.

Vergennes

7

Panton Road Crossing

LAKE CHAMPLAIN

Panton

Panton Road

Slang Rd.

22A

Jersey Street

Stone Dam

West Road

Farrell Access

Lake Street

Dead Creek

Goodrich Corners Rd.

Potash Bay

Oven Bay

Jersey St.

Addison

Farr Cross Rd.

Otter Creek

Tri-Town Water District Plant

Tri-Town Road

Atherton Road

Brilyea Access

Dead Creek Wildlife Management Area

Goose Viewing Area

17

Snake Mountain

Nortontown Road

Mountain Rd.

DAR State Park

Jersey Street

Wilmarth Rd.

Champlain Bridge

Whitney Creek

McCuen Slang

Townline Road

N

0   1   2

Miles

17

125

22A

New York

125

Bridport

Lemon Fair River

West Street

From the overlook in March view the Bald Eagle show. Eagles sit on the ice, fly overhead, or perch on white pines or other trees lining the bay. The waterfowl display here in the shallows can also be impressive: geese (Ross's and Greater White-fronted on rare occasions), Canvasback (uncommon), Redhead (uncommon), Ring-necked Duck, both scaup species, Bufflehead, Common Goldeneye, and all three merganser species. A nice diversity of dabblers can loiter along the edge of the bay to the north: Wood Duck (before the ice melts in the swamps), Gadwall, American Wigeon, American Black Duck, Mallard, Northern Shoveler (uncommon), Northern Pintail, and Green-winged Teal. Boat traffic can virtually vacate the bay of ducks.

The surrounding fields host blackbird flocks, including Eastern Meadowlark, in early spring. They also offer unobstructed views of raptors: Northern Harrier, Red-tailed Hawk, Rough-legged Hawk, and American Kestrel. Short-eared Owls sometimes hunt here before dusk.

In April and May walk into the park (pay a fee during the summer season) and investigate the cedars, thickets, and brush for songbirds, including Fox Sparrow in the area that surrounds the parking lanes east of the swimming pool.

In late summer small numbers of shorebirds sometimes gather at Button Bay's rather long shoreline: Black-bellied Plover, both yellowlegs species, Semipalmated Sandpiper, and Least Sandpiper. The beach habitat, however, can widely vary with lake level, from negligible to robust.

In fall, flocks of geese, including Snow Goose, can join the duck show. (Hunting can clear them out, however.) In November look for all three scoter species and Long-tailed Duck. Harlequin Duck visited once. Button Bay in late fall is also one of the best sites in Vermont for Common Loon, Horned Grebe, and Red-necked Grebe (bring a spotting scope). Waterfowl linger into winter until the bay freezes over.

Finally, always enjoyable is a walk to Button Point in the state park. A service road leading to the point winds through the park and along the northern edge of the bay. Look for songbirds among the mature oaks, hickories, pines, and maples. Look also in the limestone and limy shales for coral and arthropod fossils dating to the Middle Ordovician period, 440 to 500 million years ago. By the way, Button Bay is named for the buttonlike concretions formed from clay deposits found along the shoreline.

Northern Dead Creek Area

The northernmost dam over Dead Creek, **Stone Dam**, is the water's last stop before flowing north into Otter Creek and on to Lake Champlain. Many birds follow this same course, notably waterfowl and shorebirds, often pausing here on their travels.

Because of its longer legs, Greater Yellow-legs can feed in deeper water and depends less on the availability of mudflats.
Photo: Dave Hoag

From the bridge over Otter Creek in Vergennes drive south on 22A for 0.2 mile and turn right on Panton Road. Proceed 2.9 miles, turn left on Slang Road, drive 1.4 miles, and turn right on West Road. The dam is 0.7 mile ahead and a parking loop is 0.3 mile farther. WARNINGS: Slang Road can be muddy and West Road muddy to impassable and unplowed in winter. Stone Dam is sometimes a local hangout and occasionally used for target practice; don't leave a car unattended and avoid it altogether if bullets are flying.

Depending on the crops planted, the fields and shrubby borders along Slang Road and West Road can be great for sparrows from spring through fall, including Grasshopper Sparrow (uncommon). Horned Larks nest in the broad fields along the northern half of Slang Road (south of its crossing over a lobe of Dead Creek).

At the river and dam, waterfowl, particularly Wood Duck and all five eastern swallow species, gather in spring. In late summer and fall shorebirds are the main attraction, but only if wildlife managers have drawn down Dead Creek to expose the mud below. Then it can be a table set for plovers and sandpipers from July through September. Rare sightings here include Whimbrel, Hudsonian Godwit, Ruddy Turnstone, Sanderling, Wilson's Phalarope, and Red-necked Phalarope. First time visitors might glance at the mud and not see shorebirds, but another look will find them blending in among broken buttonbush roots or at the impoundment's edge. Also watch for waders —Great Blue Heron is abundant here in summer and fall, with an occasional Great Egret or Black-crowned Night-Heron. When the shorebirds seem nervous, look up for Peregrine Falcon or Merlin. Finally, in winter check Slang Road and any navigable section of West Road for Short-eared Owl (around dusk), Red-tailed Hawk, and Rough-legged Hawk.

Return to Panton Road and proceed west to where it crosses Dead Creek; this is generally called the **Panton Road Crossing**. Park at pull-offs on either end of the bridge. WARNING: Watch for speeding traffic. In spring this is a good spot for waterfowl, particularly Green-winged Teal and swallows. In late summer and fall shorebirds can gather here if mud is exposed. In July 1991 a Ruff and a Curlew Sandpiper shared some mud here for a few days.

Another spot along Dead Creek worth a look is **Farrell Access**. Bald Eagles and gulls can stop by in early spring and shorebirds can gather in late summer and fall during a Stone Dam drawdown. From the Panton Road crossing continue west 1 mile and bear left at the intersection. Continue south for 2.6 miles (despite the main road bearing right and Jersey Street changing names to Goodrich Corners Road) to the mile-long Farrell Access road on the left. Northern Shoveler often drops by in April.

Oven Bay and Potash Bay

For birdwatchers with spotting scopes, no visit to the Dead Creek region in fall or winter should exclude Lake Champlain's **Oven Bay** in Addison. Waterfowl and gulls gather here in spring. But birding here really heats up in fall and winter.

From Route 22A in Addison drive west on Route 17 for 3.7 miles to Jersey Street. Turn right on Jersey Street, proceed 0.2 mile, and turn left on Atherton Road. Drive 0.9 mile across Lake Street, where Atherton Road changes its name to Tri-Town Road. Ahead 0.6 mile Tri-Town Road bears right; continue 0.3 mile to the brick Tri-Town Water District Plant on Oven Bay. WARNING: Current from the plant's overflow pipe makes the ice here dangerously thin in winter.

In October and November Red-throated Loon (uncommon) and Common Loon stop here during their migration to the Atlantic Ocean. This is one of the best places on the lake to find Horned Grebe and, in October, Red-necked Grebe. Other highlights include all three scoter species, Long-tailed Duck, Bald Eagle (particularly on the ice at water's edge), and, with enough open water in winter, Common Goldeneye and Common Merganser in good numbers (often far from shore). This is a fairly good observation spot for the fall migration of Brant and other waterfowl, as well as hawks. Northern Gannet, King Eider, and Parasitic and Pomarine Jaegers have also visited this stretch of water. For another view of the lake a bit to the north, return to Lake Street, drive 0.6 mile north (left) and turn left on Potash Bay Road. Limited parking at **Potash Bay** is 0.1 mile ahead.

Dead Creek Wildlife Management Area

In the natural course of things Dead Creek was once only another waterway draining the west slopes of Snake Mountain and portions of the Champlain

One of New England's great avian events is the gathering of tens of thousands of Snow Geese each October at Dead Creek Wildlife Management Area in Addison.
Photo: David Jenne

lowlands. But in the 1950s and 1960s the State of Vermont dammed several spots, flooding fields and creating wetlands. Dead Creek Wildlife Management Area is anything but dead. Its sixteen dikes create a patchwork of cattail-dominated wetlands. The surrounding uplands are a mix of agricultural lands, wet meadows, grasslands, shrublands, and clay-plain forests of shagbark hickory, swamp white oak, burr oak, and white pine. Like many places in Vermont, it has its quiet days. But when it is good, it is very good—legendary among Vermont birdwatchers. Created for waterfowl protection, management, and hunting, the wildlife management area is a fine example of hunters and birdwatchers coexisting. Funding to establish Dead Creek, like most wildlife management areas in Vermont, came from fees and taxes assessed on hunters. It is a wildlife refuge, so please obey the signs and keep a respectful distance from nesting species, particularly Osprey on platforms.

Start at the **Goose Viewing Area** on Route 17. From Route 22 in Addison, go west on Route 17 for 1.6 miles to a long parking area on the south side of the road. Birders eager for an early spring might stop here for Savannah Sparrow and blackbirds in April. Grasshopper Sparrow (uncommon) comes through here in May. Bobolink is common on the north side of Route 17 if the crop that year is grass. Look for dabbling ducks in the wet fields: American Black Duck, Mallard, Northern Pintail, Green-winged Teal, and an occasional Gadwall or American Wigeon. Horned Lark breeds in the area.

In late summer and fall shorebirds can gather in wet fields or at the edges of the ponds visible from the parking area. But the fall is when this place erupts with birds. It would be a mistake to gawk at only the thousands of Snow Geese stopping here during migration from late September through November. Adding to the overwhelming bird biomass are flocks of tens of thousands of Red-winged Blackbirds and hundreds of Brown-headed Cowbirds. All the while, southbound hawks soar far overhead.

Snow Goose Spectacle

As maples begin to drop their blazing yellow and red leaves each fall, the fields of Dead Creek Wildlife Management Area begin a spectacle of their own in black and white. From late September though November Snow Geese, migrating from the Canadian Arctic to wintering grounds in the southeast, stop by the tens of thousands to rest and feed. Geese numbers peak roughly around the middle of October with as many as 15,000 to 20,000 birds. It is an event no Vermont bird-watcher should miss.

The meticulous observer might also find Ross's Goose among the masses of Snows. Look carefully for smaller birds with noticeably stubbier bills lacking a "grinning patch"—a black line along the length of the mandibles where they meet. Dead Creek has become the most reliable spot in New England, perhaps the entire East, for Ross's Goose. But it takes patience, more patience, and often a spotting scope. Beware of being fooled by the smaller race of Lesser Snow Goose (the birds here are predominantly Greater Snow Goose) and Snow Goose–Ross's Goose hybrids, which are regular. As a skilled Vermont birder once put it while gazing out at the honking mass of Snow Geese: "I know I'm looking at a Ross's Goose—I'm just not sure which one it is."

Other rare geese spotted here from time to time include Brant, Greater White-fronted Goose, and Barnacle Goose (once). Look also for the rare and smaller "Richardson's" and "Cackling" races of Canada Goose.

Note that thousands of Snow Geese and ducks here can vanish into a pond out of view in a depression in the field south of Route 17.

Perhaps recognizing this as a hunter-free zone, ducks dabbling in the ponds can include the species mentioned above plus Wood Duck, Blue-winged Teal, and Northern Shoveler (uncommon). Shorebirds here in fall can include American Golden-Plover, Killdeer, and Pectoral Sandpiper foraging the fields. Joining them can be most any other regular species around wet spots and pond edges. Hudsonian Godwit (uncommon) can sometimes wander among the geese. American Pipit and Horned Lark fly by regularly and occasionally land in view in the fields. And don't be surprised to find a Bald Eagle or, rarely, a Golden Eagle scattering the goose flocks or a Peregrine Falcon feasting on a goose downed by a hunter or dead from exhaustion.

Finally, in winter, as the geese clear out, this becomes hawk central. Red-tailed Hawk and Rough-legged Hawk can be common sentinels on perches, as Northern Harrier, which nests here, peruses the fields. Snowy Owl and Gyrfalcon are rare. (On one occasion a Gyrfalcon was seen chasing a Snowy Owl.) Watch also for flocks of Snow Bunting with attendant Lapland Longspur.

A Black-crowned Night-Heron peers from its perch at the Brilyea Access to Dead Creek. Photo: David Jenne

Not far from the Goose Viewing Area is the **Brilyea Access** to Dead Creek. With a predawn chorus of Marsh Wren, rails, and an occasional owl, this is a nice place in spring to watch the day begin. From the Goose Viewing Area continue west on Route 17 for 0.6 mile to the Brilyea Access Road on the left (immediately past the bridge over Dead Creek).

In March gulls and Bald Eagle will gather here to feed on fish that failed to survive the winter. Bufflehead and Common Goldeneye will occasionally join dabbling ducks. In May the place gets busy—listen for the distinctive vocalizations of American Bittern, Least Bittern, Virginia Rail, Sora, Common Moorhen, Marsh Wren, and Swamp Sparrow. Enjoy, and practice identifying, all five swallow species on the wing. If mud is exposed, watch for shorebirds dropping from migration for a quick meal.

Osprey nests here, and Dead Creek is one of the few places in Vermont that Northern Pintail and Green-winged Teal find good enough for nesting. Brilyea is also good enough for Eastern Screech-Owl and Great Horned Owl year-round. In June and July this is an excellent place to see the otherwise secretive Virginia Rail leading chicks on their first forays to the muddy margins. And it is a reliable spot for Black-billed Cuckoo, particularly along the access road or the paths south from the parking lots. If all that isn't enough, take some time to study the subtleties of Alder and Willow Flycatchers.

In late summer and fall Great Blue Heron and wandering Great Egret feed in the shallow waters. The shorebird show depends on the availability of muddy feeding grounds. On occasion wildlife managers draw down Dead

Creek to promote the increase of moist soil plants and invertebrates (both serving as bird food) and to provide habitat for shorebirds. The exposed muddy creek and impoundment bottoms beckon the hungry shorebirds from migration. During these legendary drawdowns shorebirds sometimes gather at the eastern end of the dam. Better yet, in the event of a drawdown, walk southwest from the first parking lot through a metal gate about 1 mile along a grassy access road to what can be a shorebird bonanza on the left. (Look carefully to see birds woven into the buttonbush roots.) The mix here can include Black-bellied Plover, American Golden-Plover, Semipalmated Plover, Killdeer, Greater Yellowlegs, Lesser Yellowlegs, Solitary Sandpiper, Spotted Sandpiper, Semipalmated Sandpiper, Least Sandpiper, White-rumped Sandpiper, Baird's Sandpiper (uncommon), Pectoral Sandpiper, Dunlin, Short-billed Dowitcher, and Common Snipe. Rarities here have included American Avocet, Willet, Western Sandpiper, Stilt Sandpiper, Buff-breasted Sandpiper, Long-billed Dowitcher, and Red-necked Phalarope. And where good numbers of shorebirds go, Merlin and Peregrine Falcon are sure to follow.

DAR State Park to McCuen Slang

Four spots close together along Lake Champlain will enhance most any birding trip to the Dead Creek region. One way to beat the birding-by-car syndrome is to spend time wandering **DAR State Park**. The park entrance is along Route 17, 1.5 miles north of the Champlain Bridge. (In the off-season park at the gate, leaving enough room for maintenance staff to swing open one side, and walk straight in toward the lake.) In spring Gray Catbirds love the tangled shrubby vegetation. The day-use area around the parking lot can be good for migrating warblers and sparrows. And the bank beyond the day-use shelter (continue from the parking lot toward the lake) can be a decent spot to watch loons in spring or anything flying down Lake Champlain in fall. This is actually one of the better migration watch sites yet discovered on Lake Champlain. As a bonus, scoters often pause here a while on their southbound trip, perhaps contemplating the possibility that they have run out of lake. (For more about lakewatching at DAR State Park, see "Lakewatching on Lake Champlain," page 24.)

The **Champlain Bridge** is 0.1 mile west of the intersection of Routes 17 and 125. Bird from below and around the base of the bridge on the Vermont side. (The parks on the New York side can offer alternate vantages when birds are too distant or aligned with the sun. There is also a small pull-off on Route 125, 0.3 mile to the east of the bridge.) Common Loons gather north of the bridge in fall. This is also one of the better spots on Lake Champlain for Red-throated Loon in fall. Waterfowl linger here (within a mile of the bridge in either direction) in early spring and late fall, particularly Ring-necked Duck, scaup, Common Goldeneye, and all three merganser species, but boat traffic can scare them off. In short, this can be a big hit or a big bust. Tricolored Heron, King Eider, Laughing Gull, and Caspian Tern have been seen here during big hit phases. And a White-winged Dove graced the entrance road in 2000. The narrowing of the lake seems to make this a good crossing spot for monarch butterflies migrating toward Mexico in September and October.

From the bridge, proceed east on Route 125 along the lakeshore for 1.2 miles to the mouth of **Whitney Creek**. Park on the left just past the creek crossing. In late summer and fall this is a relatively reliable spot for Great Egret. In fall (other than during hunting season), waterfowl gathering here can include American Black Duck, Mallard, Northern Shoveler, Northern Pintail, and Green-winged Teal. Scan the mud for shorebirds or, in October, American Pipit.

Finally, continue east on Route 125 for another 0.4 mile to **McCuen Slang**, a Vermont Fish and Wildlife Department boat launch on the right (the sign may be missing). Scan the lake from the parking lot or walk the short path southwest to another view of the lake. In spring check the lake for waterfowl and the trees for songbirds including Warbling Vireo, Yellow Warbler, and Baltimore Oriole. Orchard Oriole nested along the access road in 2000 and has been seen here in years prior. Osprey frequent the area and nest nearby. In fall, from the end of the path, look for American Coot, Ring-necked Duck, scaup species, Ruddy Duck (rare), and shorebirds in low-water years. Hudsonian Godwit and Red Knot, both hard to come by in Vermont, have stopped here. Watch also for Bald Eagle, Red-tailed Hawk, or Rough-legged Hawk in migration. McCuen Slang can also be good for the fall songbird migration, including warblers and particularly sparrows (Swamp, Song, White-throated, and White-crowned).

Farr Cross Road to Lemon Fair River

East and south of Dead Creek, a variety of birding opportunities await as well. Eastern Bluebird, sparrows (notably Vesper Sparrow), and American Pipit (in fall) frequent the fields along the one-lane **Farr Cross Road**. The road, which is closed in winter and muddy to impassable in early spring, runs east from Route 22A in Addison 0.3 mile north of Route 17. Birding can be good here from spring through fall; October is best. (Park off the road or risk an unpleasant encounter with a milk truck.)

The moderate two-mile hike up **Snake Mountain** offers beautiful views of the Champlain Valley (particularly during foliage season), migrating hawks, and the ocean of Snow Geese in the fields below. From the intersection of

Route 22A and Route 17 in Addison drive south on Route 22A for 2.9 miles, turn left on Wilmarth Road, and proceed 0.6 mile to Mountain Road. The trailhead is straight ahead, but turn left on Mountain Road and proceed 0.1 mile to the parking lot on the left. The wildflower show here is impressive in April. Avoid this area during deer hunting season, however.

In winter scan the fields or **Nortontown Road** itself, particularly after a snowstorm, for Horned Lark, Lapland Longspur (uncommon), and Snow Bunting. The stretches near the working farms are usually best. Rough-legged Hawk likes the area as well. From the intersection of Route 22A and Route 17 in Addison, go south on Route 22A for 1.8 miles and turn right onto Nortontown Road. The network of dirt roads southward between Route 22A and Lake Champlain can offer similar fare.

One of Vermont's largest springtime congregations of waterfowl is frustratingly far from view at the **Lemon Fair River** in Bridport. From Route 22A in the village of Bridport, the ambitious birdwatcher with high-powered optics and a desire for eyestrain can go east on Route 125 for 3.5 miles to its crossing over the Lemon Fair River. Proceed straight ahead here along West Street and pick a good spot to park without interfering with traffic. Scope ducks and geese in the valley (or "flooding") below. Activity here peaks in April.

🖋 Rutland Region

If Vermont had bayou country, it would be the swampy lowlands at the southern end of the Champlain Valley. The western portions of Addison and Rutland counties are flat, wide, wet, and often buggy. It's a happy place for wetland specialists. Spring arrives early here, and these lowlands are often mild enough for American Robin, Eastern Bluebird, Song Sparrow, and other hearty songbirds to overwinter. But the climate and birdlife change dramatically only twenty miles or so to the east in the unavoidable and imposing form of the Green Mountains, where spring and the chorus of high-elevation birds arrive much later. Four of Vermont's biophysical regions converge in this diverse section of the state—the Champlain Valley, the Taconic Mountains, the Vermont Valley, and the Green Mountains.

Cornwall Swamp Wildlife Management Area and Leicester Junction

The hardwood-dominated **Cornwall Swamp Wildlife Management Area** belongs to the largest interior wetland complex in Vermont. Its mosaic of tree species (red maple, elm, green ash, white cedar, and white pine) assures a

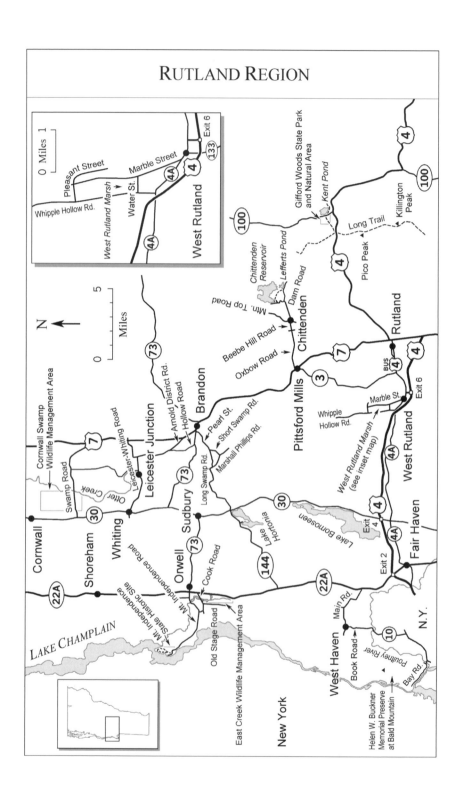

RUTLAND REGION

mosaic of birds. With the lengthening spring days the mosquito population here can become nearly sufficient to influence Earth's tides.

From Route 30 (3.4 miles south of the center of Cornwall or 3.5 miles north of the center of Whiting), go east on Swamp Road 1.8 miles to a parking lot on the right before a covered bridge. If the road is flooded, turn around, because waterfowl will be scattered throughout the area and not concentrated in the swamp.

In April, depending on ice and flooding, this can be a good spot for Pied-billed Grebe and almost all of Vermont's puddle ducks, including Wood Duck, Gadwall, American Wigeon, American Black Duck, Mallard, Blue-winged Teal, Northern Shoveler, Northern Pintail, and Green-winged Teal. The best viewing is west of the covered bridge looking north, or east of the bridge on both sides of the road. As the season progresses and noisy Warbling Vireos pepper the trees, the ducks are occasionally joined by a humble mix of shore-birds picking along the water's edge and in wet spots in the fields.

In wet springs a section of the Otter Creek near **Leicester Junction** can attract Common Snipe and a similar variety of waterfowl to that noted above. (In dry springs it can be reliably duckless.) From Route 30 in the village of Whiting, take the Leicester-Whiting Road east 2.9 miles through Leicester Junction to a bridge over Otter Creek. Check flooded areas west of the bridge and along Old Jerusalem Road, which runs north along the creek east of the bridge.

Arnold Hollow

Warblers are the legend of Arnold Hollow. Nesting along the rural, residential Hollow Road are "southern" bird species at the northern edge of their range. Some of this property is subject to housing development, which would make portions of this area inaccessible or lacking in birds.

From the northern intersection of Route 7 and Route 73 in Brandon, drive Route 7 north 1.2 miles, turn left on Arnold District Road, and proceed 1.1 miles to a left turn onto Hollow Road. (Hollow Road returns to Route 73 in 1.8 miles.)

Find safe places along the road southbound to pull over and find birds, particularly 0.6 mile down Hollow Road at the crest of a hill. While this road can be fine for a diversity of warblers during spring migration, the highlights are breeding Blue-winged Warbler, Golden-winged Warbler, and their hybrids. Prairie Warbler also nests here. Other "southerners" include Eastern Towhee and Field Sparrow. Listen and look for Brown Thrasher. Farther ahead, check the cedars for more warblers, including Yellow, Chestnut-sided, Magnolia, Black-throated Blue, Black-throated Green, and American Redstart.

An American Goldfinch stops to feed on the seeds of one of its favorite plants—thistle. Photo: Dave Hoag

Long Swamp Loop and Lake Hortonia

Long Swamp in Brandon, an extensive wetland of white cedar, red maple, black ash, and other deciduous trees, is one of Vermont's few remaining spots for Whip-poor-will. Barred Owl also likes this kind of habitat. So do mosquitoes.

One way to investigate the area in spring is to drive a triangle formed by three roads, stopping anywhere the urge strikes. From Brandon, at the northern intersection of Route 7 and Route 73, drive southwest on Pearl Street 1.6 miles to Short Swamp Road. (Pearl Street changes names to Long Swamp Road along the way.) At dusk or night here listen for Whip-poor-will. Continue along Short Swamp Road 1 mile and turn right on Marshall Phillips Road, which returns to Long Swamp Road 1.1 miles ahead. Turn right on Long Swamp Road and bird on the way back toward Brandon. Among the diverse cast of characters who live in this area are Red-shouldered Hawk, American Woodcock (displaying over the swamp), Winter Wren, Red-breasted Nuthatch, Eastern Wood Peewee, Indigo Bunting, Veery, Hermit Thrush, Wood Thrush, Golden-winged Warbler (uncommon), Northern Waterthrush, and Louisiana Waterthrush (uncommon on Marshall Phillips Road). Add Barred Owl and an occasional Great Horned Owl to the background chorus of spring peepers and mosquitoes, and the result is a symphony for (bug-dope-covered) ears. Incidentally, the patches of green lichen on the trees here form a fine display of the common *Flavoparmelia caperata*. In winter check for finches and fruit-eating songbirds.

Not far from Long Swamp, the north end of **Lake Hortonia** in Sudbury attracts waterfowl and rails in spring, including Wood Duck and Virginia Rail. Common Loon occasionally visits the open water in migration. From Route

30 drive west on Route 144 for 1 mile and turn left on a road to a state boat launch. Park at the launch 0.4 mile ahead and walk back beside the road along the wetland to a serenade of Swamp Sparrow and Common Yellowthroat.

Mt. Independence State Historic Site

American Revolutionary forces built this fort during the war on a promontory of Lake Champlain directly across from Fort Ticonderoga in New York. So imposing were the two forts that the British general Guy Carleton abandoned a planned invasion in October 1776 in favor of a quick retreat into Canada. Nowadays this state historic site offers a retreat for birds and birdwatchers, not to mention a nice walk with views of the lake. Mt. Independence is one of the lower Champlain Valley's best opportunities for major songbird fallouts during spring migration.

From Route 22A in Orwell go west on Route 73 for 0.4 mile and continue straight on the Mt. Independence Road (as Route 73 bends right). Stay on the main road for another 5.1 miles to the parking lot on the left. Trail guides, available at the trailhead or in the visitor center, reveal much of the rich history here. The visitor center is open from Memorial Day through Columbus Day (when visitors pay a small entrance fee to walk the trails) with additional historical information and displays.

In spring, Chipping Sparrows offer a welcoming trill. The trail leaving the parking lot for the top of the hill can be an excellent place to observe the songbird migration, including impressive warbler fallouts. The trail continuing along the lake toward the northern point of land (the blue trail on the official park map) can be similarly active. Return on the orange trail. Ruffed Grouse and Wild Turkey inconspicuously wander the woods. Long-eared Owl, a rare bird in Vermont, has bred in the park in the past.

East Creek Wildlife Management Area

Managed impoundments on East Creek have created an emergent marsh harboring waterfowl, herons, and other wetland species. This wildlife management area includes Vermont's largest narrow-leafed cattail marsh (the more widespread cattail species is called common cattail). This is a refuge, so please obey the signs and keep a respectful distance from wildlife.

From Route 73 in Orwell drive south on Route 22A for 0.6 mile, turn right on Cook Road at the crest of a hill, and proceed 0.3 mile to a bridge over East Creek. Ahead 0.2 mile is a Vermont Fish and Wildlife Department access to a small dam and parking on the left. At the fork 0.1 mile beyond the parking area, go left on Old Stage Road for about 0.2 mile to another view of East Creek on the left.

In spring this area is particularly good for Pied-billed Grebe, Wood Duck, and most any dabbler. Canada Goose nests here. Great Blue Herons stalk the waters. A young (white) Little Blue Heron made an appearance in 1996, and an Eared Grebe visited in 1994. From July into October, in years with very little rainfall, shorebirds sometimes gather here on exposed mud.

West Rutland Marsh

This long, narrow cattail marsh along the meandering Castleton River provides a summer home to a host of birds. Roads crossing the marsh bring birders close to waterfowl, rails, and other wetland species. Migrant songbirds also feed in trees along the marsh's eastern side.

From U.S. Route 4 take Exit 6 at West Rutland, go north 0.2 mile, turn left onto Route 4A, proceed 0.4 mile, and turn right on Marble Street. Ahead 1.2 miles is Water Street, which crosses the marsh to the left. From this road in spring watch for Pied-billed Grebe (uncommon), American Bittern, Least Bittern (rare), Green Heron, Virginia Rail, Sora (uncommon), Common Moorhen (rare), all five eastern swallow species, and ducks in open water. Marsh Wren and Swamp Sparrow breed here.

Return to Marble Street and continue north another 1.5 miles, stopping now and then (in spring) to look for Common Snipe on fence posts, warblers, and other passerines. Sedge Wren nested here, and Yellow-breasted Chat visited this area. Turn left on Pleasant Street, which crosses the marsh's northern edge, to look for more Common Snipe as well as Virginia Rail, flycatchers, Yellow Warbler, and other wetland or scrubland specialists.

Rutland East

Birdwatching is limited in and around Vermont's second largest city. But the Green Mountains rising to the east of Rutland are worth a visit—if not for birds, then for the views and simple peace of mind.

A strenuous hike south on the Long Trail from Sherburne Pass (Route 4) leads to high-elevation specialists, including Winter Wren, Yellow-rumped Warbler, Blackpoll Warbler, Purple Finch, and, in some years, White-winged Crossbill. (The Long Trail crosses Route 4 about 2.5 miles west of its intersection with Route 100.) This is also home to the state's second largest nesting population of Bicknell's Thrush. The thrushes are concentrated around **Pico Peak** and **Killington Peak** and largely absent from the saddle between the two

Cattail marshes in Vermont provide habitat for Virginia Rails and their black, downy young.
Photo: Roy Pilcher

summits. As expected, black flies can be pesky in the spruce and fir up high. Late May and June are good times here to find both birds and bugs.

Kent Pond, on the east side of Route 100 only 0.3 mile north of Route 4 in Killington, can attract an occasional Common Loon, waterfowl, and songbirds in the deciduous woods. A wayward Caspian Tern once stopped here. The trail from the parking lot, which passes through woods and along the pond edge, coincides here with the legendary Appalachian Trail. At **Gifford Woods State Park and Natural Area**, a few hundred feet north of the pond on Route 100, look for warblers among the conifers at the camping area or deciduous specialists among the old trees.

Lefferts Pond and Chittenden Reservoir

These high-elevation waters and accompanying woods and wetlands, set in a basin of the Green Mountains, offer not only fine paddling, walking, and views of the range but a nice diversity of waterfowl and songbirds. The smaller Lefferts Pond, bordered by balsam fir and red spruce, has wetlands at its eastern end. Black flies can be distracting here during their peak feeding times from around Mother's Day to Father's Day.

The approach to **Lefferts Pond** from Pittsford Mills (at the intersection of Routes 7 and 3) is the simplest. From Route 7 proceed east on Oxbow Road, which changes to Beebe Hill Road in 2.9 miles. Continue on Beebe Hill (staying straight onto pavement in 0.5 mile) into Chittenden village. Pass a statue and turn right on Mtn. Top Road, cross a bridge and take a quick left onto Dam Road. Drive 1.3 miles, turn right, and proceed about 0.9 mile to a parking lot and trailhead on the left. Additional parking near the alder wetland is about 0.6 mile ahead.

In spring investigate the pond for Pied-billed Grebe, Red-necked Grebe, Great Blue Heron (which has nested here), Wood Duck (nesting), Common Merganser, Bald Eagle, and songbirds including Swainson's Thrush and numerous breeding Northern Waterthrush (in the wetland). More passerines, including mixed flocks of migrating warblers, can be found along the road and a trail between the pond and Chittenden Reservoir. The trail leaves from the first parking area.

To reach **Chittenden Reservoir** by vehicle, return to Dam Road, turn right, drive 0.7 mile, and bear right at the fork below the dam to a parking area at water's edge. The view across the 750-acre reservoir includes the prominent summits of Mt. Carmel and Bloodroot Mountain. Common Loon, Red-necked Grebe, waterfowl, and Bald Eagle are occasional during migration. Spotted Sandpiper breeds here and Solitary Sandpiper passes through in spring and fall. Magnolia Warbler frequents this area.

Helen W. Buckner Memorial Preserve at Bald Mountain

Roughly 20 miles west of Rutland is some of Vermont's most remote territory. The lower Poultney River and southern terminus of Lake Champlain have the slow, lazy feel of southern rivers. And if woods of oak, hickory, and American hop hornbeam in the Taconic Range aren't "southern" enough, the possibility of encountering timber rattlesnake in remote parts of this region should make the point. This is where The Nature Conservancy owns and operates **Helen W. Buckner Memorial Preserve at Bald Mountain**, 3,200 acres of woods, wetlands, and fields, three miles of undeveloped shoreline on Lake Champlain, and a Peregrine Falcon nest site.

From Route 4 take Exit 2 at Fair Haven and go north on Route 22A for 2.4 miles to Main Road. Turn left on Main Road, drive 3.4 miles to West Haven, turn left on Book Road, and proceed 4.7 miles (into New York) to a "T" intersection. Turn right on Route 10 and drive 2.6 miles to an intersection with an unnamed road that goes straight as Route 10 curves left. Bear right onto the unnamed road, continue 0.1 mile across the Poultney River, turn left on Bay Road (also known as Galick Road), which is usually muddy in spring, and continue 1.8 miles to the small Nature Conservancy parking lot on the right. (Please don't park at the farmstead beyond.)

A loop trail here, less than three miles long, skirts the farmstead to a field, over the shoulder of Austin Hill and past an oak-hickory glade. A kiosk about a half mile up the trail has reserve information.

WARNING: This is eastern timber rattlesnake country. This native snake, which is most active from May to October, is not aggressive and would rather be left alone. As a precaution, however, wear long pants and hiking boots that cover the ankle. When hiking through grass or thick vegetation, carry a walking stick and part the vegetation before taking a step. Birders should watch where they sit or place their hands. Stay on trails—folks have wandered old woods roads here and gotten lost (and found again). Sections of the reserve around the cliffs and talus slope of Bald Mountain are closed to protect nesting Peregrine Falcons.

Seeing that Golden-winged Warbler frequents the reserve and a male Prothonotary Warbler spent the spring singing here in 1989, be on the lookout for other southerners, such as Yellow-billed Cuckoo, Carolina Wren, Blue-gray Gnatcatcher, and Louisiana Waterthrush. Yellow-throated Vireo can be found along Bay Road.

✒ *Southwestern Vermont*

Two distinct mountain ranges, the Taconics and the Greens, dominate the landscape in the southwestern corner of Vermont. Squeezed in between them, running north-south, is the long, low, and narrow Vermont Valley—a tempting flyway for migrants. The rolling hills of the Taconics offer leisurely woodland birding. The valley below and its milder climate attract southern species pressing the northern edge of their range. Conversely, the intrusion of conifers in the southern Green Mountains brings northern birds (moose and black flies, too) toward the southern edge of their range. This diverse region, then, is the only place in Vermont where southerners such as Eastern Towhee, Blue-winged Warbler, and Prairie Warbler can be found nesting not far from such northerners as Bicknell's Thrush, Lincoln's Sparrow, and Rusty Blackbird.

Merck Forest & Farmland Center

This environmental education center perched high in the Taconics is a study in forest management. Before he died in 1957, George Merck, president of the pharmaceutical company that bears his name, established with family money a patchwork of land as a nonprofit reserve. On display is the so-called "working landscape"—a blend of active farmland, clearcuts, sugarbush, second-growth, and older deciduous woods. The varying landscape assures a diversity of birds from spring through fall. The 3,130-acre reserve is open seven days a week. Admission is free but contributions to support the center are welcome.

From the village of East Rupert (northwest of Manchester Center) take Route 315 west for 2.6 miles to the entrance road (which can be muddy in spring) on the left. The parking lot is 0.5 mile ahead.

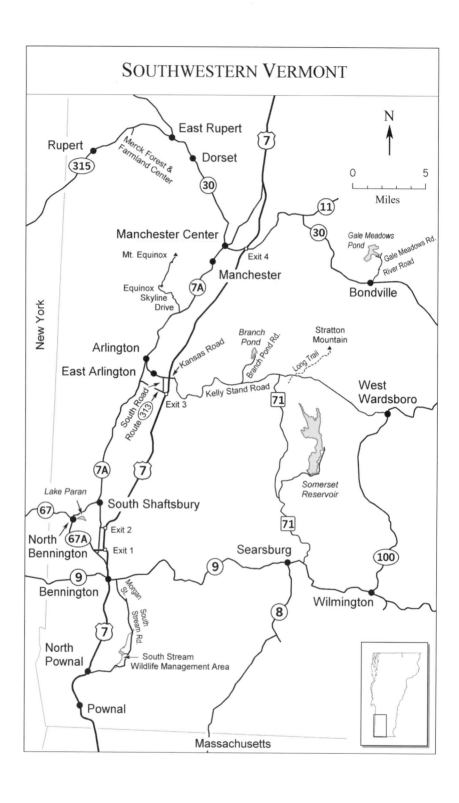

SOUTHWESTERN VERMONT

A Great Horned Owl blends into its surroundings. Vermont's largest nesting owl is more common in southern Vermont and the Champlain Valley. Photo: Steven D. Faccio

More than 28 miles of trails beckon. All of them leave from Old Town Road, the main trail south from the parking lot. Pick up a map at the reserve's visitor center. As the breeding season begins, Eastern Wood-Pewee, Red-eyed Vireo, American Redstart, Ovenbird, Scarlet Tanager, and Rose-breasted Grosbeak join the thrush quartet of Veery, Hermit Thrush, Wood Thrush, and American Robin to perform a classic Vermont woodland serenade. Bird activity can be particularly busy around the forest edges, and with so many openings here edges are easy to find. Merck Forest is a fine place to settle in and spend a long morning or an entire day on foot with songbirds.

The entrance road, with wide views to the north and west, also offers a ringside seat to the fall hawk migration. Good numbers of Red-tailed Hawk and Turkey Vulture venture by in October, and migrating geese can also be seen tracking the Hudson Valley far to the west. On at least one occasion a Golden Eagle joined the southbound flow.

Mt. Equinox

The highest peak in the Taconics is a towering example of the diversity of southwestern Vermont. The summit of Mt. Equinox (3,852 feet) is an island of spruce and fir above slopes of rich deciduous woods. The understory includes rare plants sprouting from calcium-rich soils. But Mt. Equinox also offers relatively easy (paved) access to high-elevation songbirds, including Bicknell's Thrush, that are more common in the peaks of the Green Mountains farther north. It also offers knee-weakening views across Vermont and into three other states.

From the intersection of Route 30 and Route 7A in Manchester Center, drive south on Route 7A for 5.4 miles to the well-marked Equinox Skyline Drive, a toll road on the right. The road ($6 for car and driver, $2 per passenger) is open from about 9:00 A.M. to 9:00 P.M., May through October, weather permitting. Hiking and bicycling on the toll road are prohibited (a number of hiking trails leave the pavement higher up). Don't come during the annual antique car race on the mountain, typically held during the second weekend in June. Check ahead for other special events. (Toll road information is available, when the road is open, at (802)362-1114.)

The drive winds 5.2 miles from rich deciduous woods through transitional zones (red spruce, paper birch, and mountain ash) to the spruce-fir (mostly fir) zone at the summit. Along the way, pull over and turn the parking/picnicking areas into birding areas as well. As the elevation rises, notice the cast of bird characters becoming more northern and the views more grand. To the east lie the Vermont Valley, the Green Mountains, and the White Mountains of New Hampshire. The Adirondacks rise to the northwest, and the Taconic and Berkshire Mountains of Massachusetts to the south.

At the summit is an inn owned by Carthusian monks who live in seclusion in the monastery visible on the mountain slope to the west. The inn's paved parking lot offers woodland edge access to birders who use wheelchairs. The best skyline birding is along the relatively flat "Red Trail" that runs 0.5 mile from the inn north to Lookout Rock and its remarkable mountain view. Along the way look for Winter Wren, Yellow-rumped Warbler, Blackpoll Warbler, Purple Finch, and on occasion White-winged Crossbill and Pine Siskin. Perhaps inspired by the monks, Bicknell's Thrush often remains out of sight as well. Its numbers seemed to have decreased on Mt. Equinox during the 1990s, with only a tiny population remaining. Enhancing the thrush sonata near the summit are the more populous Swainson's Thrush and Hermit Thrush.

Gale Meadows Pond

This impoundment on Mill Brook in the town of Winhall is, like the resorts nearby, a year-round destination. Visit during the spring and fall migrations and, when conifers produce a good crop of seeds, in winter for finches. The pond is a pleasant retreat by canoe or kayak. Landlubbers can use the access road and short trails leaving the parking lot.

From Route 30 in Bondville, just west of the bridge over the Winhall River, drive north on River Road for 1.8 miles (River Road changes its name to Gale Meadows Road halfway along) to a short access road on the left that leads to the boat launch and parking lot.

Common Loon has attempted to nest on this pond. Great Blue Heron had better luck. Other nesters have included Wood Duck, Blue-winged Teal, Common Merganser, Hooded Merganser, and Rusty Blackbird. Ring-necked Duck mixes with the locals during migration. Look for mixed warbler flocks in spring and fall with resident Black-throated Blue Warbler. Witch hazel, which flowers at the same time that the hawks fly south, grows along the access road. (Okay, it's not a bird, but it blooms when most everything else has given up for the year.) In winter the conifers (including tamarack and white pine) attract Golden-crowned Kinglet and finches.

Kelley Stand Road and Stratton Mountain

The 18-mile road crossing the Green Mountains between East Arlington and West Wardsboro, undeveloped and remote, provides access to an isolated pond, a high peak, and the heart of the Green Mountain Plateau. Found at this higher elevation are birds common many miles to the north. (Comparable too are the armadas of black flies.) A good time to visit is mid- to late May, when Vermont's brief spring, expiring in the valley below, is just getting underway.

From Route 7 north of Bennington take Exit 3, drive west on Route 313 for 0.2 mile, and turn north (right) on South Road. Ahead 0.7 mile turn right on Kansas Road and drive 0.6 mile to **Kelley Stand Road** (U.S. Forest Service Road 71) on the right. The road is unplowed in winter and muddy and pot-holed in spring. WARNING: Be aware that, not expecting pedestrians, drivers on this road can move surprisingly fast.

Gain altitude along Kelley Stand Road and look for safe spots to pull off. In spring, stop-and-go birding on the road along the aptly named Roaring Branch can produce everything from Barred Owl to Northern Goshawk, Yellow-bellied Sapsucker to Cape May Warbler. Thrushes sing like flutes here while Common Ravens croak overhead. Approximately 6.5 miles east from the Kansas Road intersection, Branch Pond Road leads north about 2.5 miles to its namesake, **Branch Pond** (which has deluxe wilderness amenities: a trail and an outhouse). Here and throughout this high country be on the lookout for such northerners as Black-backed Woodpecker (rare), Ruby-crowned Kinglet, Lincoln's Sparrow, and Rusty Blackbird.

About 4 miles east of its intersection with Branch Pond Road, Kelley Stand Road crosses the Long Trail. From here is a well-marked and demanding 3.8-mile hike north to the summit of **Stratton Mountain**, Bicknell's Thrush territory. Parking is available at the trailhead.

West of the Long Trail crossing, and roughly 3 miles east of the Branch Pond Road intersection, Route 71 leaves Kelley Stand Road and heads south. This remote road (closed in winter and muddy to impassable in spring)

An American Wood-cock, uncharacteristically visible, forages for earthworms with its long, probing bill. Photo: Christopher McBride

bisects the Green Mountains and provides access to hiking trails, moose, and more "northern" birding. It also provides a back door approach to Somerset Reservoir.

Somerset Reservoir

Nestled in the rolling eastern slopes of the Green Mountains, Somerset Reservoir is a full-day destination, especially for a birdwatcher with a boat. About five miles long, with sixteen miles of shoreline, this reservoir's secrets can hardly be discovered in a single outing. So pack binoculars, a spotting scope, a picnic lunch (even supper), and, in spring, a tolerance of black flies.

The access road to the reservoir leaves Route 9 about 1.6 miles east of its intersection with Route 8 in Searsburg and 5.4 miles west of Wilmington. The road (which begins as U.S. Forest Service Road 71 and is muddy to impassable in spring) winds north for 9.7 miles to a boat launch, parking, and picnic area at the reservoir's southern end. (Along the way, after a bridge over the Deerfield River, continue straight to the reservoir as Route 71 turns left toward Kelley Stand Road.) If boating, watch the weather because the reservoir's long reach can quickly turn high winds to high seas.

Watch for mixed flocks of migrating flycatchers, vireos, and warblers along the entrance road. The reservoir is typically the southernmost Common Loon nesting site in Vermont. But there is room here for more, including scoters (in fall) and waterfowl during migration. Bald Eagle stops here regularly and a summering pair has spurred speculation of future nesting. Wetlands and their characteristic species can be found in the ample curves and corners of this huge reservoir, which are most easily reached by boat. From the boat launch the access road continues north past additional picnic areas. A trail leaves from the last picnic area and runs north along the east side of the reservoir. It is a popular spot for thrushes, including Swainson's Thrush, warblers, including Northern Parula, and a myriad of other songbirds. Barred Owl oversees activities here after sunset.

Lake Paran

A dam on Paran Creek created instant birdwatching in downtown North Bennington. Open water here can satisfy a birdwatcher's duck habit from fall through spring. And the place can sing with songbirds from spring through fall.

From North Bennington, at the intersection of Routes 67 and 67A, drive south about 0.1 mile on 67A and turn left on Sage Street. Bear right 0.1 mile ahead, cross the creek, turn left on Willing Road, and proceed 0.3 mile ahead to a boat launch and parking lot. (The railroad bed and tracks here, currently idle, may be either reactivated or converted to a recreation trail. If the tracks remain, use caution.)

In winter, open water on or below the lake is a refuge for Canada Goose and Mallard. In spring and fall small numbers of other ducks in migration visit. Solitary Sandpiper finds the shoreline appealing for a little R and R (rest and refueling) during its travels. Eastern Bluebird can be seen in the area year-round. Walk the railroad bed east (away from the sluice) toward a large stand of white birch. In the shrubby buckthorn and honeysuckle look for Northern Mockingbird, Brown Thrasher, Eastern Towhee, and other thicket-lovers. A little farther along, where the railroad bed abuts a wet area, the warbler attendance can be impressive during migration in May. The typically uncommon Wilson's Warbler often joins Blue-winged Warbler (probable resident), American Redstart, and Yellow Warbler perusing the shrubs and thickets.

South Stream Wildlife Management Area

Throughout the southwestern corner of the state the long, north-south Vermont Valley tugs constantly at the birdwatcher. With the Taconic Mountains to its west and the Green Mountains to its east, the valley is a natural, narrow corridor for migrants zooming north or south. A dammed section of South Stream in the town of Pownal is an invitation to visit, particularly for waterfowl in early spring.

From Route 7 in downtown Bennington, drive east on Route 9 for 0.5 mile

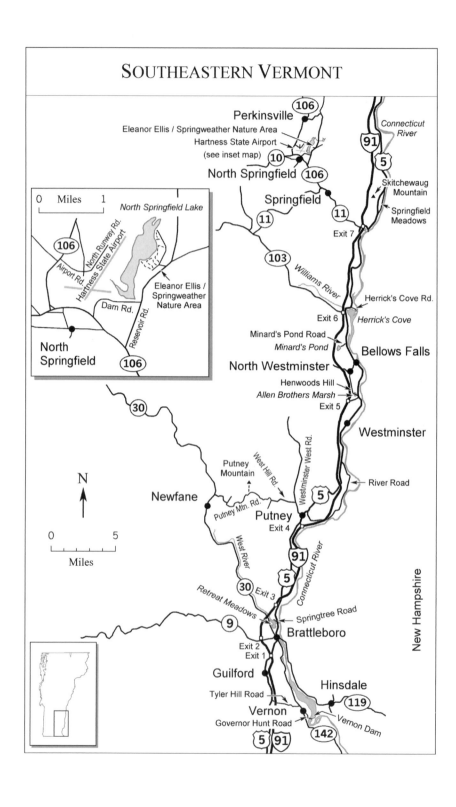

SOUTHEASTERN VERMONT

Perkinsville
Eleanor Ellis / Springweather Nature Area
Hartness State Airport
(see inset map)
106
10

North Springfield
106

Springfield
11

11
Exit 7

103

Williams River

Connecticut River

91
5

Skitchewaug Mountain

Springfield Meadows

Herrick's Cove Rd.

Exit 6   Herrick's Cove

Minard's Pond Road
Minard's Pond

North Westminster
Henwoods Hill
Allen Brothers Marsh
Exit 5

Bellows Falls

Westminster

0   Miles   1

North Springfield Lake

106
North Runway Rd.
Hartness State Airport
Airport Rd.

Dam Rd.

Reservoir Rd.

Eleanor Ellis / Springweather Nature Area

North Springfield
106

30

Putney Mountain

West Hill Rd.

Westminster West Rd.

River Road

5

Newfane

Putney Mtn. Rd.

Putney
Exit 4

West River

91
5

30 Exit 3

Retreat Meadows

Connecticut River

N

0   5
Miles

9

Springtree Road

Brattleboro

Exit 2
Exit 1

New Hampshire

Guilford

Tyler Hill Road

Vernon
Governor Hunt Road

Hinsdale
119

Vernon Dam

5 91   142

and turn right on Morgan Street. Drive south 1.7 miles, at which point Morgan merges into South Stream Road. Ahead 3.4 miles is the entrance to the wildlife management area on the right. Head down the access road and bear left at the fork to the boat launch or right toward the dam.

This is spring's point of entry into Vermont. Pied-billed Grebe, Canada Goose, Wood Duck, American Black Duck, Mallard, Ring-necked Duck, Common Merganser, and Hooded Merganser are among the first paddling visitors. Woodland birds can include Eastern Phoebe, Ruby-crowned Kinglet, thrushes, Yellow Warbler and other warblers, and Eastern Towhee. Mosquitoes can be plentiful here.

🖊 *Southeastern Vermont*

The longest waterway in New England, the Connecticut River cuts an impressive path between Vermont and New Hampshire (the river itself is New Hampshire property). That path is an important flyway for migrants. Waterfowl congregate on the river or in flooded fields as the ice breaks up in late March and early April. The land birds are next, either stopping to nest or using the valley as a route toward breeding grounds farther north. The tide turns in fall, when good numbers of raptors join the southbound traffic. Patches of open water keep a small entourage of ducks and gulls on or near the river throughout the winter.

Eleanor Ellis/Springweather Nature Area and Hartness State Airport

A joint effort of the U.S. Army Corps of Engineers and Ascutney Mountain Audubon, the **Eleanor Ellis/Springweather Nature Area** offers birds and birders alike seventy acres of fields, forests, wetlands, riparian zones, and a waterfowl-friendly reservoir. The informal refuge is busy during migration. After all, a few flaps of the wings can carry many birds from the Connecticut River flyway just inland to the rich mixture of habitats at this reserve on the Springfield-Weathersfield town line. The species list here exceeds 150 and is growing.

From Interstate 91 take Exit 7 and drive west on Route 11 for 4.3 miles into Springfield. Where Route 11 turns left at a traffic light continue straight on Route 106 for 1.9 miles, turn right on Reservoir Road, and proceed 0.8 mile to Dam Road. (Turn left on Dam Road for a big view of the reservoir and Mt. Ascutney to the northeast.) Continue another 0.7 mile (beyond Dam Road) on Reservoir Road to the reserve entrance and parking on the left. The best way to see birds here is to abandon the vehicle and walk.

During the spring rush northward, North Springfield Lake attracts waterfowl from the Connecticut River flyway, including Canada Goose, American Black Duck, Mallard, Ring-necked Duck, Bufflehead, and Hooded and Common Merganser. Osprey often stop to feed and investigate the nesting platforms erected for them. Spotted Sandpiper, American Woodcock, and Common Snipe nest and raise young from April through October. Both Great Horned and Barred Owl claim permanent residency here. Less common visitors over the years have included Little Blue Heron, Gadwall, Northern Shoveler, and Canvasback.

Songbirds can also be abundant here, so take a long walk on the trail system during spring and fall migrations, especially May and September. (Maps are available at the kiosk by the parking area.) A good portion of Ellis/Springweather is farmland returning to forest. So where Eastern Meadowlark and Field Sparrow were once common, Brown Thrasher and Eastern Towhee have moved in. A Yellow-breasted Chat once dropped by for a visit. And the omnipresent Song Sparrow has watched them all come and go. The forested areas attract vireos, thrushes, warblers, and other sparkling songbirds.

The nearby **Hartness State Airport** is worth a visit for grassland and shrubland species. From Reservoir Road, proceed north on Route 106 (which bends right in 1.3 miles) for 2.2 miles to Airport Road. Turn right, drive 0.4 mile, and continue straight along North Runway Road for another 0.5 mile. Along the way, pull over in spring for grassland specialties, including Vesper Sparrow, Grasshopper Sparrow, and, in the shrubs, Indigo Bunting.

Springfield Meadows and Skitchewaug Mountain

A private field in the Connecticut River floodplain, known locally as **Springfield Meadows**, can be a fine spot for waterfowl when it floods from late March through April. From Exit 7 on Interstate 91, go east toward the river on Route 5 for 0.5 mile and turn left to stay on Route 5 northbound. Ahead 1.9 miles park at a pull-off on the right side of Route 5. The flooded field between Route 5 and the Connecticut River can attract good numbers of Wood Duck and common dabblers. A Greater White-fronted Goose once joined the Canada Geese here in spring migration. Peregrine Falcon can sometimes be seen on and around the cliffs of **Skitchewaug Mountain** to the west. Old Connecticut River Road, on the river side of the fields, offers an alternate view of the area.

Herrick's Cove and Minard's Pond

Vermont has many welcoming places for birds, including time-tested "migrant traps"—those magical spots where migrants pour from the sky. **Her-**

Herrick's Cove in Rockingham is one of the best places in Vermont to find Palm Warbler in migration. It was recently discovered nesting in the Northeast Kingdom.
Photo: Steven D. Faccio

rick's Cove in Rockingham, at the heart of the Connecticut River flyway, is a supreme, delightful example. A peninsula cradles the mouth of the Williams River where it joins the Connecticut, forming a cove of lazy backwater—a magnet for waterfowl. But the abundant landbird visitors here can out-perform even the ducks. All told, a diverse 225 feathered species have been encountered in this relatively small area, elevating Herrick's Cove to one of Vermont's premier places for watching birds. It is a great place to spend a full morning in spring or fall. During a fallout spend the entire day.

For drivers southbound on Interstate 91, take Exit 6 and proceed south on Route 103 for 0.3 mile. Turn north (left) on Route 5 and continue 0.7 mile to a right turn onto Herrick's Cove Road. Northbound drivers on Interstate 91 also take Exit 6 and, at the end of a long exit ramp, turn left to pick up Route 5 north. After 0.5 mile go right to stay on Route 5 and continue another 0.7 mile to a right turn on Herrick's Cove Road. A parking area, boat launch, picnic grounds, and lots of birds are ahead at the end of the road.

Herrick's Cove is actually the confluence of the Williams and Connecticut Rivers. The shallow waters here have at one time or another hosted nearly every duck species seen in Vermont. Uncommon visitors to these waterways and wetlands have included Sandhill Crane, Mute Swan, Eurasian Wigeon, Redhead, Common Eider, Ruddy Duck, Fulvous Whistling-Duck (unknown if wild or escaped), American Coot, and Black-legged Kittiwake. Short-eared Owl has stopped here in migration.

The variety of vegetation at this waypoint on the flyway guarantees high songbird diversity. Passerines seen here over the years include eight of the nine regular Vermont flycatchers, all five regular vireos (plus White-eyed Vireo), all five eastern swallow species (plus Purple Martin), twenty-nine species of warbler (plus Yellow-breasted Chat), and a dozen species of sparrow (plus Henslow's Sparrow).

The park is small enough so that a birdwatcher can wander all of it, from the southern tip of the peninsula back out to the entrance road. Check water wherever it is visible. Most of the aquatic activity is in the cove rather than the Connecticut River proper.

About 3 miles south of Herrick's Cove, **Minard's Pond**, the water supply for Bellows Falls, attracts waterfowl in April and from October onward as long as its surface remains free of ice. From Route 5 at the northern end of Bellows Falls, turn west on Pond Road, go up the hill, and bear left on Minard's Pond Road to the pond and parking lot. A trail circles the pond.

Allen Brothers Marsh and River Road

A surprising diversity of marsh birds haunts **Allen Brothers Marsh**, an emergent wetland just off Interstate 91 in Westminster. Visit in spring or early summer. From Interstate 91 take Exit 5 and drive east 0.8 mile to Route 5. Turn left on Route 5 and take another quick left onto Henwoods Hill road.

This road (muddy in spring) passes through a wetland whose main attractions include American Bittern, Great Blue Heron, Great Egret (uncommon), Wood Duck, American Black Duck, Mallard, Green-winged Teal, Blue-winged Teal, Ring-necked Duck, Hooded Merganser, Northern Harrier, Virginia Rail, Sora, and Marsh Wren. Eastern Kingbird and Yellow Warbler like nesting here. Common Nighthawk sometimes vacuums the sky for insects. And Orchard Oriole has nested here. Quite rare in Vermont (even if it's not exactly a bird), Fowler's toad has been heard calling here. The road through the wetland continues on to North Westminster and can be good for migrating landbirds. Louisiana Waterthrush nests in a ravine along this road.

While in the area, **River Road** between Westminster and Putney can afford good looks at waterfowl in the flooded fields along the Connecticut River in spring. From Putney Village drive north on Route 5 for 0.5 miles to River Road on the right. Or, from the village of Westminster, drive south on Route 5 for about 3 miles to River Road on the left. The road runs along the floodplain for at least five miles. A Harris's Sparrow spent the winter of 2000–2001 in this area.

Putney Mountain

With a long north-south ridgeline in the Connecticut River flyway, Putney Mountain offers a tempting orientation to migrating birds—most notably hawks. Smatterings of migrant warblers and other songbirds can adorn the fairly easy hike to the summit. But this place is all about hawk migration. The mountain's cleared summit and commanding view attract a dedicated crew of hawkwatchers each September and October, when Putney becomes the most faithfully tended hawkwatch site in Vermont. This is a good place to pack a lunch and enjoy. Hundreds of raptors a day are possible; the nice view is guaranteed.

From Interstate 91 in Putney take Exit 4 and drive approximately 0.2 mile toward Putney to Route 5. Turn right on Route 5 and proceed 0.5 mile to the center of Putney. Turn left on Westminster West Road (unmarked), drive 1.1 miles, turn left on West Hill Road and proceed another 2.5 miles to Putney Mountain Road. Turn right on Putney Mountain Road and continue 3.3 miles to the crest of the ridge and a parking lot on the right. Behind the parking lot, hike north on the "Main Trail" along the ridge 0.6 mile to the summit. (For more about Putney Mountain and hawkwatching in Vermont, see "Hawkwatching," page 21.)

Retreat Meadows

The mouth of the West River yawns at its confluence with the Connecticut. The open water and wetlands here, just north of downtown Brattleboro, can tempt a wonderful variety of waterfowl, waders, and the occasional rarity. Retreat Meadows is one of Vermont's finest spots away from Lake Champlain for rare winter gulls. Access for birders is limited, however.

View the West River floodplain from two spots. First, from Interstate 91 in Brattleboro take Exit 2 and drive east on Route 9 for 0.9 mile to Route 5 in downtown Brattleboro. Turn left, and in 0.2 mile turn left again onto Route 30. Just ahead turn right to remain on Route 30 and continue 0.5 mile past the Brattleboro Retreat (a psychiatric and addiction treatment center) to a pull-off on the right. This is on the western shore of the West River. WARNING: Beware of the fast traffic on Route 30.

For another view, on the north side of the West River, return on Route 30 toward downtown Brattleboro and proceed north (left) on Route 5 for 0.8 mile to Springtree Road. Turn left on Springtree, which weaves between businesses, proceeds along the river, and ends 0.3 mile ahead at private land posted against trespassing.

In April and again beginning in October this can be a retreat for waterfowl. Among the common American Black Duck and Mallard, uncommon visitors here have included Brant, Tundra Swan, and Ruddy Duck. Small numbers of shorebirds show up in May but tend to be more common during the southbound migration in August and September.

Best known for their wing whistles in flight, Common Snipe also vocalize from exposed perches. This connoisseur of sound stakes out a favorite fence post.
Photo: Dave Hoag

Osprey, Bald Eagle, Northern Harrier, and Common Snipe are often seen in migration. And in spring, and from fall through winter, provided there is open water, Retreat Meadows is a popular spot for gulls. Besides Ring-billed Gull and Herring Gull, watch for Iceland Gull or Glaucous Gull. Black-legged Kittiwake made an appearance here once.

Vernon Dam

When the bulk of the Connecticut River freezes over, the desperate duck can often find open water at the big bend at Vernon Dam. The stretch of river for more than a mile downstream from the dam can be busy with waterfowl from October through April. Vernon is home to Vermont's only nuclear power plant.

From Interstate 91 in Brattleboro take Exit 1 and drive south on Route 5 for 3.5 miles to Tyler Hill Road. Turn left, drive 2.2 miles, and turn right at the "T" intersection onto Route 142. Continue 0.4 mile and go left at the "Y" intersection onto Governor Hunt Road. Now, at the "Z" intersection . . . (just kidding). Continue 0.9 mile on Governor Hunt Road to the dam and parking lot just beyond on the left. There is also parking at a small park across the road. (Neither of these parking areas is plowed in winter.) Consider also crossing the bridge in Brattleboro to New Hampshire and traveling to Hinsdale, which provides more varied views of the river south of the dam.

Fairly common here are Canada Goose, American Black Duck, Mallard, Common Goldeneye, and Common Merganser. Less common are Bufflehead, Ring-necked Duck, Hooded Merganser, and Barrow's Goldeneye. Bald Eagle, nesting nearby in New Hampshire, occasionally works the river.

🪶 Upper Connecticut River Valley

In the milder climate of the Connecticut River Valley the northern hardwoods of Vermont's Eastern Piedmont yield to oak and pine forests more characteristic of terrain farther south. The birds respond, with a few southerners using the valley as an outpost in northern New England. The Connecticut River flyway also brings waterfowl, which sometimes linger through winter in open water. And towering above the show is Mt. Ascutney, an orphan mountain in this valley that only enhances the diversity of birdlife found in this region.

Lake Morey

Lake Morey along the Connecticut River flyway attracts loons, grebes, waterfowl, and limited numbers of wetland species, but in the summer months humans are far more abundant. Camps and docks surrounding the lake limit viewing options. The best time to visit is during fall migration after summer traffic has cleared and early in the day before boaters might scatter birds.

Reach the lake from Exit 15 on Interstate 91. Turn west at the end of the exit ramp onto Lake Morey Road (unmarked), which runs 1.6 miles along the lake's west shore to a boat launch on the right. Birds typically gravitate toward the center of the lake. Visitors have included Common Loon, Horned Grebe, Red-necked Grebe, Bufflehead, Common Goldeneye, and all three scoter species. On much less typical days, Lake Morey has hosted Great Cormorant, Brant, Long-tailed Duck, and Black-legged Kittiwake.

Union Village Dam and Mystery Trail

A back road winding through a quiet hollow offers some of this region's most pleasant birdwatching. The road passes through a park, actually a flood-control project of the U.S. Army Corps of Engineers. In 1950 the corps completed the **Union Village Dam** on the Ompompanoosuc River in Thetford. **Buzzell Bridge Road**, along the river between Thetford Center and the dam (in Union Village), has become a popular recreation spot. Best of all it is closed to vehicles from late summer through early spring, presenting a fine opportunity for leisurely birdwatching through varied habitats. Gates on either end are opened to vehicles daily (7 A.M.–7:30 P.M.) from the third Saturday in May through the Sunday after Labor Day. But arrive early, leave the car, and walk.

Visit from Thetford Center. From Interstate 91, take Exit 14 in Thetford and proceed west on Route 113 for 1.9 miles to Buzzell Bridge Road on the left.

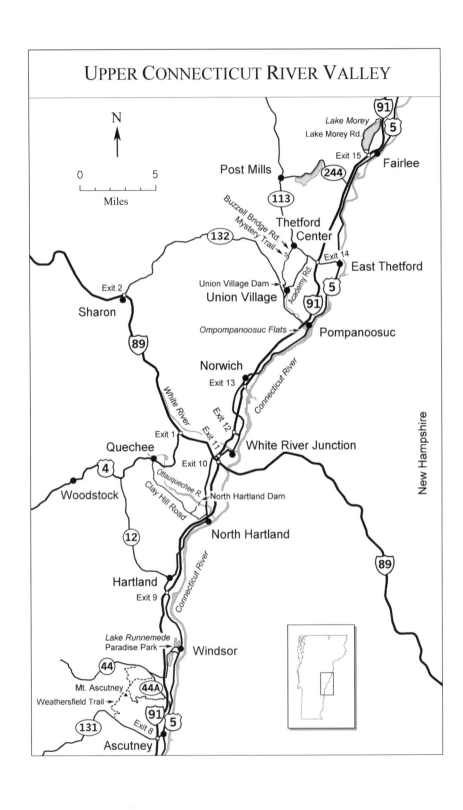

UPPER CONNECTICUT RIVER VALLEY

Epitomizing the union of bird and habitat, a female Ruffed Grouse (known to many Vermonters as partridge) blends into the woods to hide herself and her eggs.
Photo: Dave Hoag

Park either at the gate or in a lot 0.4 mile ahead. From here to the dam (about 2.5 miles away), Buzzell Bridge Road has picnic areas, swimming, and loop trails.

Not to be missed along Buzzell Bridge Road is the **Mystery Trail**. This short loop passes through wetland and woodland, with opportunities for seeing American Bittern, Great Blue Heron, Green Heron (uncommon), Wood Duck, Hooded Merganser, Red-shouldered Hawk (uncommon), Barred Owl, Common Snipe, American Woodcock, Alder Flycatcher, and Nashville, Black-throated Blue, Yellow-rumped, Black-throated Green, and Black-and-white Warblers. Among migrating songbirds, Blue-winged and Wilson's Warblers are uncommon here. In late summer, migrating Common Nighthawks seem to use the river as a corridor toward the Connecticut River and points south. Consider skiing or snowshoeing the route for winter songbirds, including both nuthatch species, Golden-crowned Kinglet, Dark-eyed Junco, Purple Finch, and, in years with a good conifer cone crop, White-winged Crossbill and Pine Siskin.

To reach the Union Village Dam at the southern end of Buzzell Bridge Road (if Buzzell Bridge Road is closed), return to Route 113, drive east for 1.2 miles, and turn right onto Academy Road. Continue 2.9 miles, pass through a covered bridge, and turn right to reach the U.S. Army Corps of Engineers recreation area, which has picnic tables, restrooms, a ranger's office, and access to the dam.

Ompompanoosuc Flats

The mouth of the Ompompanoosuc River, at its confluence with the Connecticut River, can attract waterfowl and shorebirds during migration. Near busy roads, this is hardly a quiet place for birds. But so rare is good shorebird habitat in Vermont that the flats are worth a visit, particularly in late summer and fall. Note that the shorebird show depends on the Wilder Dam, downstream on the Connecticut, for lower water and exposed mud. In other words: "If you *lower* it they will come."

From Interstate 91 take Exit 13, drive east to pick up Route 5 north, and continue 6 miles ahead to Route 132. Turn left and park on the wide shoulder before passing beneath the interstate. Deeper water here can attract waterfowl in spring and fall such as American Black Duck, Mallard, Green-winged Teal, Hooded Merganser, and Common Merganser. Exposed mud can bring shorebirds (even American Pipit) out of migration to feed. American Golden-Plover can sometimes be seen here with Black-bellied Plover, as well as more common shorebirds such as Killdeer, Semipalmated Plover, Semipalmated Sandpiper, Least Sandpiper, Pectoral Sandpiper, and Dunlin.

North Hartland Dam

When the U.S. Army Corps of Engineers in 1961 completed a flood-control dam on the Ottauquechee River in Hartland, the byproduct was 1,711 acres of recreation area—mixed woods, wetlands, and fields. Because this is a popular spot, the best times to visit are before or after the swimming and boating seasons.

From Route 5 in North Hartland (just north of where it passes under Interstate 91), drive west on Clay Hill Road 1 mile to an access road (on the right) that ends at the dam and a wildlife overlook. From high on the dam itself, look in spring for Great Blue Heron (from a nearby rookery), Common Merganser, Hooded Merganser, and other waterfowl, even a flyby Bald Eagle and nesting Common Raven. Back on Clay Hill Road, a few hundred feet east of the dam access road, is a parking lot with a short trail to a platform overlooking a beaver-engineered wetland. Wood Duck, one of the most highly decorated waterfowl, nests here.

Paradise Park and Lake Runnemede

William Maxwell Evarts, attorney general under President Andrew Johnson, named Lake Runnemede in honor of the Magna Carta, which was signed at Runnymede near Windsor, England, in 1215. Once held in the Evarts family, this lake and adjacent forest north of the village of Windsor is now a 225-acre recreation area going by the name "Paradise Park." The best times to visit are during migration, from late March through late May and late August through October. Finding a diversity of habitat, birdwatchers parking themselves here for a morning just might find avian paradise.

Paradise Park lies north of State Street and west of Route 5 (Main Street) in the village of Windsor. Access to the lake itself is best from Route 5, but parking can be hard to find. Try parking near the Old Constitution House or nearby along Route 5 (mostly on the west side) and walking north along the road or lakeshore to a park entrance at Eddie's Place Road. The best access to the forested area is from County Road (see below). Before setting out, pick up a park map, which shows entrances, parking spots, and trails, from the Windsor Town Hall or at the entrances off County Road or Eddie's Place Road.

After the ice breaks up on this impounded lake (usually by late March), waterfowl begin to trickle in. Later visitors include Common Loon and American Bittern. In April early flying insects run the gauntlet of all five eastern swallow species. During the spring landbird migration, warblers and other songsters (including the fairly regular Palm Warbler) feed among the thickets of sumac, dogwood, and highbush cranberry. Some of the more common nesters here include Alder Flycatcher, Willow Flycatcher, Eastern Bluebird, Gray Catbird, Yellow Warbler, and Common Yellowthroat. Continue along the lakeside trail toward the hills and into the woods, where Pine Warbler and Louisiana Waterthrush nest and other songbirds can be abundant during migration.

For a direct route into the 117-acre woods, from Route 5 (Main Street) head west on West State Street past the school, turn right (north) on County Road, and, just before reaching the hospital, park at a trailhead lot on the right.

Mt. Ascutney

Mt. Ascutney appears odd and alone in the Connecticut Valley. This 3,144-foot peak is a monadnock—a mound of granite (born from molten volcanic rock) that intruded into rock from below, only to be exposed when the upper layer eroded away. Younger than the Green Mountains to the west, Ascutney is more closely related to the White Mountains of New Hampshire. Various routes to the top pass through mixed deciduous woods below and conifer-dominated forest above. The result is a fine mix of woodland birds from mid-May through mid-September. Openings and a fire tower provide good hawk-watching potential from late August through November.

From Interstate 91 take Exit 8 in Ascutney and drive east 0.5 mile on Route 131 to Route 5. Go north on Route 5 for 1.1 miles, bear left on Route 44A, and continue another 1.1 miles to the entrance to Ascutney State Park. A park road

Downy Woodpecker is common across Vermont and a frequent visitor to feeders.
Photo: Ted Murin

leads to a parking lot at a saddle between the south peak and the true summit. A trail runs the final 0.8 mile to the summit and a fire tower with panoramic views (broken only by telecommunications towers on the mountain). The park is normally open from two weekends before Memorial Day through the Tuesday after Columbus Day. The road is open from 10 A.M. to a half hour before dark.

Better yet, hike one of the several trails to the summit. One favorite is the Weathersfield Trail on the mountain's southwest side. In spring the trail passes through a songbird serenade of Great Crested Flycatcher, Winter Wren, Hermit Thrush, Black-throated Blue Warbler, Ovenbird, and other woodland species.

For a trail map and guide, inquire at the park headquarters inside the entrance gate or at the Springfield district office of the Vermont Department of Forests, Parks and Recreation, (802)885-8855.

Connecticut River Birding Trail

Scores of birdwatching areas along the Connecticut River from Woodsville, New Hampshire, to Rockingham, Vermont, comprise the Connecticut River Birding Trail. Contact the trail office at (802)291-9100 for details and a map of the forty-six birding sites in Vermont and New Hampshire.

✒ North Central Vermont

Forests, farmland, wetlands, lakes, rivers, and the state's highest peak offer the birdwatcher in this region a diverse encounter with Vermont. Deciduous and mixed woods dominate the eastern foothills here. But the Green Mountains, on the western edge of this area, offer trails to high-elevation spruce-fir forests and their own avian specialties. The mountains also influence the climate, which is colder and wetter than much of Vermont. The birdwatching hotspots are dispersed in this region. Migrant traps and flyways are a bit harder to find. But, like so much of Vermont, all of that forest, water, and varying elevation means birds can turn up virtually anywhere.

Mt. Mansfield and Camels Hump

Vermont's highest and most massive peak, **Mt. Mansfield**, with a long ridgeline and classic bald summit, hosts one of the state's largest nesting populations of Bicknell's Thrush. This tiny songbird that sings like a flute shares the mountain with a barrage of development—ski trails and lifts, radio towers, and even a visitor's center. The Stowe Mountain Resort's 4.5-mile toll road toward the top offers access to Bicknell's Thrush and other high-elevation songbirds. While Mt. Mansfield welcomes a diversity of birds during the warmer months, Bicknell's Thrush is most active and evident during the first two weeks of June.

From the village of Stowe, take Route 108 (Mountain Road) north for 5.8 miles to the toll road parking lot on the left (not shown on map). Watch carefully for the sign. Call the resort at (802)253-3000 to see if the toll road is free of snow and open for the season. The toll is $14 per carload for up to six people. Hours for vehicles are from 9 A.M. to 5 P.M.—convenient for a picnic but not ideal for finding birds. Walking the steep road early and in the dark is a viable (but ambitious) option. Prepare for clouds, relentless wind, colder temperatures, and snow on top, even when it is warm and sunny below. Also be prepared for black flies, which are most tenacious on calm, humid days. Another approach is a strenuous hike to the summit along one of the mountain's numerous trails. The Long Trail south from Route 108 in Stowe or the Sunset Ridge Trail from Underhill State Park are among the best options. Contact the Green Mountain Club in Waterbury at (802)244-7037 for maps and details.

The ascent of Mt. Mansfield passes through several life zones. The various habitats guarantee high bird diversity. During a single outing on this mountain, for example, it would be possible to locate every eastern North American thrush (except Gray-cheeked), from Eastern Bluebird and Veery below to

NORTH CENTRAL VERMONT

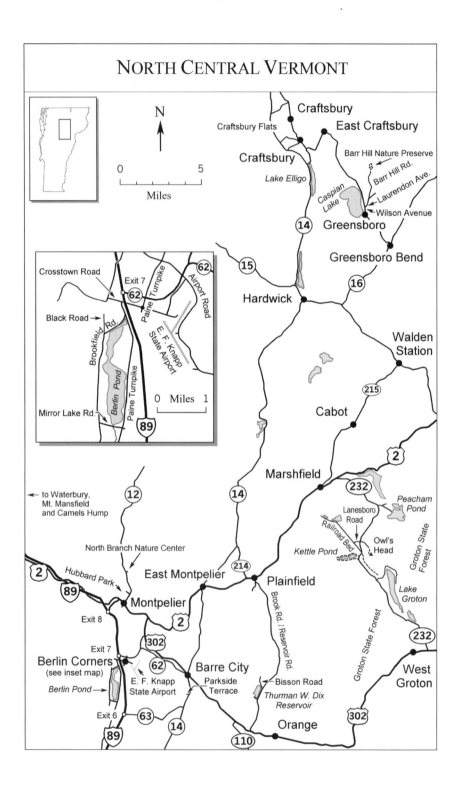

N

0   5

Miles

Craftsbury

Craftsbury Flats

East Craftsbury

Craftsbury

Barr Hill Nature Preserve

Lake Elligo

Barr Hill Rd.

Laurendon Ave.

Caspian Lake

Wilson Avenue

14   Greensboro

15

Greensboro Bend

Hardwick

16

Walden Station

Crosstown Road

Exit 7

62

62

Airport Road

Paine Turnpike

Black Road

Brookfield Rd.

E. F. Knapp State Airport

Berlin Pond

Paine Turnpike

Mirror Lake Rd.

89

0   Miles   1

215

Cabot

Marshfield

232

Peacham Pond

Lanesboro Road

Railroad Bed

Owl's Head

Groton State Forest

to Waterbury, Mt. Mansfield and Camels Hump

12

14

North Branch Nature Center

Kettle Pond

Lake Groton

2

Hubbard Park

89

East Montpelier

214

Plainfield

Groton State Forest

Montpelier

Exit 8

2

Brook Rd. / Reservoir Rd.

232

Exit 7

302

Berlin Corners
(see inset map)

62

Barre City

West Groton

Berlin Pond

E. F. Knapp State Airport

Parkside Terrace

Bisson Road

Thurman W. Dix Reservoir

302

Exit 6

63

14

Orange

89

110

Beauty, or mediocrity, is sometimes only feather deep. Vermont's state bird, the Hermit Thrush, got the job for its sweet, ethereal song rather than its (unassuming) plumage.
Photo: Steven D. Faccio

Swainson's Thrush and Bicknell's Thrush on top. Forests of sugar maple, yellow birch, American beech, and other hardwood species dominate below. Songbirds here include Great Crested Flycatcher, Red-eyed Vireo, Black-throated Blue Warbler, Ovenbird, Scarlet Tanager, and Rose-breasted Grosbeak. Red spruce, paper birch, and mountain ash enter the picture somewhat higher, along with Red-breasted Nuthatch, Winter Wren, Golden-crowned Kinglet, Hermit Thrush, Magnolia Warbler, Black-throated Green Warbler, and Dark-eyed Junco. And finally, taking over near the summit are the stunted, contorted balsam fir and black spruce known as *krummholz*, the German word for crooked wood.

Good places to stop for Bicknell's Thrush include the parking area below the Octagon (3.9 miles from the toll gate) and the summit station at the end of the 4.5-mile road. On windy days investigate leeward areas of the mountain. On calm days the thrushes sometimes sing between dawn and dusk. But the ideal time is the crepuscular hours, even just before dark. Listen for the raspy and Veery-like *preer*.

Also expect nesting Common Raven, Winter Wren, Swainson's Thrush, Yellow-rumped Warbler, Blackpoll Warbler, Purple Finch, and, depending on the fir cone crop, White-winged Crossbill and Pine Siskin.

No matter which birds show themselves, an ascent of Mt. Mansfield is one of the most rewarding encounters with Vermont and points beyond. Views from the top include Lake Champlain to the west, the northern Green Mountains (and Montreal on a clear day) to the north, the White Mountains (and Vermont's Worcester Range) to the east, and the southern Green Mountains to the south. From this high place in Vermont a visitor can sense the curvature of the Earth.

Note that the area near the top of the toll road is within a thrush research site. While birding here, please stay on the road or marked trails. Near the summit of Mt. Mansfield, a 1.4-mile hike along the Long Trail from the upper parking area, is an alpine meadow, one of only three Vermont sites for this rare natural community. While these alpine plants, including Bigelow's sedge, alpine bilberry, and mountain sandwort, can tolerate the thin soils and harsh conditions here, they are vulnerable to human boots. Please step only on bare rocks in this zone.

Another classic Vermont summit, this one without the toll road and development, is **Camels Hump** (not shown on map). Bicknell's Thrush and the other Mansfield residents nest here as well. Choice trails up this peak, a prominent landmark in much of central Vermont, include the Monroe Trail from Duxbury and the Burrows Trail from Huntington Center. The same warnings about weather and alpine plants apply. To reach the Monroe Trail, take Exit 10 from Interstate 89 and go south on Route 100 for a few tenths of a mile, turn left on Route 2, and drive 0.2 mile to Winooski Street. Turn right on Winooski Street, cross over the Winooski River, turn right on River Road, and drive 3.9 miles to the Camels Hump Road on the left. The trailhead parking lot is 3.6 miles up this road at its end. It is a 3.4-mile hike to the summit. To reach the Burrows trailhead, take Camels Hump Road east from Huntington Center for 1.9 miles. Turn right across a bridge and continue 1.6 miles to the end of the road. The 2.4-mile hike to the summit begins at the back of the parking lot. Both hikes up the mountain are fairly strenuous.

Montpelier-Barre Area

Two miles north of downtown Montpelier, at a big slow bend in the North Branch of the Winooski River, is a small refuge with a big heart. The Vermont Institute of Natural Science's **North Branch Nature Center** is a reserve of grassland and floodplain forest. The best time to visit is spring through fall.

From State Street (Route 2) in Montpelier, drive north on Elm Street (Route 12) for 2 miles to the nature center, an old sheep farm, on the right. Stop in to visit the staff naturalists or the entertaining "Critter Room," or to pick up a field guide in the gift shop. A short nature trail passes through open habitat for American Kestrel, Common Snipe, Eastern Bluebird, Savannah Sparrow, and Bobolink. Closer to the river, watch for Spotted Sandpiper, Belted Kingfisher, Cedar Waxwing, Alder Flycatcher, Veery, Yellow Warbler, Chestnut-sided Warbler, and American Redstart. More unusual visitors have included Bald Eagle, Upland Sandpiper, and Carolina Wren. The butterfly garden is always worth a stop for Monarch, Great Spangled Fritillary, Red Admiral, and other delights with four wings. The reserve has a public restroom.

Elsewhere in Montpelier, **Hubbard Park** offers walking trails and decent birding within city limits. There is access to the park from the North Branch Nature Center, or from Route 2 go about 0.4 mile north on Elm Street, turn left on Winter Street, and go up the hill into the park. Hermit Thrush, Wood Thrush, a smattering of warblers, including Pine Warbler, and other songbirds are reliable in the city park during spring migration.

In **Barre City**, a recreation path above the Stevens Branch offers city songbirding. From Main Street in downtown Barre, at the small park with a statue and gazebo, drive south on South Main (Route 14) for 1.1 miles, turn right on Parkside Terrace, and continue ahead 0.2 mile (crossing the recreation path) to the parking lot for the Barre City Elementary and Middle School. Walk the path southbound for songbirds in May. Another short trail in the same direction, along the riverbank, leaves from the parking lot and picnic area just below the school (across from the tennis courts). Belted Kingfisher, Least Flycatcher, American Redstart, and Common Yellowthroat are among the riverside visitors.

Berlin Pond and E. F. Knapp State Airport

An Osprey smacks crystalline waters and emerges with a fish wiggling in its talons. Two Virginia Rails, staking out turf among a cattail marsh, grunt their comical *ki-ki-ki-ki-KEER*! A Common Loon investigates a nest site. And off in the woods, waves of warblers descend from the sky like manna from heaven.

Another spring day dawns at **Berlin Pond**, a unique refuge only a few miles from two of Vermont's largest cities. Rare is an undeveloped pond in Vermont. This one has a list of more than 157 species. So what's a pond with an undeveloped shoreline doing a mere five miles from the Capitol dome and four miles from Barre's granite sheds? The pond is the city of Montpelier's drinking water supply. As a result it is off limits to fishing, boating, and swimming, making it a de facto refuge. The best times to visit are from mid-April through June and during the fall waterfowl migration in October and November. Most of the access to birding is from a rural residential road that circles the pond. WARNING: The road is relatively quiet but not without the occasional speedster. Runners, families on bicycles, dogwalkers, and birders frequent the five-mile loop around the pond.

To reach the pond, take Exit 7 from Interstate 89. Turn right at the first stoplight onto Paine Turnpike. Drive 0.2 mile and turn right on Crosstown Road (near a flagpole and large boulder monument on the right). Immediately after passing under the interstate, turn left onto a dirt road and drive a few tenths of a mile to the pond. Investigate the pond in a 5.6-mile counterclockwise loop. Remember to watch for traffic, be aware that the shoreline is off limits, and please respect private property.

A pair of Hooded Mergansers plies calm water. Like many bird species, the female's drab plumage makes her less obvious to predators during nesting.
Photo: Ted Murin

Starting at the pond's north end near Interstate 89, drive south on Brookfield Road (with the pond to the left) and park at a widening in the road only one-tenth of a mile ahead. From here walk a half mile or so on the road along the shoreline. Scan the pond for Common Loon, Pied-billed Grebe, Wood Duck, Ring-necked Duck, and Hooded Merganser. Practice identifying all five eastern swallow species on the wing. Osprey or Bald Eagle (uncommon) perch on shoreline trees across the pond.

Linger at the cattail marsh up ahead. Virginia Rail, Yellow Warbler, Common Yellowthroat, and Swamp Sparrow nest here. American Bittern is usually around in early May. In the willow-alder stand across the road, with a backdrop of tall conifers, Ruby-crowned Kinglets flash their crowns in late April; and later in May this is a reliable spot for Alder Flycatcher. In the conifers, look for Olive-sided Flycatcher (surprisingly reliable), Cape May (rare), and other warbler species.

Continue driving south 0.6 mile and turn right onto the narrow, dead-end Black Road. Drive ahead another 0.4 mile past Black Cemetery to a tiny parking spot on the right. The road and cemetery area attract passerines. Winter Wren, Veery, Hermit Thrush, and Wood Thrush are reliable, as are warblers including Chestnut-sided, Yellow-rumped, Black-throated Green, Blackburnian, and Canada.

Turn around and return to the pond loop road. Continue south 0.2 mile to another wide spot with a pull-off on the right. Listen for both kinglet species, Northern Parula, Black-throated Blue Warbler, and other songbirds. Broad-winged Hawk sometimes nests near here.

Continue south another 1.3 miles past a number of homes with limited birding opportunities (watch for Eastern Bluebird on fence posts, though). Turn left on Mirror Lake Road and proceed 0.3 mile to the most magical spot on the pond, an open wetland with views of the pond's southern end. Park at a widening in the road. Scope the lake for Common Loon, waterfowl, and swallows, then walk Mirror Lake Road through a wetland of alder, willow, and black ash. Highlights here include nesting Yellow Warbler and Baltimore Oriole. Flocks of Rusty Blackbirds maraud through the ash from late April to early May. Northern Waterthrush, which nests here, perches in the open and belts out its song. The poplar and willow stands at the end of Mirror Lake Road attract Least Flycatcher, Warbling Vireo, Veery, American Redstart, and Baltimore Oriole. Meanwhile, Common Snipe display high above while an Osprey circles the pond. Rarer visitors over the years have included Wilson's Warbler and Yellow-throated Vireo.

Continue (east now) along Mirror Lake Road another 0.2 mile to the four corners. Either turn right and explore roadside woods and wetlands for several miles or turn left (north) on Paine Turnpike and proceed close to the shoreline. Pull aside with caution in another 0.2 mile and check for loon or waterfowl. Red-necked Grebe occasionally stops here during migration. From here the birding thins out. Continue circling the pond to the starting spot.

Not far from the pond, the **E. F. Knapp State Airport** in Berlin has hosted nesting Upland Sandpiper and other grassland species. From Exit 7 on Interstate 89, continue 1.2 miles on the exit road (Route 62), turn right on Airport Road, and drive 1.2 miles to the airport parking lot on the right. Scan the openings for the sandpipers (sometimes even walking runway edges), Northern Harrier, American Kestrel, Savannah Sparrow (on the chainlink fencing), Bobolink, and Eastern Meadowlark. The airport has a restaurant and public restrooms.

Thurman W. Dix Reservoir

The source of Barre City's drinking water is another de facto refuge off limits to swimming, boating, and fishing. And belying its location in Orange County, the reservoir's border of mature conifers and wetlands makes the place seem farther north by nature. The best time to visit is spring through fall.

To reach the reservoir from Plainfield Village, turn south off U.S. Route 2 at the blinking yellow light onto School Street, take an immediate right on Mill Street, and drive past the church 0.2 mile to Brook Road on the left. (Note that the road sign to the right says Barre Hill Road.) Turn left on Brook Road and drive 7 miles to the north end of the reservoir. (Brook Road changes its name to Reservoir Road along the way.) Alternatively, reach the reservoir from U.S. Route 302 in Orange. Pick up Reservoir Road 1.1 miles east of Route 302's intersection with Route 110 and proceed north for 1.9 miles to the reservoir's southern end.

Common Loon usually nests at Dix Reservoir. Osprey stop for visits. Expect the unusual: a Red-throated Loon, rarely seen in Vermont away from Lake Champlain, once stopped on the reservoir. The best land birding is at the northern end. From Reservoir Road (at the northern end of the reservoir), turn west onto Bisson Road and pull off at a widening 0.2 mile ahead on the right. Scope the open water for waterfowl, including Wood Duck, Green-winged Teal, Ring-necked Duck, Common Merganser, and Hooded Merganser. Both kinglet species and Yellow-rumped Warbler are common in the coniferous woods. Cape May Warbler is relatively reliable from mid- to late May. Watch for river otter munching fish out in the reservoir. In fall, the reservoir attracts waterfowl and, during periods of low water, an occasional shorebird on the exposed mud flats.

Groton State Forest

Vermont's second largest tract of public land, Groton State Forest is 26,000 acres of woods, bogs, ponds, and developed state parks. Beneath it all is granite—the Groton area's shared bedrock with the White Mountains to the east. Black bear, moose, white-tailed deer, mink, beaver, otter, fisher, and bobcat wander this state forest. Birds, by the way, are abundant.

Groton State Forest is hardly pristine, however. Intensive logging here began in 1873 and continues to a lesser extent today. And with no fewer than seven parks within its boundaries (Big Deer State Park, Boulder Beach State Park, Kettle Pond Group Camping Area, New Discovery State Park, Ricker State Park, Seyon Ranch State Park, and Stillwater State Park), campsites and trails abound. Groton is arguably the closest wild retreat from the cities of Barre, Montpelier, and St. Johnsbury.

Spring migration in May is the best time to visit, when it is possible to encounter seventeen or more warbler species in a single morning. The woods here are varied. Deciduous woods offer their own specialties, including Red-eyed Vireo, Black-throated Blue Warbler, Rose-breasted Grosbeak, and Scarlet Tanager. Stands of conifers offer theirs, including Red-breasted Nuthatch, Golden-crowned Kinglet, and Hermit Thrush. Lakes and wetlands offer herons, waterfowl (not very common in this region), and specialists such as Lincoln's Sparrow or Rusty Blackbird.

The easiest ways to find birds in Groton State Forest is to stop the car anywhere along the many unpaved roads, to hike the numerous trails, or even to explore by mountain bike, with birdsong signaling each stop. Route 232, which bisects the forest, is the perfect entryway. From Marshfield Village drive east on Route 2 for 1.1 miles to Route 232. Proceed south 3.1 miles and turn left on the Peacham Pond Road. Drive 0.2 mile, bear right at the fork, and continue 0.8 mile to a boat launch at **Peacham Pond**. Common Loon nests here, and the forest edges along the pond can be speckled with warblers in spring. Return to Route 232 and continue south 2.5 miles to an access road on the left for **Owl's Head**, a granite pluton affording striking views of the region. From spring through fall (it's closed in winter), drive the road 0.8 mile to a parking area, from which there is a short, steep hike to the top. Better yet, hike the entire access road and trail to look and listen for songbirds. In fall Owl's Head is great for viewing foliage and an occasional migrating hawk.

Directly across Route 232 from the Owl's Head access road is Lanesboro Road. Walk or drive it 0.5 mile to the old **Montpelier to Wells River Railroad Bed**, the best birding in Groton State Forest. Walk, bike, or drive the rail bed to the right (northwest) and watch for Olive-sided Flycatcher, Blue-headed Vireo, northern nesting warblers, and perhaps a Peregrine Falcon, which nests on Marshfield Cliffs towering to the northeast. **Marshfield Pond**, a beautiful spot with occasional waterfowl, is 1.9 miles ahead, and **Bailey Pond**, sometimes good for moose, is farther ahead another 0.4 mile. Retrace your path to Route 232.

One mile south of the Owl's Head access road is the parking lot (on the right) for **Kettle Pond**, a kettle hole (formed by a big chunk of leftover glacial ice) where Common Loon often nests. The open birch-maple deciduous woods near the parking lot can attract warblers during spring and fall migrations. Walk the 2.7-mile loop around the pond, emerging at the group camping area from which it is a short walk north on Route 232 back to the parking lot.

Barr Hill Nature Preserve and Craftsbury Flats

At the foothills to the Northeast Kingdom, The Nature Conservancy's **Barr Hill Nature Preserve** is an island of boreal habitat. The panoramic views alone from this high 256-acre reserve are worth the visit.

Leave the village of Greensboro northbound on Wilson Avenue and bear right at the Town Hall on Laurendon Avenue. Travel 0.6 mile (passing the Greensboro Elementary School on the left) to bear left at a fork onto Barr Hill Road (muddy in spring). Proceed another 1.2 miles past a farm to a sign at the reserve's entrance. Drive a bumpy road to the parking lot about a half mile uphill.

In spring, pick up a trail guide at the trailhead and walk the loop trail 0.8 mile through woods dominated mostly by red spruce, white spruce, and balsam fir. Listen for Cape May Warbler at the edge of the open area near the start of the trail. Magnolia Warbler, Nashville Warbler, Blackburnian Warbler, Yellow-rumped Warbler, and Chipping Sparrow are among the common species here. Boreal Chickadee is uncommon along the trail.

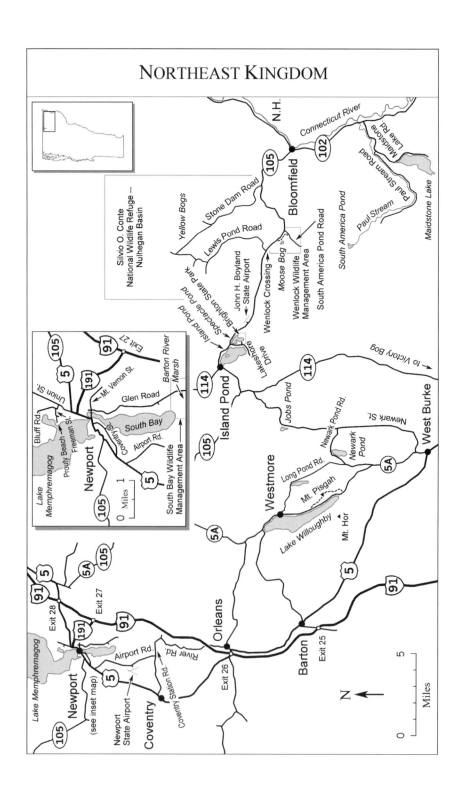

NORTHEAST KINGDOM

To the northwest, not far from Barr Hill and Greensboro, is **Craftsbury Flats**, a floodplain of the Black River along Route 14 beginning just north of the north end of Lake Eligo. From Hardwick, drive west on Route 15 for 1.2 miles, turn right (north) on Route 14, and drive 7.5 miles just past the north end of Lake Eligo. Explore the area using the roads that cross the flats to the east from Route 14 north of the lake. Waterfowl and, on occasion, shorebirds visit the flooded fields in spring. The flats can also host Rough-legged Hawk, Northern Shrike, and Horned Lark in winter, and American Pipit in migration.

🖊 *Northeast Kingdom*

Colder and wilder than most of the state, the northeastern corner is Vermont's boreal playground. Granite bedrock exposes this region's connection to the White Mountains of New Hampshire and Maine. Extensive spruce-fir forests and remote bogs and other wetlands evoke images of places much farther north. The spring migration here is impressive. But a winter visit, by ski or snowshoe, can be one of Vermont's most delightful birding experiences. At any time of year the Northeast Kingdom, resistant to suburban sprawl and wary of popular culture, is not only a place for solitude but also home to boreal species found nowhere else in Vermont.

Lake Memphremagog Area

"Memphremagog" descends from the original native name meaning "vast open lake." To be sure, **Lake Memphremagog**, the state's second-largest lake (straddling the Vermont-Quebec border), is a temptation for migrating loons, grebes, and waterfowl. As the ice breaks up in April, the lake itself hosts Bufflehead, Common Goldeneye, Common Merganser, Hooded Merganser, and other waterfowl. Yet some of the best birding here is in the marshes around the lake's South Bay. Accidental to this area have been Yellow Rail, White Pelican, and Franklin's Gull.

From the western intersection of Route 105 and Route 5 in Newport, go south on Route 5 for 0.9 mile and turn left on Airport Road. Airport Road crosses a wetland and the Black River here at **South Bay Wildlife Management Area**. Continue 0.4 mile to a pull-off on the right just past the Black River bridge. In spring this is a fine spot for viewing (or more often hearing) Pied-billed Grebe and other wetland specialists. Common Snipe struts the sky here, with the wind across its out-turned tail feathers generating its comical (and diagnostic) winnowing sound. Occasionally several birds at once

Solitary Sandpiper often upholds its name, typically appearing unaccompanied during migration.
Photo: Dave Hoag

can perform this aerial roller-coaster display, perhaps raising air traffic control issues at the nearby airport.

Continue south on Airport Road another 2.2 miles to the **Newport State Airport** and the surrounding fields, where Upland Sandpiper and other grassland species nest. From the airport continue south on Airport Road for another 1.4 miles. Turn left on Coventry Station Road and go 1.3 miles to the intersection with River Road on the right. River Road follows the Barton River, which in spring can fill the floodplain and attract waterfowl and gulls in migration.

Another access to South Bay is from the east. From just south of the Route 105/5 bridge in the center of Newport, turn east at the busy intersection onto Mt. Vernon Street. Go 0.2 mile across the Mt. Vernon Street bridge, turn right on Glen Road, and continue 2.0 miles to a pull-off just before a small oil storage depot on the right (past the railroad yard). Walk a short way to the railroad bed southbound into the **Barton River Marsh**, cornerstone of the South Bay Wildlife Management Area. WARNING: These are active tracks so use caution and always have an escape route while birding here. Notable marsh species here in spring include Pied-billed Grebe, American Bittern, Virginia Rail, Sora, Common Moorhen (uncommon), and Black Tern (uncommon and threatened in Vermont, so please give them a wide berth during the nesting season). Find all five eastern swallow species, Baltimore Oriole, and a vibrant display of Yellow Warbler. Look for marsh ducks in the open water.

Boaters can get another perspective on South Bay. During late summer and early fall, particularly in dry years, boats can reach exposed mud flats where shorebirds sometimes stop and feed. From the western intersection of Route 105 and Route 5 in Newport, go south on Route 5 for 0.6 mile and turn left on Coventry Street, which leads to a boat launch on the right. WARNING:

Later in fall, South Bay becomes the busiest waterfowl hunting site in northeastern Vermont and is best avoided during the hunting season.

Downtown Newport's newly renovated waterfront offers a good vantage of **Lake Memphremagog**. Watch for waterfowl and gulls in spring and fall. Continuing north on Route 105/5 (Main Street) across the bridge, the shopping center parking lot on the left is another good spot for scoping the lake. Unusual species visiting the lake and South Bay can include Red-necked Grebe, all three scoter species, and Barrow's Goldeneye. In fall, Lake Memphremagog is perhaps the best place in Vermont away from Lake Champlain to enjoy the flight and chatter of Bonaparte's Gull.

Finally, **Prouty Beach**, a city park, can attract ducks and shorebirds in spring and fall. From the Route 105/5 bridge in the center of Newport, go north on Route 105/5 for 0.3 mile and continue straight on Union Street (as Route 105/5 turns right) for 0.4 mile. Turn left on Bluff Road, proceed 0.2 mile, turn left on Freeman Street, and continue 0.2 mile to the park entrance on the right.

During migration the view of the southern portion of the lake here can include waterfowl and gulls. An inlet to the north can harbor dabbling ducks, Osprey, and, in the cattails, Virginia Rail and other wetland specialists.

Lake Willoughby–Mt. Pisgah Area

The drive or mountain bike ride over rugged dirt roads from Lake Willoughby to Jobs Pond covers varied habitat in Westmore and Newark. The route provides ample opportunities for viewing Common Loon and woodland birds including Winter Wren, both kinglet species, Hermit and Swainson's Thrushes, Magnolia, Blackburnian, and other sparkling warblers, and Scarlet Tanager. In early spring the roads can be muddy to impassable. Late May through early June, when black flies abound, is the best time to visit.

WARNING: Common Loon, endangered in Vermont, often nests in the remote ponds along this route. The birds choose the ponds largely due to the minimal human activity. Please appreciate the loons from afar (a spotting scope is recommended) and never approach a nest. If they retreat or repeatedly vocalize, they are stressed and need more space. Any energy spent tending to humans is energy lost from rearing chicks and can make the difference between nesting failure and success.

Begin the trip at the intersection of Routes 16 and 5A in Westmore, where the town beach offers a great view of **Lake Willoughby** framed by Mt. Pisgah and Mt. Hor. Common Loon frequents the lake in migration. Go south on Route 5A for 1.4 miles into the village and turn left on Long Pond Road. From here it is 2.1 miles to a Vermont Fish and Wildlife Department boat launch and a view of **Long Pond**. From the access continue on Long Pond Road (not plowed in winter) through mixed woods with songbirds about 3.8 miles to where it joins with Newark Pond Road. Take the hard left onto Newark Pond Road and continue about 1 mile to the **Newark Pond** boat-launch parking lot on the left.

Finally, from here continue east on Newark Pond Road 1.5 miles to Newark Street. Turn left and drive 3.0 miles to a Vermont Fish and Wildlife Department boat launch to **Jobs Pond** on the left. Peregrine Falcon has nested behind the pond on the cliffs of Jobs Mountain.

Mt. Pisgah, which towers over Lake Willoughby, offers an invigorating hike, beautiful views, and the possibility of seeing Peregrine Falcons flying below. The most popular trail leaves the east side of Route 5A about 0.4 mile south of the lake. Check around the village of Westmore for trail maps published by the Lake Willoughby Association.

Island Pond Area

A commercial center (where snowmobiles seem to outnumber automobiles in winter) is the village that shares a name and shoreline with **Island Pond**. Approaching town, a sign accurately states "Speed limit strictly enforced." Heed the warning. Even slow to a stop to find Cliff Swallow touring the village. Island Pond Lakeside Park, at the north end of the village along the shoreline, offers a nice view of the pond. Lodging is available in the village.

Brighton State Park has camping (Memorial Day to Labor Day), trails, and songbird diversity during spring migration and beyond. Common Loon has nested on Spectacle Pond and Bay-breasted Warbler has nested in the park. From the old railroad depot in the village (at the intersection of Routes 114 and 105), drive east on Route 105 for 1.7 miles and turn right at the crest of a hill onto Lakeshore Drive. The park entrance is 0.7 mile ahead on the left. An excellent view of Island Pond itself, where loons regularly visit and feed, is at a picnic area and beach 0.5 mile south of the park entrance.

Finally, the **John H. Boyland State Airport**, 3.6 miles east of the village on Route 105, hosts nesting Vesper Sparrow among the wild strawberry and blueberry. A pull-off 0.4 mile beyond the airport entrance is available on the left. The quaking Nulhegan Bog behind the airport has hosted nesting Northern Harrier. Moose tracks are fairly common here. Most, but not all, are created at night.

Moose Bog

The highlight of any birding trip to the Northeast Kingdom, the quintessential Vermont boreal experience, is a visit to Moose Bog in Wenlock Wildlife

The Northeast Kingdom is a breeding ground for boreal species rarely found elsewhere in Vermont, including this Black-backed Woodpecker.
Photo: Roy Pilcher

Management Area. The forest here includes black, red, and white spruce, balsam fir, and white pine, all mixed with white birch and aspen species. Interspersed are sphagnum bogs and spruce-fir-tamarack wetlands. Moose and black bear roam the woods and wetlands. And boreal bird species attract birdwatchers from Vermont and points south. This is a remote and delightful place, explored best on foot or by ski or snowshoe.

Much of the prime lowland boreal habitat is remote and inaccessible for all but the insect-tolerant bushwhacker. A notable exception is Moose Bog, one of Vermont's most magical places. Here an observant non-bushwhacker can locate (with more luck than skill) the boreal grand slam: Spruce Grouse (rare), Black-backed Woodpecker (rare), Gray Jay (uncommon), and Boreal Chickadee (sparse but fairly common). Keep in mind that playing a recorded bird song ("taping") to attract an endangered or threatened species such as Spruce Grouse can be construed as harassment and, as such, is illegal in Vermont. All these birds are here, so relaxed, patient exploration is the best approach.

From the old railroad depot in Island Pond, drive Route 105 east for 9.4 miles and turn right onto the unmarked and unpaved South America Pond Road. Pass through a metal gate and park in a small pull-off ahead on the right. (This road is unplowed in winter, but a cautious driver can sometimes find a spot along Route 105 about one-quarter mile east of South America Pond Road. Or about 1 mile west is a parking lot on the north side of Route

Self-Preservation in the Kingdom

Birdwatchers who like the idea of returning to their families (or at least a nice meal) after an outing might consider the following advice when visiting the Northeast Kingdom:

- Wander off-trail at your own risk (even when chasing a Gray Jay). Otherwise have a sense of where you are and carry a map and compass. Getting misplaced in the dense woods can be surprisingly simple.
- Watch for moose in the road, especially from dusk until dawn. Moose are built a good deal like a bulldozer on stilts (with the bulldozer part fixed precisely at windshield height).
- Logging still happens here. Stay to the right of the road (especially on hills) and yield to logging trucks, which can't easily stop.
- Spring floods often wash out roads here. Some logging and federal roads are gated and locked in May until their annual repairs.
- Expect black flies and mosquitoes on a mission in late May and June, to be joined by deer flies later on.
- If you happen upon moose or bear, give them plenty of room; they'll typically leave you alone.

105 just east of a bridge. From this parking lot it is about 0.25 mile to the western end of the Moose Bog trail—see text below.)

In spring the excitement begins with the first step away from the car (where a Gray Jay might greet a lucky visitor). Walk the road toward an open spruce wetland a few tenths of a mile from the parking area. Nashville Warbler, Magnolia Warbler, and Yellow-rumped Warbler are common nesting species. Shy Boreal Chickadees sometimes join the more inquisitive Black-capped Chickadees. And Gray Jays sometimes float ghostlike over the road. At the wetland look carefully for Black-backed Woodpecker, which has nested here.

While walking to the wetland, notice on the right (west) side of the road large boulders blocking a path through the woods. This is the Moose Bog trail—three-quarters of a mile of delightful walking and birding. Dense with conifers, this trail passes through good habitat for Spruce Grouse (especially near the start and end of the trail), Gray Jay, and Boreal Chickadee, in addition to the aforementioned warblers. Ruffed Grouse lives here as well. Cape May Warbler and Bay-breasted Warbler make appearances here on occasion in late May. Both kinglet species nest here, as does Yellow-bellied Flycatcher. The nomadic and sporadic White-winged Crossbill can be abundant and nests here from winter to spring during heavy cone years.

Approximately two-thirds of a mile down the trail from South America Pond Road (past a small stand of white cedar on the right) are a few well-worn (and not-so-well-worn) paths on the left leading to the bog. (Not very far beyond the paths, a large boulder blocks the other end of the trail near Route 105. Missing the paths to the bog might not be a bad idea, however, since Spruce Grouse can be found toward the main trail's terminus.)

Moose Bog, only a few hundred feet from the main trail, is a classic black spruce woodland bog—a dreamy place at dawn. At the opening's edge is a floating mat of sphagnum and woody peat, featuring Labrador tea, bog rosemary, and other bog specialists, including the unusual (and carnivorous) pitcher plant and sundew. (Don't worry, they only eat humans indirectly via black flies and mosquitoes.) Expect wet feet. Look for Common Raven overhead and Boreal Chickadee in the woods around the bog. Black-backed Woodpecker and Gray Jay can sometimes be found in the woods here or among the bog's scattered black spruce and snags. Cedar Waxwing loves it here, and Lincoln's Sparrow belts out its bubbly song. A late May or early June visit to the bog includes the dramatic pink bloom of rhodora (a rhododendron), providing a distraction from the equally dramatic bloom of mosquitoes.

"Thkee Toed Road" AREA
Silvio O. Conte National Wildlife Refuge—Nulhegan Basin

Once the property of the Champion International Corporation, these vast timberlands were purchased and protected in one of the Northeast's largest conservation deals. A region of 26,000 acres north of Route 105, comprising much of the town of Lewis, is part of the Silvio O. Conte National Wildlife Refuge. The area includes the Nulhegan Basin and Yellow Bogs, a vast wetlands complex with some of Vermont's richest natural diversity. This is a Vermont stronghold for Spruce Grouse (endangered) and Black-backed Woodpecker, and a recently discovered nesting place for Palm Warbler. As pointed out earlier, the "taping" of endangered species such as Spruce Grouse can be considered illegal in Vermont.

Access to much of this refuge requires a map, a compass, and plenty of bug dope. But two access roads (when passable—call (877)811-5222 for road conditions) penetrate the refuge and offer ample birding. Don't expect a pristine experience, because much of the area is still recovering from timber cutting. But do expect Scarlet Tanager, Rose-breasted Grosbeak, and other residents of deciduous woods, along with boreal and other northern nesting specialties frequenting patches of conifers. Roughly twenty warbler species are possible during a drive, long walk, or mountain bike trip along these roads in late May. The best technique is to listen for chickadee flocks or other vocal songbirds. Migrating warblers often form around a chickadee flock nucleus or wander around in flocks of their own, with occasional vireos thrown in for good measure.

The first access into the refuge is **Lewis Pond Road**, which leaves on the north side of Route 105 at Wenlock Crossing, 7.9 miles east of the Island Pond 114/105 intersection (at the old railroad depot). Another access, 4.9 miles east of Wenlock Crossing on Route 105, is **Stone Dam Road**, which goes north along the Black Branch of the Nulhegan River.

3 Toed Road

Victory Bog

A road and a river transect some of Vermont's wildest boreal habitat at Victory Basin Wildlife Management Area, often simply called Victory Bog. About two-thirds of this 4,970-acre property is forested, and the remaining third is a varied wetland complex of ponds, bogs, wooded swamps and sedge meadows. Options for walking off-road are limited but nevertheless enjoyable. Because this is remote country, lock the car and carry valuable items. Black flies and mosquitoes can be bad here in late May and June. WARNING: Birders should note that this wildlife management area is popular with hunters, particularly from late September through November.

From Route 2 in North Concord (about 4.4 miles east of Concord and 10 miles west of Lunenburg), turn north on Victory Road opposite a general store (a good stop for restrooms and provisions). Proceed 3.5 miles on Victory Road to where it changes names to River Road. Continue straight for another 2.1 miles to a parking lot on the left before a bridge (not shown on map).

While the birding can be good anywhere along River Road (particularly during migration), the parking area, adjacent open wetland, and trail are almost always busy with birds. A walk westward from the parking lot along the trail (which can be wet or flooded in spring and summer) can reveal Saw-whet Owl (uncommon), breeding Black-backed Woodpecker (uncommon), Yellow-bellied Flycatcher, abundant migrant and breeding warblers, Rusty Blackbird, and Purple Finch, to name a few. Boreal Chickadee is in the basin but can be surprisingly hard to find.

At the bridge by the parking area, look over the wetland (no access) for American Bittern, Green Heron, American Woodcock (which displays here at dusk in early spring), Lincoln's Sparrow, and other wetland and shrubland species.

From the bridge, a walk, bicycle ride, or slow drive northbound will produce more birds, sometimes including Black-backed Woodpecker. One of Vermont's most reliable spots for Gray Jay is a parking lot on the right 2 miles north of the bridge. Look for color bands on the legs of these research subjects. Another 1.3 miles beyond this is a trailhead on the left. The trail leads to the pipeline clearing and continues along it. Cape May Warbler inhabits this

Saw-whet Owls have a varied diet, including insects, birds, and a mainstay of small rodents like the one locked in this owl's talons.
Photo: Ted Murin

area during spring migration or even the breeding season (along with mink frog croaking in the open water).

In the winter, particularly one with a bumper conifer cone crop, the basin is a finch playground. Purple Finch, White-winged Crossbill, and Pine Siskin can be abundant in the treetops.

Paul Stream

Paul Stream Road, along the remote Paul Stream in the towns of Brunswick, Maidstone, and Ferdinand, passes through coniferous and deciduous woods and wetlands that attract migrant songbirds and nesting northerners in spring. This is a distant stream in a remote section of Vermont—the state's West Mountain Wildlife Management Area. Warning: Drivers stuck in the mud here might wait a long time for help.

From Route 105 in Bloomfield, go south on Route 102 (along the Connecticut River) for 5.1 miles. Turn right on Maidstone Lake Road and drive 2.4 miles to Paul Stream Road on the right. A drive, bicycle ride, or long walk along Paul Stream Road can reveal flocks of migrating songbirds, notably warblers in late May. As evidence of this place's potential, Black-backed Woodpecker has nested along this roadside and Bay-breasted Warbler has visited in good numbers.

VERMONT STATE PARKS AND LONG TRAIL

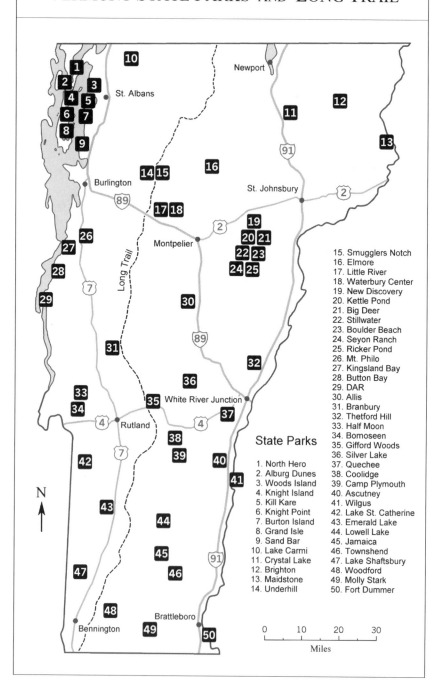

Newport

St. Albans

Burlington

89

Montpelier

Long Trail

7

St. Johnsbury

2

91

2

89

White River Junction

Rutland

4

4

7

91

N

Brattleboro

Bennington

15. Smugglers Notch
16. Elmore
17. Little River
18. Waterbury Center
19. New Discovery
20. Kettle Pond
21. Big Deer
22. Stillwater
23. Boulder Beach
24. Seyon Ranch
25. Ricker Pond
26. Mt. Philo
27. Kingsland Bay
28. Button Bay
29. DAR
30. Allis
31. Branbury
32. Thetford Hill
33. Half Moon
34. Bomoseen
35. Gifford Woods
36. Silver Lake
37. Quechee
38. Coolidge
39. Camp Plymouth
40. Ascutney
41. Wilgus
42. Lake St. Catherine
43. Emerald Lake
44. Lowell Lake
45. Jamaica
46. Townshend
47. Lake Shaftsbury
48. Woodford
49. Molly Stark
50. Fort Dummer

State Parks

1. North Hero
2. Alburg Dunes
3. Woods Island
4. Knight Island
5. Kill Kare
6. Knight Point
7. Burton Island
8. Grand Isle
9. Sand Bar
10. Lake Carmi
11. Crystal Lake
12. Brighton
13. Maidstone
14. Underhill

0   10   20   30

Miles

Vermont State Parks

Birds thrive in the varied habitats of Vermont's state parks. They are gateways to lakes and rivers, forests and wetlands, summits and grasslands alike. Buffeted by the march of suburbanization and sprawl, state parks in some sections of Vermont afford the only public land available for birdwatching.

Perhaps best of all, state parks are by definition special Vermont places, worth visiting even without their birdlife. While some bustle with campers, many are slow and serene—designed for escaping the car and spending a long morning, an entire day, or even longer observing birds by foot, by canoe, or simply sitting and soaking in the surroundings. Fortunately, the best birdwatching in state parks, in spring and fall, comes before and after the busy season.

Vermont's state parks are generally open from mid-May through either Labor Day or Columbus Day, when day-use and camping fees apply. State parks depend on visitor revenues. If entering before park hours, please stop and pay on the way out—help keep the parks in business.

Maps, brochures, and park details are available from the Vermont Department of Forests, Parks and Recreation, 103 South Main Street, 10 South, Waterbury, VT 05671-0603, or (802)241-3655 or <www.vtstateparks.com>. Park entrances are normally gated during the off season but remain available for public use. Birdwatchers who park and walk in should not block entrance gates (leaving access for emergency and maintenance vehicles) and should carry out their trash.

Wildlife Management Areas

The Vermont Fish and Wildlife Department owns or maintains 85 wildlife management areas. These varied habitats—about 119,000 acres in total—are managed for everything from waterfowl to white-tailed deer. Many lend themselves to birdwatching, and are featured in this book. Others are among the unexplored frontiers of birding in Vermont. But access is restricted and hunting is commonplace in many. For more information about locations and accessibility contact the Vermont Fish and Wildlife Department at (802)241-3700.

The Long Trail

Vermont's most remote birdwatching experience lies along the famous 271-mile footpath into the wild, the Long Trail, which traverses the spine of the

Green Mountains between Canada and Massachusetts. While it is hardly renowned as a birdwatching hotspot, the trail is a kaleidoscope of woods and wetlands, meadows and (mostly) mountains.

During migration the trail nearly anywhere can be loaded with woodland birds. At lower elevations expect Ruffed Grouse, Hairy Woodpecker, Downy Woodpecker, Least Flycatcher, Eastern Wood-Pewee, Black-capped Chickadee, White-breasted Nuthatch, Veery, Red-eyed Vireo, Black-throated Blue Warbler, Ovenbird, American Redstart, Scarlet Tanager, Rose-breasted Grosbeak, and other specialists of deciduous woods. The trail also climbs to Vermont's highest places with their resident birds, including hawks in migration, Common Raven, Red-breasted Nuthatch, Winter Wren, Golden-crowned Kinglet, Bicknell's Thrush, Swainson's Thrush, Hermit Thrush, Yellow-rumped Warbler, Blackpoll Warbler, Dark-eyed Junco, and White-throated Sparrow.

The Long Trail and its side trails are generally closed before Labor Day because they are muddy and subject to damage and erosion under a hiker's (or birder's) boot. By June black flies and mosquitoes can be abundant and annoying. The best Long Trail birding comes in September, when chickadee flocks are accompanied by good numbers of southbound migrants, notably Ruby-crowned Kinglet and warbler species that include Magnolia, Black-throated Blue, Yellow-rumped, Black-throated Green, Blackpoll, and Ovenbird. The presence of White-throated Sparrows and Dark-eyed Juncos can often alert a hiker to the less-obvious warbler flocks in the trees. Hiking without binoculars, one author of this book noted sixty-three species during an end-to-end Long Trail trek in September 1998.

For guidebooks, maps, and anything else to do with the Long Trail, contact the Green Mountain Club (see "Resources" at the back of this book).

CHAPTER 5

Species Accounts

Anyone who enjoys the flap of feathered wings eventually comes to realize that the pursuit of birds often involves being in the right place at the right time. Birds are creatures of habit—and habitat—and their abundance in a given place is remarkably predictable. Of course birds can occasionally be in the "wrong" place at the "wrong" time. It is one of their best qualities. Yet knowing when and where to look can be as important as a good pair of binoculars. This chapter is a guide to which birds live in Vermont, when they are here, and the habitats they prefer.

More than 350 bird species have been documented in Vermont. They either reside permanently, migrate here for the nesting season, visit for the winter only, pass through in migration, or arrive wholly by accident.

✎ *Regular Species*

This section offers brief written and graphical accounts for the 296 species that occur in Vermont regularly—meaning at least once every five years for the past fifteen years. It includes a few species (Fish Crow and jaeger species) that have only recently demonstrated a likelihood of being regular in Vermont.

Each account describes the species' preferred habitat and, in some cases, its distribution across the state. Each nesting species or suspected nester is identified with a 🪺 after its name. The account may also include a note on a bird's behavior or, for less common or unevenly distributed species, good (but not guaranteed) locations for finding them. Information about a few species, marked with a (†), comes from *The Atlas of Breeding Birds of*

A Spruce Grouse (endangered in Vermont) displays for a female at Yellow Bogs in the Northeast Kingdom. Photo: Ted Murin

Vermont, edited by Sarah B. Laughlin and Douglas P. Kibbe and published in 1985 for the Vermont Institute of Natural Science by University Press of New England.

Although it is dominated by forests, Vermont is a mosaic of habitats. And birds are selective about their habitats—Boreal Chickadee in boreal woods, for example, or Swamp Sparrow in a wetland. So a bird described in a species account simply as "widespread" is one that is well distributed across Vermont *in its appropriate habitat.* Yet even the most typical habitats can be devoid of their typical birds. And to keep things interesting, birds can also visit—or even nest in—uncharacteristic places. But generally, if it walks like a duck and squawks like a duck, it probably won't be walking or squawking on the top of a mountain. And speaking of mountains, many songbird species drop in abundance with rising elevation, something that isn't necessarily pointed out in each account.

Each species account also includes a graph representing the species' status throughout the year. The graphs depict abundance—the relative quantity of a given species in its proper habitat across Vermont. For the most part, the relative abundance shown in the graphs correlates with the likelihood that an observer will actually encounter the species. But that's not always the case. Limiting factors include the skill and patience of the observer, the time of day, the weather, and other field conditions. In addition, some species are inherently more conspicuous than others, and some become secretive during their breeding cycle. Some birds also shift their distribution. After the nesting season, for example, Tree Swallows gather by the thousands in the southern Champlain Valley. The species is still classified in this book as "abundant" but is no longer widely distributed throughout its habitat.

Below is the key to the abundance charts. Each definition describes a species' abundance in Vermont and the likelihood it can be found by a skilled observer under good field conditions. Like they say in the weight-loss ads, your results may vary.

Abundant — Present in very large numbers. Can be found in a great majority of suitable habitat, or at least one hundred individuals can be encountered in a day.

Common — Present in large numbers. Can be found in a majority of suitable habitat, or at least ten individuals can be encountered in a day.

Fairly Common — Present in good numbers. May require some effort, but at least one individual can be encountered in a day.

Uncommon — Present in limited numbers and often unevenly distributed. Usually not seen in a day, but can be found with several days of birding.

Very Uncommon — Almost certainly present somewhere in Vermont in small numbers, but highly unlikely to be encountered.

Rare — Not necessarily present in Vermont, but occurs in some years in low numbers. Extremely unlikely to be encountered.

Irregular — Diagonal lines indicate that abundance and presence can vary widely from year to year.

While the vast majority of birds occur according to these charts, they can occur rarely outside the indicated periods as well. Seasonal abundance can also vary by a week or two depending on weather, food supplies, and other factors. The graphs were developed with data from two sources: twelve years of records of Ted Murin's own observations and twenty years of sightings recorded in *Records of Vermont Birds*, a quarterly publication of bird sightings from hundreds of observers across Vermont. (Some information from the publication is also incorporated into written accounts.) The scientific method does not live within these charts. If it were applied, however, the authors would like to think the results would look something like this.

Loons

Red-throated Loon

A regular visitor to Lake Champlain, most reliably seen flying southbound in late fall. Rarely splashes down on other large bodies of water. Patience and a scope are helpful to find and enjoy this often-distant bird. Any location on Lake Champlain is fair game, particularly near congregations of Common Loon.

Common Loon

Endangered in Vermont, nesting mostly in the Northeast Kingdom. Visits other lakes and ponds during migration, especially Lake Champlain. A calm November day can reveal gatherings at the Champlain Bridge and Oven Bay in Addison, Button Bay in Ferrisburgh, and Charlotte Town Beach.

Grebes

Pied-billed Grebe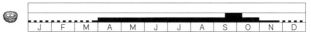

Nests sparingly in marshes. More widespread in migration on lakes and ponds, preferring vegetative cover nearby. Two strongholds are Missisquoi National Wildlife Refuge in Swanton and the South Bay wetlands of Lake Memphremagog in Newport.

Horned Grebe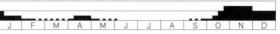

Frequents Lake Champlain in migration, including Oven Bay in Addison, Button Bay in Ferrisburgh, and Charlotte Town Beach. Much less common on other flat water. Some ply the shallows, though most linger far from shore. Very rare in summer.

Red-necked Grebe

Virtually identical to Horned Grebe in its use of Vermont, though appearing in smaller numbers. Sightings increased during the 1990s.

Gannets and Cormorants

Northern Gannet

Young birds occasionally stray inland on their first southbound migration, usually during the second half of October. Most wander Lake Champlain; a few others have run out of steam and touched down in unlikely locations, from front lawns to the summit of Killington Peak.

Double-crested Cormorant

One of Vermont's few nesting seabirds. First appearing in 1975; now tending large Lake Champlain rookeries. Widespread but sparse on flat water elsewhere. Population is controlled by Vermont wildlife biologists. The banning of the pesticide DDT, southern fish farms (which help winter survival), and an abundance of smaller prey fish may be among the reasons for its expansion.

Great Cormorant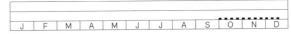

A very rare, usually immature visitor. Although seen on Lake Champlain, most have appeared at random along the Connecticut River and on lakes and ponds of the Northeast Kingdom.

Waders

American Bittern

Widespread in cattail marshes of any size, including those listed for Least Bittern. Also prowls open fields with tall grass. More often heard than seen, usually at dawn and dusk.

Least Bittern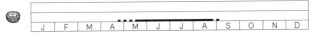

Highly elusive. Resides in cattail and sedge marshes. One of Vermont's rarest known breeders. Some known haunts include Mud Creek Wildlife Management Area in Alburg, Dead Creek Wildlife Management Area in Addison, and West Rutland Marsh. To find this bird, scrutinize cattail edges and hope for a miracle.

Great Blue Heron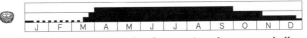

Vermont's most common and widespread wader, frequenting almost any shallow water. The largest nesting colony has been in Missisquoi National Wildlife Refuge in Swanton, but smaller rookeries occur throughout the state.

Great Egret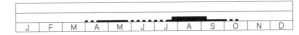

Visits mostly the Connecticut River and Champlain Valleys, including Dead Creek Wildlife Management Area and Whitney Creek in Addison. Nesting pairs in Quebec and on Lake Champlain's Four Brothers Islands in New York in 2000 suggest Vermont may be next.

Snowy Egret

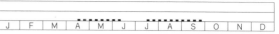

Once a rare nester on Lake Champlain, now seen sparingly in shallow waters and wetlands.

Little Blue Heron

Scarce in wetlands and shallow waters. These visitors are overshooting migrants in spring and post-breeding wanderers, often young, in fall.

Cattle Egret

Once nested in small numbers on Lake Champlain's Young Island in Grand Isle. Nesting birds at the lake's Four Brothers Islands in New York occasionally feed in fields in Shelburne and Charlotte in association with livestock. Sometimes gathers at Shelburne Bay in late summer.

Green Heron

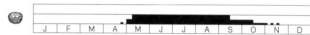

Frequents varied wetland habitats, including swamps, across much of Vermont. No particular stronghold, but reliable spots include Mud Creek Wildlife Management Area in Alburg, Dead Creek Wildlife Management Area in Addison, and West Rutland Marsh.

Black-crowned Night-Heron

May nest in Vermont, but a colony on New York's Four Brothers Islands probably accounts for many sightings. Hunts in marshes and swamps near Lake Champlain, often in late afternoon. Reliable spots include LaPlatte River Marsh Natural Area in Shelburne and Dead Creek in Addison.

Glossy Ibis

Nested recently on New York's Four Brothers Islands (Lake Champlain). Feeds in marshes, flooded fields, and shallow shorelines. Most often seen in spring in the Champlain Valley. Visitors are usually over-enthusiastic migrants in spring and post-breeding wanderers in fall.

Vultures

Turkey Vulture

Recently expanded into Vermont, nesting around rocky slopes and cliffs. This fair-weather flier, thriving on carrion and thermals, is found teetering over open country across the state.

Greater White-fronted Goose

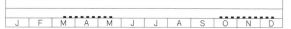

Occasionally associates with other geese, usually Canada Goose, in fields or flat waters during migration through the Champlain and Connecticut River Valleys and the Vermont Valley.

Snow Goose

With the Champlain Valley hosting the bulk of the traffic, Dead Creek Wildlife Management Area in Addison is the showplace, but flocks drop into fields and open waters elsewhere during migration.

Ross's Goose

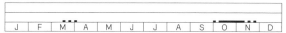

Mingles in small numbers with Snow Goose at Dead Creek Wildlife Management Area in Addison and occasionally elsewhere. Hybrids with Lesser Snow Goose are almost as common. To find one, scan Snow Goose flocks patiently and thoroughly. Like locating the period in a bowl of commas.

Canada Goose

Introduced as a nester at Dead Creek Wildlife Management Area in 1956.[†] Breeding range in Vermont has expanded ever since. (A separate arctic population visits in migration.) Winter population depends on open water and scant snow cover. Small, rare arctic races found more often with Snow Goose than Canada Goose flocks.

Brant

Seen most often on the wing southbound over Lake Champlain but occurs in the Connecticut River Valley as well. Erratic; can appear in good numbers on a single "flight day" and be completely absent the day after. Some have appeared in summer.

Mute Swan

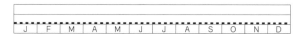

Introduced to North America as a status symbol in the 1800s and now crowds native waterfowl from breeding habitat. Has nested in Vermont but the Vermont Fish and Wildlife Department probably won't allow a repeat performance. Periodically found on larger bodies of water such as Lake Champlain and the Connecticut River.

Tundra Swan

Prefers flat water and farm fields, mostly in the Champlain and Connecticut River lowlands, but no location is reliable. Sometimes appears in family groups. Occasionally associates with Canada Goose.

Ducks

Wood Duck

Widespread cavity nester preferring deciduous swamps, but often visible nesting and swimming at water's edge in small ponds and marshes with brushy cover. In spring, before swamps thaw, joins other dabblers in open water.

Gadwall

Rare breeder, has been found nesting only in the Champlain Islands. In migration prefers flooded fields or open water, predominantly in the Champlain Valley. One of the few dabblers comfortable in the middle of Lake Champlain.

Eurasian Wigeon

When encountered, it is almost exclusively with American Wigeon and in the Champlain Valley. Like its American cousin, prefers calm waters, flooded fields and, before inland ponds thaw, Lake Champlain. Seen more than once at Tabor Road in Swanton and the Colchester Railroad Causeway.

American Wigeon

 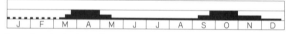

Nests rarely, known to breed only in northwestern Vermont. During migration congregates with other dabblers in flooded fields, marshes, or open water, mostly in the Champlain Valley, occasionally elsewhere.

American Black Duck

While it nests across the state in wetlands with emergent vegetation and other cover, it is fond of wide open water during migration. As with most wintering waterfowl, winter attendance depends on the extent of open water on lakes (particularly Lake Champlain) and rivers.

Mallard

Widespread during migration and breeding seasons in open water, wetlands, flooded fields, farmland, and public parks (everywhere except your bathtub). Some birds have learned to dive for zebra mussels on Lake Champlain.

Blue-winged Teal

Relatively inconspicuous. Nests in marshes mostly in the Champlain Valley. Seen in migration in valleys on west and east sides of the state. Reliable spots include Dead Creek Wildlife Management Area in Addison and South Slang area in Ferrisburgh.

Northern Shoveler

Possible but undocumented nester in northwestern Vermont. Prefers marshes and shallow water. Can occur "inland," but seen mostly in the Champlain Valley and, to a lesser extent, the Connecticut River Valley. In spring, occasionally visits Farrell Access to Dead Creek in Addison.

Northern Pintail

Sporadic nester in marshes or grasslands of the Champlain Valley. Often consorts with American Black Duck and Mallard in flooded fields, marshes, and open water. Reliable spots include Lemon Fair River in Cornwall in spring and Addison's Dead Creek Wildlife Management Area in fall.

Green-winged Teal

Rare nester in Champlain Valley marshes or ponds with dense vegetation, including Dead Creek Wildlife Management Area in Addison. Widespread in migration in flooded fields, marshes, and open water, with highest number in the Champlain Valley.

Canvasback

Sightings declined markedly in Vermont during the 1990s. Almost exclusive to Lake Champlain, rarely visiting the Connecticut River Valley. Unpredictable in winter. Colchester Railroad Causeway in early spring is among the more reliable locations. Sometimes mingles with scaup.

Redhead

Less common than Canvasback, favoring Lake Champlain and, rarely, the Connecticut River and large inland lakes and ponds. Often hobnobs with scaup. Seen on occasion at Colchester Railroad Causeway, McNeil Cove in Charlotte, and Button Bay in Ferrisburgh.

Ring-necked Duck

Probable but rare nester in northern Vermont. Widespread in spring migration, favoring open water, often at the edge of retreating ice. In fall large numbers gather at Missisquoi National Wildlife Refuge in Swanton and near Sandbar State Park in Milton.

Greater Scaup

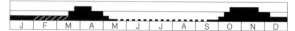

A diver into the open waters of larger lakes, primarily Lake Champlain but also Lake Memphremagog. Occasional on other inland lakes and the Connecticut River. Mid-winter abundance depends on the availability of open water.

Lesser Scaup

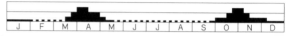

A juvenile seen recently in summer (in Missisquoi National Wildlife Refuge in Swanton) was intriguing, but nesting remains undocumented. Similar to Greater Scaup in its use of Vermont, but visits smaller inland lakes and ponds as well.

King Eider

Extremely rare; the few recent sightings are from Lake Champlain. Never predictable and often vanishes shortly after appearing. Sometimes buried in scoter flocks.

Common Eider

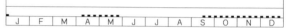

Only slightly more common than King Eider (which isn't saying much). Has appeared on Lake Champlain and in the Connecticut River Valley during spring and fall migrations. One first-year male overwintered on Lake Champlain in 1998–1999.

Harlequin Duck

Only slightly more common than Common Eider (which still isn't saying much). Usually seen on Lake Champlain, and occasionally large rivers as well, including the Connecticut and Missisquoi. Has visited Charlotte Town Beach several times.

Surf Scoter

Vermont's least common scoter. Stops during southbound migration on Lake Champlain, often far from shore, but also sporadically on other lakes and ponds and, rarely, the Connecticut River. Often flocks with other scoters. Periodically visits Shelburne Bay.

White-winged Scoter

Widespread on Lake Champlain during fall migration, usually far from shore. Stops on larger inland lakes as well. Flocks can include other scoter species. DAR State Park in Addison, Charlotte Town Beach, and Shelburne Bay are a few of the more reliable locations.

Black Scoter

More abundant than it might seem because large rafts roam far offshore on Lake Champlain, often between Burlington and Ferrisburgh (requires patience and a scope). Good numbers will sporadically drop into other ponds and lakes, such as Lake Willoughby in Westmore and Lake Morey in Fairlee.

Long-tailed Duck

Fairly widespread in small numbers during migration on lakes and ponds. Most abundant far from shore on Lake Champlain in fall, where larger flocks careen southbound low over the surface. Often seen at Shelburne Bay and DAR State Park in Addison. Formerly called Oldsquaw.

Bufflehead

Nested once recently in the Champlain Islands. Fairly widespread on lakes and ponds in migration, most abundant on Lake Champlain. Sightings increased during the 1990s. Overwinters regularly in Charlotte from Converse Bay to Charlotte Town Beach.

Common Goldeneye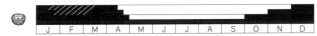

Uncommon cavity nester in woodlands adjacent to northern reaches of Lake Champlain. Resides in summer at Missisquoi National Wildlife Refuge in Swanton and near Sandbar State Park in Milton. One of the two most abundant ducks wintering on Lake Champlain; most depart if the lake freezes over.

Barrow's Goldeneye

Winters on Lake Champlain in small numbers, almost exclusively among Common Goldeneye. Often visits Blodgett's Beach in Burlington and the Colchester Railroad Causeway. Rare elsewhere in the state, including Lake Memphremagog in Newport and Vernon Dam. Patiently scope flocks of Common Goldeneye.

Hooded Merganser

Cavity nester in woods near open waters or wetlands, sometimes sharing sites with Wood Duck. Widespread during migration on lakes, ponds, and broad rivers. Often remains near shore. A likely spot in winter is McNeil Cove in Charlotte.

Common Merganser

Scattered in breeding season, with diverse nesting habits near water, including tree cavities, among rocks, and in chimneys. As a migrant, frequents almost everything but the kitchen sink (and small, stagnant ponds). One of the two most abundant wintering ducks on Lake Champlain.

Red-breasted Merganser

Rare breeder on lakes or ponds; known to nest in recent years on the Champlain Islands. Migrates along Lake Champlain, less often seen on other lakes and along the Connecticut River. Favored spots include Button Bay in Ferrisburgh and Charlotte Town Beach. Tiny numbers winter on Lake Champlain.

Ruddy Duck

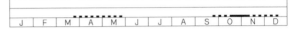

Stops in migration on Lake Champlain and, much less reliably, on other open inland waters. Has visited Herrick's Cove in Rockingham and Lake Memphremagog in Newport. Most often encountered at McCuen Slang in Addison and Shelburne Bay.

Hawks and Falcons

Osprey

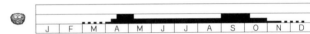

Likely to be moved from "endangered" to "threatened" status in Vermont. Recovery is due in part to the banning of DDT and placement of nesting platforms by the Vermont Fish and Wildlife Department. Nests near water, mostly in the Champlain Valley, including the Kingsland Bay Region in Ferrisburgh and Missisquoi National Wildlife Refuge in Swanton. Widespread in migration.

Bald Eagle

Endangered in Vermont but increasing in recent years, so nesting is expected soon. Frequents open water on Lake Champlain in March, usually at ice edge between Addison and Charlotte. A visitor to hawkwatches statewide during fall migration. Overwinters at open water on Lake Champlain and the Connecticut River.

Northern Harrier

Widespread but sparse nester in suitable grassland habitat and marshes, largely in the Champlain Valley and Northeast Kingdom. More cosmopolitan during migration. Overwintering birds prefer southern half of the Champlain Valley.

Sharp-shinned Hawk

Widespread in low numbers during nesting season in mixed woods with dense evergreen cover.† More obvious during fall migration, when hawkwatch counts are highest in the Connecticut River Valley. Lurks at bird feeders throughout Vermont in winter.

Cooper's Hawk

Less common than Sharp-shinned Hawk throughout the year, and more inclined to nest in deciduous woods.† More evenly distributed than Sharp-shinned Hawk during fall migration. Also hunts at bird feeders statewide in winter.

Northern Goshawk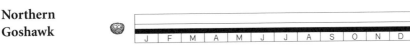

Sparse and scattered breeder in a variety of mature woods. The least-often encountered of all Vermont's accipiters. Occasionally and best found at hawkwatches in November. Inhabits wooded and open habitats in winter.

Red-shouldered Hawk

Nests sparingly in deciduous or mixed woods near wetlands across Vermont. Its diet includes amphibians. More often encountered on hawkwatches during fall migration in mid-October.

Broad-winged Hawk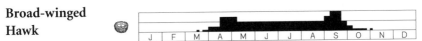

Nests widely in deciduous or mixed woods away from the Champlain lowlands. The most abundant and gregarious hawk during fall migration, peaking abruptly in mid-September. Fall flights depend entirely on weather—hundreds can move one day and none the next.

Red-tailed Hawk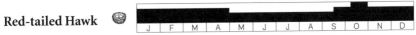

Vermont's most evident hawk throughout the year. Nests primarily in open and semi-open country across Vermont. Broad fall migration period peaks in late October. Overwinters in good numbers in open country of the Champlain Valley.

Rough-legged Hawk

Occasionally found in any open country, though most winter in the southern Champlain Valley. Concentrations vary and may coincide with meadow vole populations. Assumes more treetop perches and diagonal posture than Red-tailed Hawk, and hovers longer over open fields.

Golden Eagle

Adept at wandering great distances, this bird has been seen soaring over virtually every part of Vermont, particularly at hawkwatches in late October. Extremely rare in winter and summer. Often confused with young Bald Eagle.

American Kestrel

Nests in tree cavities adjacent to open country across Vermont, often seen perched on power lines. Seen at hawkwatches migrating in ones and twos rather than kettles. Most overwintering birds are found in the Champlain Valley.

Merlin

Only recently discovered nesting in north central Vermont, at the southern end of its breeding range. Encounters are sometimes unexpected and brief. Hunts small birds in clearings, shorelines, and other open areas. Frequently hugs the terrain, even during migration. Uncommon but regular at hawkwatches.

Gyrfalcon

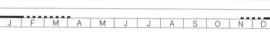

A rare northern visitor to open country, with most encounters in the Champlain Valley. Gray morph is most common. Rarely lingers for a second look.

Peregrine Falcon

Pesticides eliminated this endangered predator from the East, but state and federal agencies collaborated with nonprofit organizations on a successful reintroduction program. At least twenty-five pairs staked out nesting cliffs across Vermont in 2001, according to the state's peregrine biologist. (Unfortunately, this success has spurred falconers' desire to capture and own these birds.) Occasionally seen at hawkwatches in migration.

Grouse and Relatives

Gray Partridge

Dwindling and restricted to fields, pastures, and hedgerows of Alburg, St. Albans, and Swanton. Usually seen in winter on snow-covered fields. Pattern of sightings suggests only one nomadic flock of this non-native species may remain.

Ring-necked Pheasant

This non-native species was once heavily stocked. Recent sightings of birds lacking street sense, including one chasing cars in Charlotte, suggest escapes and releases continue. Sightings of winter birds and females with young suggest wild breeding also occurs. Seen mostly in overgrown fields in southern Vermont and the southern Champlain Valley.

Ruffed Grouse

Widespread throughout mixed or deciduous woods, often with birch or aspen and dense undergrowth. Often first detected by the sound of its drumming or its flutter when flushed.

Spruce Grouse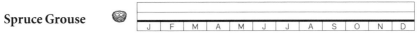

Endangered in Vermont. Sparse resident of spruce forests in the Northeast Kingdom, often near bogs or open woods. Usually seen along Moose Bog trail in Ferdinand and at Yellow Bogs in Lewis.

Wild Turkey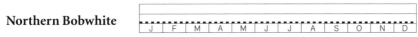

Extirpated with the extensive logging of Vermont in the 1800s. First reintroduced in 1969 and 1970 in the Taconics,[†] now widespread in deciduous woods and pressing into the Northeast Kingdom. Most often seen in spring and fall, foraging in farm fields.

Northern Bobwhite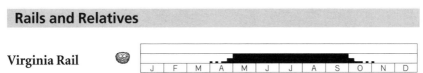

Origins uncertain. Most birds are probably escapees or released. Lifespan outside the barnyard fence may not last the winter. Preferred habitat includes open woodlands near fields with brushy cover.

Rails and Relatives

Virginia Rail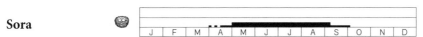

Vermont's most common and vocal rail nests widely in cattail marshes. A patient observer can spot it walking or sprinting across wetland openings. Most outspoken at dawn.

Sora

Less common and harder to see than Virginia Rail in the same cattail habitat. Sometimes forages along open water at marsh's edge. Most often encountered at larger marshes such as Mud Creek Wildlife Management Area in Alburg and Dead Creek Wildlife Management Area in Addison.

Common Moorhen

Nests in larger marshes with open water, mostly in the Champlain Valley. Occurs at Mud Creek Wildlife Management Area in Alburg, Barton River Marsh in Newport, Dead Creek Wildlife Management Area in Addison, and West Rutland Marsh.

American Coot

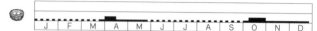

Possible nester in Missisquoi National Wildlife Refuge in Swanton. Prefers lakes, ponds, and wetlands with emergent vegetation for cover. Can turn up anywhere during migration, particularly in the Connecticut River Valley and Champlain Valley. Frequents McCuen Slang area in Addison in fall.

Sandhill Crane

No reliable pattern to its infrequent Vermont visits. Some sightings are flybys, but others linger to feed in agricultural fields. One bird (most likely the same individual) spent at least three consecutive summers along the Upper Connecticut River in Barnet.

Shorebirds

Finding Shorebirds

With only five shorebird species nesting in Vermont, the abundance of others depends largely on available habitat during migration. In years with low water, the exposed, muddy habitat along Lake Champlain and the Connecticut River can attract shorebirds in good numbers. A drawdown of impoundments at Dead Creek Wildlife Management Area in Addison is the classic example; it can seduce most any shorebird species found in Vermont. Periodically reduced water levels near dams on the Connecticut River can have a similar but less dramatic effect. Otherwise, migrating shorebirds drop in small numbers into wet farm fields, pond and lake edges, and "inland" mud flats (or they don't stop at all). In other words, shorebirding in Vermont is usually famine and only occasionally feast.

Black-bellied Plover

Visits open shorelines, mud flats, and wet fields with little or no vegetation. Occasionally seen at Button Bay in Ferrisburgh and Dead Creek Wildlife Management Area in Addison.

American Golden-Plover

Limited almost exclusively to the Champlain Valley. Sometimes associates with Killdeer. Visits shorelines, short, grassy fields, and freshly plowed or harrowed farmland. Seen regularly at Dead Creek's Goose Viewing Area in Addison.

Semipalmated Plover

Uses a variety of habitats, from gravelly shorelines to weedy wetland margins and mud bars. Can be found at most any shorebird gathering in Vermont. Customary at Blodgett's Beach in Burlington and St. Albans Bay when lake levels allow.

Killdeer

Nests in open places with sparse vegetation, including gravel driveways and construction sites. Often seen near water or in open fields. Numbers peak during migration in early April and late September through early October.

Greater Yellowlegs

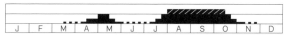

Often feeds in the open in deeper water. This makes it slightly more dependable during migration than shorter-legged shorebirds, which prefer shallow water habitat not available in some years. Tends to be more vigorous in its feeding style than Lesser Yellowlegs. Widespread in the Champlain Valley.

Lesser Yellowlegs

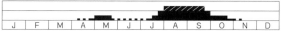

Sometimes joins in flocks with its larger cousin. More dependent on exposed mud and low water levels. Occasionally appears in large groups.

Solitary Sandpiper

As its name implies, usually seen alone or in pairs. Frequents shorelines of ponds, lakes, and rivers, and visits emergent wetlands. More evenly distributed in Vermont than most sandpipers.

Willet

Recorded a number of times on or near Lake Champlain in the early to mid-1980s, yet only twice in the 1990s. About half of these birds were seen at Dead Creek Wildlife Management Area in Addison.

Spotted Sandpiper

Widespread along shorelines of lakes, ponds, and larger streams. Well represented across much of Vermont. Does not depend on low water to find suitable habitat.

Upland Sandpiper

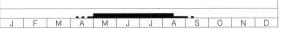

Threatened in Vermont (proposed for endangered status), its numbers appear to be dwindling due to housing and commercial development in its grassland habitat. Nests sparsely in the Champlain Valley and other scattered locations, including E. F. Knapp State Airport in Berlin and near the Newport State Airport.

Whimbrel

Unreliable; most of the recent sightings are from the Champlain Valley. As comfortable in a grassy field as along a shoreline. Often seen only in flight.

Hudsonian Godwit

Seen nearly every year; vast majority are seen in the Champlain Valley. Has appeared repeatedly at the Goose Viewing Area at Dead Creek Wildlife Management Area in Addison, where it sometimes wanders among Snow Goose flocks.

Ruddy Turnstone

Visits rocky shores of small islands on Lake Champlain. Less common on "mainland." Blodgett's Beach in Burlington is among the more reliable locations.

Red Knot

Hardly predictable. Stops on small islands on Lake Champlain, more often when the lake level is low. Infrequent along Lake Champlain shoreline. Has also appeared at Prouty Beach in Newport.

Sanderling

Runs along sandy beaches, gravel shorelines, or exposed mud, mostly along Lake Champlain. Occasionally seen at Blodgett's Beach in Burlington.

Semipalmated Sandpiper

Visits mud flats, pond edges, wet fields, and shallow water in almost any place shorebirds are seen. More common in the Champlain Valley, but migrates along the Connecticut River Valley as well.

Western Sandpiper

Seen infrequently in the Champlain Valley, even less so elsewhere. Associates with Semipalmated Sandpiper and Least Sandpiper. Bill length of some can be similar to that of Semipalmated Sandpiper, making identification difficult. Juveniles comprise most sightings.

Least Sandpiper

The most consistent and reliable "peep" in Vermont. Present in the Champlain and Connecticut River Valleys alike. Somewhat more comfortable than Semipalmated Sandpiper in grassy or weedy vegetation.

White-rumped Sandpiper

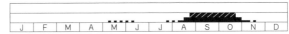

Frequents mud, shallow water, and shorelines. As with most sandpipers, adults tend to move through before juveniles in fall. Look for this slightly larger and longer "peep" among flocks of Semipalmated and Least Sandpipers and, later in the season, among Dunlin.

Baird's Sandpiper

Similar to White-rumped Sandpiper in its travels through Vermont. Can also use drier habitats. Has made repeat appearances at Blodgett's Beach in Burlington.

Pectoral Sandpiper

Visits mud, shallow water, and shorelines, often gravitating toward vegetation. Comfortable in grassy fields up to its head (or pectorals). The Goose Viewing Area at Dead Creek Wildlife Management Area in Addison is an excellent spot for this species in fall.

Purple Sandpiper

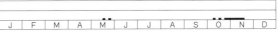

Exclusive to Lake Champlain; almost always on rocky shores of small islands. Rarely seen from shore. Has been seen more than once on the rocks of Blodgett's Beach in Burlington.

Dunlin

Widespread in the Champlain Valley's various shorebird habitats, preferring shorelines and other open areas. Like most shorebirds in Vermont, rarely seen in breeding plumage.

Stilt Sandpiper

Seen in muddy, vegetated areas or shallow water. Vast majority of sightings are from the Champlain Valley, the majority of those from Dead Creek Wildlife Management Area in Addison and Panton. Has appeared along the Connecticut River.

Buff-breasted Sandpiper

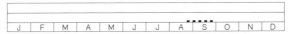

Prefers muddy, vegetated shorelines and fields that are plowed, harrowed, or feature short grasses. Found near Lake Champlain, sometimes loosely associating with Killdeer and American Golden-Plover.

Short-billed Dowitcher

Often feeds sewing-machine-style in water up to its belly. Favors Dead Creek Wildlife Management Area in Addison but can be found at many spots with shallow water in the Champlain and Connecticut River Valleys, including Herrick's Cove in Rockingham.

Long-billed Dowitcher

Undependable on exposed mud and shorelines and in shallow waters of the Champlain Valley. Distinguished from Short-billed Dowitcher with care and patience. Has visited Dead Creek several times in Addison and Panton.

Common Snipe

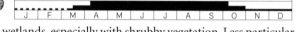

Widespread nester in wetlands, especially with shrubby vegetation. Less particular in migration, when it also uses weedy shorelines, wet fields, and ditches. Most obvious during spring "winnowing" courtship display or when calling from posts, snags, or other exposed perches.

American Woodcock

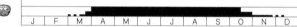

Display flights in full swing from late March to early April at dusk over wet clearings with nearby thickets or wet woods. Widespread in Vermont and particularly abundant at Missisquoi National Wildlife Refuge in Swanton.

Wilson's Phalarope

Has nested on the New York side of Lake Champlain. The rarest phalarope in Vermont, most visits are to shallow waters or muddy edges in the Champlain Valley. Has put in repeat appearances at Dead Creek Wildlife Management Area in Addison and Missisquoi National Wildlife Refuge in Swanton.

Red-necked Phalarope

The most common phalarope in Vermont (relatively speaking). Prefers similar habitats to Wilson's but also visits the offshore waters of Lake Champlain. Rarely strays outside the Champlain Valley. Has made several stops at Dead Creek Wildlife Management Area in Addison.

Red Phalarope

The most pelagic of the shorebirds. Seen rarely on the Connecticut River and larger lakes around the state. Typically found on Lake Champlain, sometimes spinning contentedly far out to "sea." Like Red-necked Phalarope, can tend floating debris lines after a storm. Has visited Shelburne Bay more than once.

Jaegers, Gulls, and Terns

Pomarine Jaeger

Jaegers have recently been discovered using Lake Champlain as a southbound flyway. Their rare appearance often correlates with north winds. This species may be the most irregular of the three. (See "Lakewatching on Lake Champlain," page 24, for details.)

Parasitic Jaeger

Moves southbound along Lake Champlain in low numbers, probably every year. Like the two other jaeger species, most are young birds, which are difficult to identify. (The easiest way to identify young jaegers may be to follow them until they grow up.)

Long-tailed Jaeger

Like the other two jaeger species, this one has been discovered moving south along Lake Champlain in fall, perhaps annually. Continued lakeside observations should shed more light on the passage of these and other arctic nesting birds that winter at sea.

Laughing Gull

Highly infrequent, sightings in Vermont are too few to predict any geographic pattern to its visits. Majority of records are from the Champlain Valley.

Little Gull

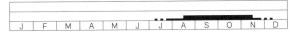

Adults and young birds visit Lake Champlain, almost always in the company of Bonaparte's Gull. Roughly one in every eight hundred Bonaparte's Gulls is actually a Little Gull—how they decide which one it will be is a well-kept secret. Often visits St. Albans Bay.

Black-headed Gull

Another rare associate of Bonaparte's Gull, but can be somewhat independent as well. All sightings, mostly of adults, are from Lake Champlain, where it is seen nearly every year. Two mid-winter records exist.

Bonaparte's Gull

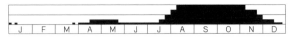

Prefers Lake Champlain's Inland Sea far from shore, but flocks wander elsewhere on the lake. Fond of St. Albans Bay. Small numbers occasionally visit "inland" waters, including Lake Memphremagog. A substrate for rarities, these flocks are always worth a close look for other small gulls.

Ring-billed Gull

First reported to have bred in Vermont in the mid-1900s. The majority now nest on Young Island in Grand Isle and New York's Four Brothers Islands. Widespread in migration, preferring farm fields, landfills, slow water, and fast food. Less common far from breeding grounds in late spring. Concentrates at the Burlington Waterfront in mid-winter.

Herring Gull

Most nest on Young Island in Grand Isle and occasionally other smaller islands on Lake Champlain. Widespread in small numbers (usually near water) away from the lake during migration. Winters on open water on Lake Champlain and, in lower numbers, along the Connecticut River.

Iceland Gull

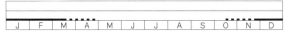

A regular visitor to Lake Champlain and, less often, the Connecticut River, often associating with Herring Gull. The best time and place to see this gull is when it stops briefly at the Burlington Waterfront during southbound migration in early December.

Lesser Black-backed Gull

Though increasing in North America, still a very rare visitor here, with only one seen on the Connecticut River and a handful scattered around Lake Champlain, including two at the Burlington Waterfront.

Glaucous Gull

Lake Champlain, mostly at the Burlington Waterfront, and the Connecticut River are the haunts for this white-winged gull. Often associates with Great Black-backed Gull. Usually seen during migration in December and late March through early April.

Great Black-backed Gull

Very few nest on Young Island in Grand Isle and New York's Four Brothers Islands in Lake Champlain. Non-breeding birds summer on the lake. Found during migration and winter on large bodies of water, primarily Lake Champlain and particularly the Burlington Waterfront.

Sabine's Gull

Sightings have been exclusively on Lake Champlain, primarily from mid- to late September and nearly always juveniles loosely associated with Bonaparte's Gulls. May occur annually, as encounters have been nearly that frequent. Use care distinguishing from juvenile Little Gull and Black-legged Kittiwake at a distance.

Black-legged Kittiwake

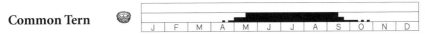

Most sightings, mainly of young birds, are confined to the Connecticut River and Lake Champlain. Probably occurs on the lake every year, where it often associates with Bonaparte's Gull. Most have been seen from October through November.

Caspian Tern

Suspected to have nested in 2000 on Lake Champlain at Popasquash Island in St. Albans and/or Young Island in Grand Isle. Almost all sightings are from Lake Champlain, mostly its northern sections.

Common Tern

Endangered in Vermont. A small, recovering, but still vulnerable population nests on Popasquash Island in St. Albans and other small islands in Lake Champlain's Inland Sea. It is recovering with help from Audubon Vermont, Green Mountain Audubon, and the Vermont Fish and Wildlife Department. Regularly seen from shore at St. Albans Bay.

Forster's Tern

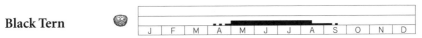

Seen in various locations on Lake Champlain from Missisquoi National Wildlife Refuge in Swanton to the Champlain Bridge in Addison, including twice in Shelburne Bay. Most don't linger, though one stayed a week at Delta Park in Colchester.

Black Tern

Threatened in Vermont, its breeding range shrank during the 1990s to the northern end of Lake Champlain, primarily Missisquoi National Wildlife Refuge in Swanton. Nests in cattail marshes. Occasionally visits large inland lakes during migration. Can forage far out over Lake Champlain in fall.

Doves and Cuckoos

Rock Dove

J F M A M J J A S O N D

Found throughout the state, usually not far from large structures such as barns, bridges, or commercial buildings. Fond of relatively warm silo and roof tops in winter.

Mourning Dove

J F M A M J J A S O N D

Widespread nester in a variety of open or semi-open habitats. A member of the suburban ecosystem. Frequents bird feeders in winter.

Black-billed Cuckoo

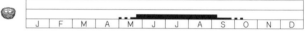
J F M A M J J A S O N D

Widespread but spotty, preferring to nest in shrubby woodlands, edges, or overgrown pastures. Abundance may correlate with caterpillar outbreaks, including eastern tent caterpillar. Brilyea Access in Dead Creek Wildlife Management Area in Addison is a relatively reliable spot.

Yellow-billed Cuckoo

J F M A M J J A S O N D

Scattered mostly in lowland areas of southern Vermont and northward into the Champlain Valley.† Prefers thickets and other dense vegetation in either open woods, riparian zones, or overgrown fields. Recent sightings have been few, suggesting this species may be declining in Vermont.

Owls

Barn Owl

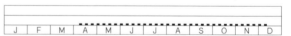
J F M A M J J A S O N D

So rare and scattered are encounters with this species that little is known about its status in Vermont. The first and last confirmed nestings, in 1976 and 1983, respectively, were established by the Vermont Breeding Birds Atlas Project in the Southern and Central Champlain Valley Regions.

Eastern Screech-Owl

J F M A M J J A S O N D

A cavity nester limited largely to the deciduous lowlands (often with or near cedar) of the Champlain Valley. Sometimes at home in rural residential areas. Prevalent in the Champlain Islands and Dead Creek Wildlife Management Area in Addison.

Great Horned Owl

The most widespread owl on the continent is more common in the Champlain lowlands and across southern Vermont; scattered elsewhere. Often nests in mature white pines in riparian areas and woodlands adjacent to openings for hunting.

Snowy Owl

An irruptive species whose abundance varies from year to year. Invariably seen during the day in open country, often on the ground or on low perches. More prevalent during movements in November and March. The Burlington Waterfront is one of the more reliable spots in late fall.

Northern Hawk Owl

Irruptive and scarce around the state in semi-open country with trees for its daytime perches. At least one has been discovered in roughly half of all recent Vermont winters. Some birds settle in an area for the entire winter.

Barred Owl

Vermont's most common owl nests in coniferous or mixed woods and swamps across the state and is least abundant in the Champlain Valley. Occasionally active during the day, particularly in some winters.

Great Gray Owl

Sporadic and extremely rare, sightings of this diurnal owl are mostly from the semi-open hill country of north central Vermont. Rarely seen after the initial encounter. Barred Owl at first glance can be occasionally misidentified as this species.

Long-eared Owl

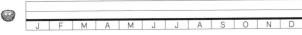

Highly secretive and nocturnal, it prefers stands of conifers near openings for nesting and communal winter roosts. Little is known about its status, but most sightings are from the Champlain Valley.

Short-eared Owl

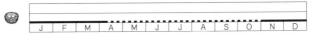

Floats low over grasslands, primarily in the Champlain Valley, often at dusk. A reliable (and possible breeding) area ranges from Slang Road in Panton to the Goose Viewing Area at Dead Creek Wildlife Management Area in Addison.

Northern Saw-whet Owl

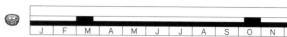

Scattered in coniferous woods across the state, this tiny owl's repeated short whistle often betrays its whereabouts in early spring. Migrants move through in March and October, sometimes stopping in deciduous thickets.

Nightjars

Common Nighthawk

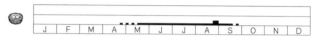

Confined largely to cities, including Montpelier, Barre, and Bellows Falls, where flat-topped buildings provide gravel "habitat" for nesting. A drop in sightings during the 1990s suggests a dramatic decline in this nocturnal, insect-eating machine. Seen during the day in fall migrating south along waterways.

Whip-poor-will

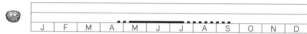

Reports of this vociferous nightjar have been in serious decline. Prefers dry deciduous or mixed woods near openings. Heard (and heard and heard) more often than seen. Scarcity of encounters after mid-July can be attributed either to silence or departure. Long Swamp in Brandon has been a consistent haunt.

Swifts, Hummingbirds, and Kingfishers

Chimney Swift

Seen singly or in large, swirling colonies across the state, often in cities where chimneys provide suitable breeding "habitat." Otherwise, prefers tree cavities for nest sites.

Ruby-throated Hummingbird

Widespread in woodlands and residential settings with suitable nectar sources, notably red and orange flowers such as bee balm and jewelweed ("touch-me-not"). Feeds on nectar and insects at blooming apple trees while moving north in spring.

Rufous Hummingbird

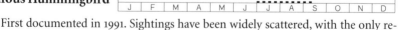

First documented in 1991. Sightings have been widely scattered, with the only repeat appearances in West Arlington and the island of Grand Isle. All reports have been of males.

Belted Kingfisher

Found throughout the state near flat water with adjacent trees or utility wires for perches. Nests in burrows, sometimes within Bank Swallow colonies. A few over-winter near available open water.

Woodpeckers

Red-headed Woodpecker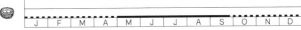

Only known to nest in Bridport in recent years, but also seen at scattered locations around the state, mostly in the Champlain Valley. Prefers open country with open deciduous woodlots and dead trees for nest sites.

Red-bellied Woodpecker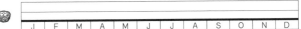

Expanding its range northward, appearing first in the 1970s and regularly since the late 1980s. First confirmed nesting in 2001. The only "southern" species seen more often in winter, usually at feeders, than summer. Found mostly in the Champlain Valley and southern Vermont.

Yellow-bellied Sapsucker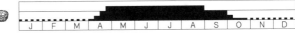

Widespread nester in deciduous and mixed woods across Vermont, less common in the Champlain Valley. Its telltale array of sap holes and a drum that slows to-ward its finale are indicators of this woodpecker's presence.

Downy Woodpecker

One of Vermont's most widespread birds, it nests in deciduous woods, mixed woods, or most any other place with trees. A regular visitor to feeders.

Hairy Woodpecker

This widely distributed relative to Downy Woodpecker requires more extensive woodlands of all kinds for nesting. Drawn to feeders. It often advertises its pres-ence with a sharp *keek!*

Three-toed Woodpecker

Last known to have nested in the Northeast Kingdom in 1981 during the Vermont Breeding Bird Atlas Project. Current status is unknown. Prefers dying or dead conifers in boreal forests but can disperse to other forest types in winter. Encounters are exceptionally rare.

Black-backed Woodpecker

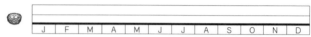

Prefers boreal spruce, fir, and tamarack, sometimes at bogs, with dead trees for nest sites. Stronghold is the Northeast Kingdom, including Wenlock Wildlife Management Area in Ferdinand, Yellow Bogs in Lewis, and Victory Bog, but has been found in the southern Green Mountains as well.

Northern Flicker

Nests across Vermont in open country at deciduous forest edges or in small woodlots, orchards, and rural settings. Often feeds on the ground. Migrant flocks can be conspicuous during the second half of September.

Pileated Woodpecker

Widespread in varied forest types with at least some mature trees, its presence is often revealed by large oval cavities formed during excavation for carpenter ants. Sometimes feeds at the base of a tree or on a fallen log. Not uncomfortable in residential settings.

Flycatchers

Olive-sided Flycatcher

Prefers coniferous woods with exposed perches, usually near water, but stops in various wooded edge habitats during migration. Most nest in the Northeast Kingdom and portions of the Green Mountains.

Eastern Wood-Pewee

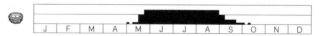

Widespread in deciduous or mixed woods, often with open understories. One of the last migrants still singing in fall. Often heard before it is seen.

Yellow-bellied Flycatcher

Inhabits boreal woods or coniferous woods at higher elevations, mostly in the Northeast Kingdom or Green Mountains. Less selective about woodland habitat during migration. Breeds at Moose Bog in Ferdinand, Victory Bog, and Camels Hump.

Alder Flycatcher

J F M A M J J A S O N D

Prefers alder swamps or similar brushy habitat in or along water. Fairly widespread, but more common in the northern part of the state. *Ray-BEER* may be a better description of the song than the oft-cited *wee-bay-oh*.

Willow Flycatcher

Inhabits open, brushy fields and edges, occasionally near water but usually higher and drier than the habitat of its close relative, Alder Flycatcher. The two species can be compared at Dead Creek Wildlife Management Area. Appears to be increasing.

Least Flycatcher

J F M A M J J A S O N D

Widespread in a variety of deciduous habitats or mixed woods, including second growth. Seems to have a proclivity for woods near water during migration. Vermont's most common *Empidonax* flycatcher.

Eastern Phoebe

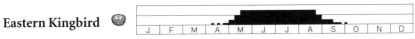

Comfortable nesting on homes, barns, wood sheds, bridges, and other structures. Prefers edges and open situations. Found throughout Vermont.

Great Crested Flycatcher

J F M A M J J A S O N D

Prefers mature deciduous woods with cavities for nest sites, but will use younger woods as well. More common in lowland settings. Migration peaks during second half of May. Loud *reeep* call is a giveaway.

Eastern Kingbird

J F M A M J J A S O N D

Conspicuous in open country across Vermont. Often selects low perches such as thickets, hedges, fencing, cattails, and weeds. Can gather in loose groups in late summer.

Shrikes

Loggerhead Shrike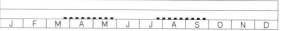

Endangered in Vermont, last known to nest in the late 1970s.[†] This dwindling hunter prefers grasslands with shrubs and small trees for perches and caching prey. Recent sightings have been restricted to the Champlain Valley, including South Slang in Ferrisburgh.

Northern Shrike

An arctic visitor whose abundance can vary from winter to winter. Scattered in open and semi-open areas across Vermont. Assumes a diagonal posture on treetop perches. Can hunt songbirds at feeders. Abundance peaks with movements in early November and late March.

Vireos

White-eyed Vireo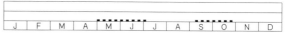

Very rare in shrubby situations and at edges of second-growth woods. Most encounters have been from river valleys and the Champlain Valley, including once at Button Bay State Park in Ferrisburgh and twice at Herrick's Cove in Rockingham.

Yellow-throated Vireo

Fairly well distributed around Vermont, except the Green Mountains and Northeast Kingdom. Nests in mature riparian and wet deciduous woods, occasionally visiting other woods during migration. Herrick's Cove in Rockingham and the lower Poultney River area in West Haven can be among the more reliable spots.

Blue-headed Vireo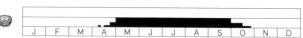

Nests in coniferous or mixed woods throughout Vermont; less common in the Champlain lowlands. Widespread during migration, visiting deciduous woods as well. The most conifer-preferring and cold-tolerant of our vireos. Formerly called Solitary Vireo.

Warbling Vireo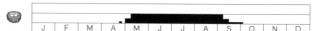

Widespread in stands of mature or middle-aged deciduous woods along lakes, ponds, and slow rivers. The energy of its zig-zagging song compensates for a blatant shortage of field marks.

Philadelphia Vireo

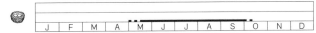

Nesting is largely limited to the Northeast Kingdom and Green Mountains in open successional woods, sometimes near water.[†] More widespread but sparse during migration. Perhaps occasionally overlooked due to the similarity of its song to that of Red-eyed Vireo.

Red-eyed Vireo

One of Vermont's most widespread and vocal songbirds, singing even on the hottest summer days. Frequents deciduous and mixed woods of varied class and age. Often high in the canopy and hard to see.

Jays, Crows, and Ravens

Gray Jay

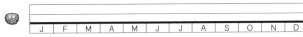

Sparse and largely limited to the Northeast Kingdom, which is near the southern end of its range. Often encountered at Moose Bog in Ferdinand and Victory Bog. Wanders on rare occasions in winter to other portions of the state.

Blue Jay

One of the most widespread year-round Vermont residents. Found in most habitats, including backyards. Gets quiet during nesting season.

American Crow

Widespread across Vermont, although less common in large, unbroken forests. Thousands can be seen moving south in late October. Wintering birds often form roosts numbering in the hundreds. Still shot for "sport" in Vermont.

Fish Crow

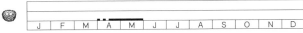

Expanding northward. First documented in Brattleboro in 1992. Nested at Red Rocks Park in South Burlington in 1998 and has visited the Burlington region every year since. Prefers urban/suburban areas with white pines for nesting, not far from major waterways. Use caution distinguishing its voice from those of courting female and young American Crow. Presence outside the breeding season is unkown.

Common Raven

After an extended absence, has repopulated Vermont during the past few decades. Now found statewide, more commonly in large unbroken forests at higher altitudes and in the Northeast Kingdom. Nests on cliffs and high in large trees.

Larks and Swallows

Horned Lark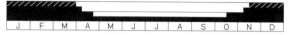

Nests in expansive grasslands with some bare ground nearby, mostly in the Champlain Valley. Frequents recently plowed or harrowed fields. Can be found on the plains of Addison County, particularly after a snowstorm when birds feed along roadsides.

Purple Martin

Nesting primarily limited to martin houses in the Champlain Valley, which provides the required open, lowland habitat near water. Also seen during migration in the Connecticut River Valley. Has nested regularly along Lake Champlain in Addison south of the Champlain Bridge.

Tree Swallow

A widespread cavity nester near open areas or water. The most common swallow in migration, with flocks numbering in the thousands during spring and fall. Can be abundant in southern Addison County in August, when it can be absent from other parts of Vermont.

Northern Rough-winged Swallow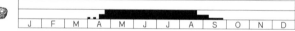

The most solitary of the swallows is well distributed across Vermont, nesting near water in pre-existing burrows and a variety of crevices, including openings in rock, cracked concrete, even drainpipes.

Bank Swallow

A colonial nester in bare river banks, sand deposits, or town sand piles. Like all its relatives in migration, often joins large flocks that can include all five Vermont swallow species. Unevenly distributed; can be abundant near a colony and absent not far away.

Cliff Swallow

Almost haphazard in its distribution; turns up across Vermont colonizing farms, bridges, commercial buildings, maybe even cliffs. Can nest at a site one year and be gone the next. A fairly large colony has nested for several years on the Rouses Point Bridge in Alburg.

Barn Swallow

Nests wherever it can find barns and other outbuildings, most often in agricultural settings. Will also colonize porches and garages at rural homes and the undersides of bridges. Frequents lakes and ponds during migration, often with Tree Swallows.

Chickadees, Nuthatches, and Creepers

Black-capped Chickadee

Perhaps the most evenly distributed year-round bird in the state. On a calm day, a Vermonter is never far from the sound of a chickadee.

Boreal Chickadee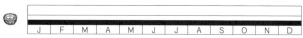

Nests in the boreal woods of Vermont's Northeast Kingdom. Occasionally irruptive farther south in winter. Associates with Black-capped Chickadee. Found reliably at Moose Bog in Ferdinand and occasionally at Barr Hill Nature Preserve in Greensboro.

Tufted Titmouse

A cavity nester expanding its range northward into lowland deciduous and mixed woods. Abundance declines toward Vermont's northernmost latitudes and higher altitudes. Has an aversion to deep woods and a preference for suburbia, city parks, and wooded residential areas.

Red-breasted Nuthatch

Widespread in coniferous and mixed woods across Vermont, a bit less common in the Champlain Valley. Can be irruptive and locally abundant during the first few weeks of September. A feeder visitor.

White-breasted Nuthatch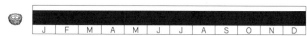

Prefers deciduous or mixed woods, often inhabiting forest edges, small patches of trees, or residential areas. Can become less common in winter in the higher, colder regions of the Eastern Piedmont, Green Mountains, and Northeast Kingdom. Caches seeds.

Brown Creeper

A cosmopolitan resident of various mature forest types—deciduous, mixed, and coniferous woods across the state. Usually seen singly or in pairs. Often inconspicuous, becomes more obvious when singing begins in late March.

Wrens

Carolina Wren

A rare, vocal nester. Prefers tangled, scrubby, brushy vegetation. More dependable toward the southern part of Vermont. Population appears to build and then crash during a severe winter. Visits feeders in winter.

House Wren

Prefers deciduous woods with low, scrubby understory, but has adapted well to backyard living. More common in the Champlain Valley and in southern Vermont. Industrious males will commandeer cavities and build several nests as part of courtship.

Winter Wren

A tiny bundle of energy inhabiting coniferous and mixed woods across most of Vermont, even at high elevations. Stops in other wooded habitats during migration. One hint for finding this elusive creature is to *spish* for the naïve and inquisitive youngsters in summer.

Sedge Wren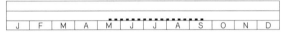

Endangered in Vermont. May have nested in the Dead Creek region of Addison County in 2000. Most reports of this rarity are from the wet fields and swales of the Champlain Valley. Like other wrens, males build multiple nests, so the presence of a nest does not confirm breeding.

Marsh Wren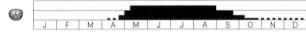

Nests in large—but not all—cattail marshes around Vermont. Patience is usually rewarded with a bird fluttering over the marsh or perching in full view. Excellent locations include Mud Creek Wildlife Management Area in Alburg, Dead Creek Wildlife Management Area in Addison, and West Rutland Marsh.

Kinglets and Gnatcatchers

Golden-crowned Kinglet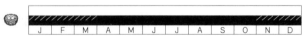

A widely distributed resident of coniferous woods, mostly spruce and fir. Less common in the Champlain Valley. Can also frequent mixed woods, including patches of hemlock in northern hardwoods. Migration peaks in April and October. Abundance can vary in winter.

Ruby-crowned Kinglet

This frenetic musician nests in spruce and fir, mostly in the Northeast Kingdom and Green Mountains. It also frequents deciduous woods and wet, shrubby habitats during the peaks of spring and fall migration. *Spishing* often gets its attention.

Blue-gray Gnatcatcher

Has expanded northward into Vermont's floodplain forests and other wet, wooded situations, primarily in the Champlain Valley and Connecticut River Valley. Infrequently seen elsewhere. Reliable locations include Porter Bay in Ferrisburgh and the lower Poultney River area in West Haven.

Thrushes

Northern Wheatear

A very rare visitor, usually to fields in the Champlain Valley. Typically gone soon after arriving, this misplaced migrant has occasionally lingered for several days.

Eastern Bluebird

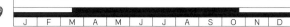

Widespread in open and semi-open areas, mostly agricultural land. Generally overwinters in southern Vermont but can linger farther north in the Champlain Valley with available food. Often perches on fence posts and telephone lines. Competes with Tree Swallow for nest boxes.

Veery

Widely distributed across Vermont in deciduous and mixed woods, at times preferring damp sites. Abundance can decline quickly with rising altitude. Like other thrushes, it frequently sings at dusk.

Gray-cheeked Thrush

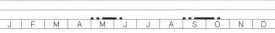

A rare migrant hard to distinguish from its close relative, Bicknell's Thrush. Its migratory status in Vermont is gradually becoming clarified now that Bicknell's Thrush is no longer considered a subspecies of this species.

Bicknell's Thrush

A specialized breeder in montane fir forests generally above 3,000 feet. Under pressure from winter range deforestation and the effects of global climate change. Resides on most high mountains, including Mt. Mansfield, Camels Hump, and Stratton Mountain. Singing males occasionally attend exposed perches, usually at dawn and dusk.

Swainson's Thrush

Breeds primarily in coniferous and mixed woods in the Northeast Kingdom and at high elevations in the Green Mountains. Widespread but scattered in other wooded habitats during migration.

Hermit Thrush

Vermont's state bird didn't get the job for its looks. Its ethereal song is among the most pleasant sounds in the Vermont woods. Prefers mixed or coniferous woods, often at higher elevations, throughout the state. Also widely distributed in deciduous woods or valleys during migration. A ground-nester, it is commonly seen at eye level or below.

Wood Thrush

Prefers older deciduous or mixed woods across Vermont, especially damp areas. Abundance drops with rising elevation. This distinctly spotted thrush has an airy song and a sputtered *whit-whit* call. Can join Hermit Thrush and Veery in an enchanting chorus at dusk.

American Robin

This widespread, versatile thrush prefers dense conifers for nesting but adapts to whatever is available, including buildings. Abundance drops with increasing elevation. Wintering population, most common in the Champlain Valley, varies with available wild fruit.

Varied Thrush

A rare western visitor to scattered locations across Vermont, often at feeders. Prefers dense conifers. Can linger at a food supply for weeks (one bird stuck around until June).

Mimics and Starlings

Gray Catbird

Well distributed throughout the lowlands of Vermont in thick, brushy habitats including deciduous woodland edges. Can be fairly numerous in migration in May and September. Very rare in mid-winter.

Northern Mockingbird

Prefers thickets and other shrubby growths in open and semi-open country, primarily in the Connecticut River and Champlain Valleys. Occasionally seen in "inland" lowlands. This conspicuous mimic frequents farms and residential areas. Sometimes sings at night. Vulnerable in harsh winters.

Brown Thrasher

Thinly spread in shrubby areas of open and semi-open country and thick under-growth in deciduous woodland edges. Often sings from high perches in trees.

European Starling

This cavity-nester likes open and semi-open areas including farmland, parks, and cities. Abundant year-round but concentrates in winter, often forming large flocks on working farms.

Pipits and Waxwings

American Pipit

Visits shorelines and fields with low or no vegetation, primarily in the Champlain Valley. Also can be found on open mountain summits. Harder to find in spring, but gathers in good numbers in fall, notably at the Goose Viewing Area at Dead Creek Wildlife Management Area in Addison.

Bohemian Waxwing

Regular and widespread visitor, but numbers vary tremendously from year to year. Nomadic flocks seek fruits from cedars, ornamentals, and other trees and shrubs, often in cities or residential areas. Can mix with Cedar Waxwings.

Cedar Waxwing

Widespread inhabitant of various woodland and open habitats, showing some preference for riparian and other wet areas. Numbers are variable in winter, when birds can flock and roam in search of fruit. Winter flocks occasionally include Bohemian Waxwing.

Warblers and Tanagers

Blue-winged Warbler

Nests in fields overgrown with shrubs and small trees, and along shrubby wet-lands, yet limited in Vermont, which is at the northern edge of its range. Most sightings are from lowland areas of southern Vermont.

Golden-winged Warbler

Similar to Blue-winged Warbler in its habitat choices, preferring drier ground; the two species readily hybridize (interbreed), and their offspring cannot be identified by song alone. Most reports are from lower elevations of western Vermont except the Champlain Islands.

Tennessee Warbler

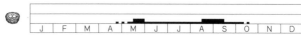

Breeds in limited numbers in coniferous bogs of the Northeast Kingdom. Migrants can turn up in varied woodland and wet habitats. Sightings declined dramatically during the 1990s. Explosive song belies this warbler's non-explosive plumage.

Orange-crowned Warbler

A very rare migrant in spring. Prefers shrubby edges and weeds. Can associate in the fall with migrating flocks of Yellow-rumped Warbler and Palm Warbler. Sightings have been from scattered Vermont locations.

Nashville Warbler

A ground-nester in coniferous woods at varied elevations and coniferous wetland edges, largely outside of the Champlain Valley. Widespread in varied woodland settings during migration.

Northern Parula

Prefers coniferous or mixed woods, mostly in the Green Mountains and Northeast Kingdom. Breeding distribution depends on the availability of its primary nest material, a lichen of the genus *Usnea* known commonly as "old man's beard." Widespread in woodlands and at edges in migration.

Yellow Warbler

Glows yellow in or near shrubby wetlands and wet, brushy, overgrown fields across Vermont. One of the most visible warblers. Robust nesting populations have resided at Windmill Point Road in Alburg, Berlin Pond, and West Rutland Marsh.

Chestnut-sided Warbler

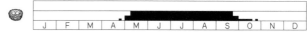

Widespread in brushy growth at woodland edges and clearings. Can sit still and sing more than the average warbler. One of the few warblers to benefit from forest fragmentation.

Magnolia Warbler

Nests in coniferous and mixed woods, mostly in the Green Mountains, Eastern Piedmont, and Northeast Kingdom. More widespread and in varied woodland habitats during migration.

Cape May Warbler

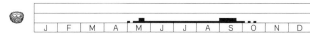

A sparse breeder in spruce-fir woods, primarily in the Northeast Kingdom. Reports have declined, but it can turn up most anywhere in migration, often at or near the top of a conifer. Found regularly at Barr Hill Nature Preserve in Greensboro and Victory Bog, and occasionally at the Thurman W. Dix Reservoir in Orange.

Black-throated Blue Warbler

Nests in shrub layers in deciduous and mixed woods across much of Vermont; less common in the Champlain Valley. More widespread in migration. Almost any walk in the Eastern Piedmont or lower elevations of the Green Mountains includes encounters with this warbler.

Yellow-rumped Warbler

Vermont's most common warbler in migration nests primarily in coniferous and mixed woods, even at high elevation. It turns up virtually anywhere during migration, from front lawns to city streets to shorelines. Cedar groves along Lake Champlain can host wintering birds.

Black-throated Green Warbler

Prefers to nest in mixed woods across the state, less commonly in the Champlain Valley. More widely distributed during migration. Next to Yellow-rumped Warbler, it can be the majority species in a mixed warbler flock during fall migration.

Blackburnian Warbler

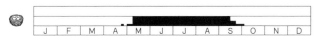

Nests in conifer treetops in mixed and coniferous woods, less so in the Champlain Valley. More widespread in similar canopy habitat during migration. Often hard to see buried high in a conifer but can drop to offer a gratifying view on an exposed perch.

Yellow-throated Warbler

Strays from the pine woods of the South, occasionally visiting feeders in winter. Has appeared in the Burlington region several times.

Pine Warbler

 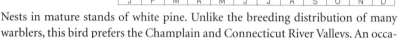

Nests in mature stands of white pine. Unlike the breeding distribution of many warblers, this bird prefers the Champlain and Connecticut River Valleys. An occasional breeder elsewhere. Good locations include Red Rocks Park in South Burlington and Paradise Park in Windsor.

Prairie Warbler

Restricted to southern Vermont and southern sections of the Connecticut River and Champlain Valleys. Prefers fields overgrown with brush, shrubs, red cedar, or other small trees.

Palm Warbler

 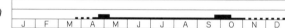

Recently discovered nesting in spruce bogs of the Northeast Kingdom. A scattered migrant, mostly through the Connecticut River and Champlain Valleys. Often found with migrating Yellow-rumped Warblers in fall. Good locations in migration include Herrick's Cove in Rockingham and Button Bay in Ferrisburg.

Bay-breasted Warbler

Nests in boreal woods, Vermont being the southern edge of its breeding range. Remains a welcome surprise in other woods during migration. Reports have declined in recent decades. Seen at Victory Bog and Paul Stream Road in Maidstone and Ferdinand.

Blackpoll Warbler

A common nester in dense spruce and fir at high elevations in the Green Mountains, less so in the foothills and the Northeast Kingdom. Widespread in migration, often moving near water. Mt. Mansfield and Camels Hump are two of many reliable spots for this warbler.

Cerulean Warbler

A rare nester in mature, deciduous and mixed woods, often on hillsides with huge, old growth trees. Difficult to see; most encounters with this canopy-lover have been in the Champlain Valley and Rutland regions. This declining species has been proposed for protection under the federal Endangered Species Act.

Black-and-white Warbler

Widespread in mixed or deciduous woods. Rarely occurs in large numbers in any given place, even during migration, yet a prevalent Vermont warbler nonetheless. Often crawls like a nuthatch on branches and tree trunks.

American Redstart

Widespread in a variety of woods, preferring deciduous growth, including shrubby successional habitats, sometimes near water. Song can be variable, often ending abruptly or with a harsh note.

Worm-eating Warbler

Very rarely encountered in Vermont. Prefers ravines, often skulking low in the underbrush. Two of the scant records have been from the Brattleboro area.

Ovenbird

One of Vermont's most widely distributed woodland birds; prefers deciduous woods but can be found in mixed woods as well. In spite of a loud song its stealthy behavior can make it hard to locate. This ground-nesting bird walks rather than hops.

Northern Waterthrush

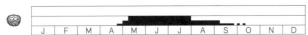

Reliable across Vermont in alder and other scrubby wetlands, also along swamp and pond edges with brushy cover. Best views are in early May, when males sing explosive songs from exposed perches. The southern end of Berlin Pond and Lefferts Pond in Chittenden are among many nesting locations.

Louisiana Waterthrush

Much more common in the southern half of the state alongside wooded streams and rivers, including ravines. The lower Poultney River area in West Haven and Henwoods Hill road in Westminster are among popular places for this bird.

Connecticut Warbler

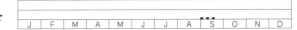

An elusive migrant that inhabits dense undergrowth. Most often encountered in southern Vermont. Its repeated occurrence in the mist nets at the Vermont Institute of Natural Science's banding station in Woodstock suggests that this bird may be more widespread and often overlooked.

Mourning Warbler

Sprinkled across Vermont in early successional, thick deciduous growth, often at the edges of clearings. Can appear shortly after land is cleared but be absent several years later owing to the regeneration of trees. Often uses overgrown clearcuts, utility rights of way, and roadsides.

Common Yellowthroat

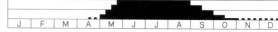

Widespread in shrubby wetlands and wet, overgrown fields and edges. While preferring the undergrowth, males sometimes sing from conspicuous perches.

Wilson's Warbler

Rare breeder in shrubby wetlands of the Northeast Kingdom. Prefers similar habitat during migration but can visit woods as well. Can be regular during migration in the thickets east of Lake Paran in North Bennington.

Canada Warbler

Vocal but sometimes hard to locate in shrubby deciduous growth, sometimes at edges. Widespread during migration but less common in the Champlain Valley during the breeding season.

Yellow-breasted Chat

A very rare visitor to dense, tangled thickets, including regenerating clearings and edges. Most of the widely scattered and infrequent reports are from southern Vermont.

Scarlet Tanager

Widespread across Vermont, preferring mature deciduous or mixed woods. Often high in the canopy, this knockout is sometimes hard to locate. Perhaps the best method is knowing its song, which sounds like an American Robin with a sore throat.

Sparrows and Relatives

Eastern Towhee

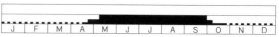

Fairly common and widespread in the southern half of Vermont, diminishing in abundance northward. Inhabits dense brushy edges and thickets, often on small mountains and hillsides.

American Tree Sparrow

Vermont's most common winter sparrow. Fond of low growth such as hedgerows, marshes, and overgrown fields. Visits feeders and roadsides; avoids deeper woods.

Chipping Sparrow

Widespread inhabitant of openings with scattered conifers for nest trees. Prefers suburban lawns, parks, and certain grassy woodland openings.

Clay-colored Sparrow

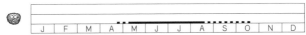

A rare breeder and migrant preferring brushy or overgrown fields with scattered trees. Recently discovered nesting in Grand Isle; only sporadically seen elsewhere around the state.

Field Sparrow

Prefers weedy, overgrown fields, mostly across southern Vermont and dropping in abundance northward. Sparsely distributed in the Champlain Valley.

Vesper Sparrow

Prefers fields with hedgerows and young trees for singing. Most common in the Dead Creek region of Addison County but pops up elsewhere, notably the dairy country of the Northeast Kingdom. Farr Cross Road in Addison and the John H. Boyland State Airport in Brighton are good locations.

Savannah Sparrow

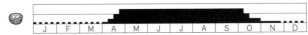

One of Vermont's most overlooked songbirds. Frequents large hayfields and pastures as well as airports across the state. Often flits into adjacent hedgerows, fencing, and trees. Its buzzy song is a hallmark of the plains of Addison County.

Grasshopper Sparrow

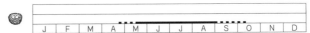

Threatened in Vermont; prefers fields with short or sparse grass and scattered patches of clover or similar clumps of taller growth. Loss of agricultural land threatens this species. Most likely to be found in the Champlain Valley. A reliable location is the Franklin County State Airport in Highgate, where mowing practices have been altered to protect grassland birds.

Fox Sparrow

Often found at feeders during spring and fall migrations but also prefers patches of shrubs and woodland edges. Can be detected by its sweet, whistled song or hearty chip note. Button Bay State Park in Ferrisburgh is a regular waypoint.

Song Sparrow

Vermont's most common and widespread sparrow nests in overgrown fields, hedgerows, residential areas, and at edges of wetlands, forests, and waterways— nearly anywhere but deep woods and high elevations. Reliable sites include your backyard.

Lincoln's Sparrow

Prefers bogs, wet fields, and other openings with shrubby growth, mostly in the Northeast Kingdom or at higher elevations in the Green Mountain Plateau in southern Vermont. Probably overlooked in migration owing to its reclusive nature and similarity to Song Sparrow. There are a few winter records.

Swamp Sparrow

More widespread in cattail marshes (even small ones) and their brushy edges than swamps. Occasional in other wet, shrubby situations. Best located by scanning the tips of cattails or higher shrubby perches for singing males.

White-throated Sparrow

Nests across Vermont in mixed or coniferous woods with shrubby undergrowth, including at high elevations; less often in the Champlain Valley. Encountered during migration in a variety of wooded and shrubby habitats. Variable numbers overwinter in lowland areas. Its song signifies the north woods.

White-crowned Sparrow

Often found at feeders, hedgerows, and patches of shrubs across Vermont. Sings occasionally during spring and even fall migration. The spring passage of most birds can be particularly abrupt.

Dark-eyed Junco

A widespread ground-nester in coniferous and mixed woods, including high peaks. During migration large flocks can also appear in deciduous habitat or at feeders. Overwinters in varying numbers, mostly in southern Vermont.

Lapland Longspur

Usually forages with Snow Bunting and Horned Lark, less commonly alone. Found in farm fields throughout the state, mostly in the Champlain Valley, especially Addison County. Occasionally found on the Lake Champlain shoreline in fall.

Snow Bunting

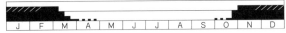

Widespread in open country across Vermont, sometimes in flocks of hundreds. Winter abundance can vary from year to year. Although flocks can be nomadic, Addison County is a relatively reliable stronghold.

Cardinals and Buntings

Northern Cardinal

Nests in dense, tangled shrubs, but is quite obvious in hedgerows, edges, and suburban and urban settings, mostly at lower elevations and away from the Northeast Kingdom. Bird feeders may have assisted its expansion northward into Vermont during the last few decades.

Rose-breasted Grosbeak

Nests in mature deciduous woods and less commonly in mixed woods across Vermont. Often forages in the canopy. Song resembles that of an American Robin in overdrive, but a trademark squeak note can also reveal its presence when the canopy won't.

Blue Grosbeak

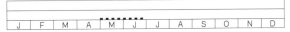

Rarely encountered in Vermont and easily confused with the far more common Indigo Bunting. Prefers open country with scattered trees and shrubby edges. Most reports are from lowland areas of southern Vermont.

Indigo Bunting

Prefers fields in the early stages of reforestation across Vermont. Often sings from a high perch on hedgerows and apple and larger tree species. Occasionally visits feeders.

Dickcissel

A rare visitor to feeders and farms, often in the company of House Sparrow. May be overlooked due to the failure to scrutinize House Sparrow flocks.

Bobolink

A widespread and showy resident of large meadows. Males can begin their molt to femalelike plumage as early as July (males caring for young keep breeding plumage longer). Premigratory flocks begin forming in mid-July. Loss of habitat and early cutting of hay threaten this species.

Red-winged Blackbird

Prefers wetlands and other open areas virtually everywhere in Vermont except at high elevation. Forms huge flocks (sometimes with other blackbird species and European Starling) in fall. Individuals occasionally overwinter at feeders or among starling flocks.

Eastern Meadowlark

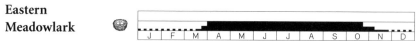

Scattered in grasslands and farm country across Vermont. Like other grassland species, under pressure from the conversion of farmland to housing. Sometimes sings from wires or other high perches. A few individuals occasionally overwinter in milder sections of Vermont.

Rusty Blackbird

Nests at bogs, ponds, and shrubby or wooded wetlands, primarily in the Northeast Kingdom and Green Mountains. Often seen elsewhere near water, including swamps, during migration. Spring migration peaks in late April. Fall migrants are most common in the swamps of the Champlain Valley.

Common Grackle

Widespread in open country, wetlands, or woodlands near water. Often seen foraging for aquatic insects and other food along water's edge. Like other blackbirds, gathers into huge wandering flocks in late summer and fall, so while still abundant, its distribution can be limited.

Brown-headed Cowbird

Widespread in a variety of open and semi-open habitats, often at forest edges. Often maligned for doing what it has evolved to do—lay eggs in the nests of other songbirds—even though increased forest fragmentation has fostered opportuities for this behavior.

Orchard Oriole

Has nested occasionally in or near orchards and similar settings, most often in the southern Champlain Valley. Nested alongside Baltimore Oriole at McCuen Slang in Addison in 2000.

Baltimore Oriole

Widespread in semi-open country and riparian woods across Vermont. One indicator in winter of its past presence is its dangling, hammocklike nest woven from plant fiber. Reliable spots are abundant, including South Bay Wildlife Management Area in Newport, Berlin Pond, and Porter Bay in Ferrisburgh.

Finches

Pine Grosbeak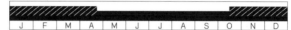

An occasional winter visitor. During "invasions," flocks can overrun crabapples and other ornamental trees, making cities and residential areas some of the more reliable locations for this docile species. Sometimes visits feeders.

Purple Finch

Nests at all elevations in coniferous and mixed woods, less often in the Champlain Valley. Winter abundance varies statewide with conifer cone crop and other food sources. Unlike House Finch, it is infrequent at "urban" feeders.

House Finch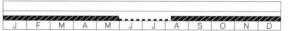

First recorded in 1968, nearly thirty years after its importation to the eastern United States from the West. Found statewide, though usually not far from its namesake and people. Fond of nesting in hanging baskets, old wreaths, or any other suitable tangle near a house.

Red Crossbill

An erratic and nomadic visitor, perhaps nesting from time to time when food supplies are adequate. Prefers to dine on pine as opposed to the seeds of the smaller conifers. Occasionally mixes with White-winged Crossbill.

White-winged Crossbill

An irruptive visitor in coniferous woods at all elevations, less so in southern Vermont, during winters with prolific cone generation. Nesting is likely (even in mid-winter), particularly during surges in food supply. In irruption years, the Northeast Kingdom can be a good location, including Moose Bog in Ferdinand and Victory Bog.

Common Redpoll

A highly irruptive species, found in Vermont one winter and absent the next. Flocks can overrun feeders and gather in large numbers in open country to feed on seeds, including those from the catkins of birch species.

Hoary Redpoll

Found rarely among flocks of Common Redpoll, usually in large invasion years. A genuine challenge to distinguish from its highly variable relative.

Pine Siskin

Another wanderer in coniferous or mixed woods at all elevations. Abundance depends on the availability of food from conifers. An occasional, sparse, and scattered nester. Can associate with American Goldfinch, including during forays to feeders.

American Goldfinch

Widespread in open and semi-open country, particularly near overgrown fields with thistle, dandelion, goldenrod, and other food sources. Commonly visits feeders. Winter abundance varies, probably with food supply.

Evening Grosbeak

Widespread but variable in abundance from year to year in coniferous woods, mixed woods, and open country with supplies of box elder seeds, a favorite food. Less common in the Champlain Valley. Winter use of feeders varies, perhaps with abundance of wild food.

House Sparrow

Found statewide and, as the name implies, rarely far from humans and homes. Particularly fond of urban settings and working farms.

🪶 *Accidental Species*

Surprise is one of the joys of watching birds. Arriving every so often are birds that have no business being here; these are "accidentals." They show up in Vermont but display no pattern of regular occurrence (have not been encountered at least once every five years for the past fifteen years). These are birds that get phones ringing, e-mail flowing, and binoculars bustling.

Below is the complete list of Vermont's accidental species. It represents more than a century of rare birds documented by hundreds of observers and researchers. Each report has been reviewed and accepted by the Vermont Bird Records Committee. In some instances the first sighting of a species in Vermont comes from a lone observer lacking supporting evidence (such as a photograph or corroboration from another person); these written reports, deemed "hypothetical," are designated by an asterisk (*). Records from 1980 through 2000 come from the Vermont Institute of Natural Science's quarterly publication *Records of Vermont Birds*. Julie Nicholson of the Vermont Bird Records Committee provided earlier records. Except where noted, the list does not include birds judged to have escaped from captivity. Of course, the odds of actually finding any of these birds in Vermont are just a little better than being hit by lightning while winning the lottery.

Pacific Loon or Arctic Loon
- Nov. 2–12, 1989: Lake Champlain Bridge, Addison.

Pacific Loon*
- Dec. 15–18, 1993*: Retreat Meadows, Brattleboro.
- Oct. 27, 1998*: Oven Bay, Lake Champlain, Addison.

Eared Grebe
- Oct. 4, 1874: Lake St. Catherine, Poultney.
- Dec. 14–15, 1984: Button Bay, Lake Champlain, Ferrisburgh.
- Dec. 15, 1990: Kellogg Bay, Lake Champlain, Ferrisburgh.
- Sep. 24–28, 1994: East Creek, Orwell.

Western Grebe or Clark's Grebe*
- Nov. 30, 1962*: Kingsland Bay, Lake Champlain, Ferrisburgh.

Northern Fulmar
- Dec. 4, 1976: Bennington. Rehabilitated and released.
- Nov. 23, 2000: A light morph southbound over Lake Champlain, Charlotte. (Author's sighting not yet reviewed by Vermont Bird Records Committee.)

Cory's Shearwater
- Sep. 22, 1938: Wheelock. Hurricane-related.

Greater Shearwater
- Sep. 21, 1938: Rutland. Hurricane-related.
- Jun. 16, 1976: Appletree Bay, Lake Champlain, Burlington.
- Aug. 3, 1992: Off Ladd Point, Lake Champlain, Grand Isle.

Leach's Storm-Petrel
- Aug. 1902: Fairlee.
- Aug. 25, 1933: Bennington.
- Sep. 22, 1938: Barre. All 1938 records were of hurricane-bullied birds.
- Sep. 22, 1938: Norwich.

- Sep. 22, 1938: Rutland.
- Sep. 22–24, 1938: St. Johnsbury.
- Sep. 21, 1989: Lake Champlain, off east coast of Grand Isle.
- Sep. 16, 2001: Charlotte Town Beach, Lake Champlain. (Author's sighting not yet reviewed by Vermont Bird Records Committee.)

White-tailed Tropicbird
- Sep. 22, 1938: North Danville. These 1938 records were hurricane-related.
- Sep. 22, 1938: Woodstock.

American White Pelican
- Aug. 1, 1944: Missisquoi Bay, Lake Champlain, Highgate.
- Aug. 19, 1954: Keeler Bay, Lake Champlain, North Hero.
- Aug. 20–Sep. 19, 1974: Dead Creek Wildlife Management Area, Addison.
- May 3–6, 1990: An adult at South Bay, Lake Memphremagog, Newport.
- May 21–22, 1998: Two adults at Shelburne Bay, Lake Champlain, Shelburne.

Tricolored Heron
- Aug. 17, 1980: Shelburne Farms, Shelburne.
- Aug. 15, 1983: On the shore of Lake Champlain by the Lake Champlain Bridge, Addison.

Yellow-crowned Night-Heron
- Early Aug. 1958: Addison.
- May 19, 1984: An adult in Weybridge.
- Jul. 28, 1984*: Dead Creek Wildlife Management Area, Addison.
- Aug. 8, 1993: An immature at Dead Creek Wildlife Management Area, Panton.
- Sep. 12, 1998: An adult at LaPlatte River Marsh, Shelburne.

White Ibis*
- Summer 1878*: South Woodstock.
- Late Aug. 1975*: An immature in Grand Isle.

Wood Stork
- Aug. 1897: A pair in Williston.

Black Vulture
- Jul. 11, 1884: Woodbury.
- Jul. 7, 1912: Pawlet.
- Jun. 26, 1954: Royalton.
- Sep. 9, 1983: Vernon.
- Sep. 3, 1999: Colchester.

Fulvous Whistling-Duck
- Oct. 13, 1990: Legally shot near Missisquoi National Wildlife Refuge, Swanton.
- Aug. 8, 1998*: Three birds at Herrick's Cove, Connecticut River, Rockingham.

As exotic waterfowl are sometimes kept in captivity, an occasional escape is inevitable. Hence additional scrutiny is afforded waterfowl as to probable origin. The 1990 bird was accepted as wild, the 1998 birds as origin unknown.

Pink-footed Goose*

- Mar. 31, 1999*: Grand Isle. On Lake Champlain ice with large flock of Snow Geese. Considered to be a wild bird.

Barnacle Goose*

- May 14-19, 1990*: Maidstone.
- Apr. 1–19, 1996*: With Canada Geese on Lake Champlain, Grand Isle. A captive bird had recently escaped nearby.
- Oct. 20, 1996*: With Snow Geese at Dead Creek Wildlife Management Area, Addison.
- Oct. 23, 1998*: Two birds southbound over Lake Champlain, Charlotte.

All but the escapee were recorded as origin unclear. Considering Vermont's appeal to arctic goose populations, however, the late October records are intriguing.

Garganey

- May 21–Jun. 5, 1988: An adult male at East Creek, Orwell. Thought to be a wild bird.

Tufted Duck

- Apr. 7, 2000: An adult male with small flock of Ring-necked Ducks at Shelburne Bay, Lake Champlain. Presumed to be a wild bird.

Swallow-tailed Kite

- Apr. 26, 1913: Waitsfield.
- May 26, 1983: Middlebury.
- Mar. 28, 1986: At an elevation of about 1500 feet in Washington.

Swainson's Hawk

- May 23, 1915: Hartland.
- Sep. 5, 1980: Over a hawkwatch in Winhall.

Yellow Rail

- Jul. 18, 1887: Mount Holly.
- Oct. 20, 1913: Windsor.
- Jun. 3, 1975: South Bay, Lake Memphremagog, Newport.
- Sep. 10, 1977: Swanton.

Clapper Rail

- Date unknown (prior to 1902): Burlington. Specimen at University of Vermont.

King Rail*

- Aug., 1961*: Addison.
- May 17–18, 1994*: Dead Creek Wildlife Management Area, Addison.

Status of these records is under review by the Vermont Bird Records Committee, since their disposition is unclear.

Pacific Golden-Plover*

- Sep. 6, 2000*: A juvenile on Young Island, Grand Isle.

Piping Plover
- Oct. 2, 1908: Bennington.
- Sep. 3–6, 1952: Burlington.

American Avocet
- Sep. 22, 1978: Addison.
- Aug. 5–19, 1994: A pair at Dead Creek Wildlife Management Area, Addison.
- Jul. 20–22, 1999: Lake Lamoille, Morrisville.

Curlew Sandpiper
- Jul. 13, 1991: A male in breeding plumage at Dead Creek, Panton.
- Aug. 28, 1994: Dead Creek Wildlife Management Area, Addison.

Ruff
- Sep. 19, 1974*: Addison.
- Jul. 6–14, 1991: An adult male at Dead Creek, Panton.

Franklin's Gull
- Aug. 31–Sep. 21, 1968: Lake Memphremagog, Newport.

Thayer's Gull*
- Mar. 5, 1983*: A first-winter bird at the Burlington Waterfront, Lake Champlain.
- Dec. 19, 1989*: An adult at the Burlington Waterfront, Lake Champlain.
- Dec. 3–5, 1996*: An immature at the Burlington Waterfront, Lake Champlain.

Ivory Gull
- Apr. 21, 1982*: Near Oakledge Park, Lake Champlain, Burlington.
- Mar. 3, 1983*: At a now-closed landfill in South Burlington.
- Jan. 4, 2000: A first-winter bird on the iced shore of Lake Champlain, Grand Isle.
- Nov. 6, 2000: A first-summer bird flying north along Lake Champlain, Charlotte. (Author's sighting not yet reviewed by Vermont Bird Records Committee.)

Arctic Tern
- May 12, 1981*: Reading.
- May 13, 1981: East Barnard.
- May 11, 1988: An adult at Retreat Meadows, Brattleboro.

Sooty Tern
- Sep. 6, 1876: Rutland.
- Sep. 6, 1979: Hartland. All the 1979 birds were associated with a hurricane.
- Sep. 7, 1979: Sandgate.
- Sep. 7, 1979: McIndoe Falls.
- Sep. 8, 1979: Hartford.
- Sep. 12, 1979: Weathersfield.

White-winged Tern
- Jun. 12, 1987: At a small pond in Hartford.

Dovekie
- Feb. 16, 1905: Location unknown.
- May 31, 1910: Bennington.
- Nov. 26, 1978: Rochester.

Common Murre
- Mar. 14, 1905: East Wallingford.
- Nov. 25, 1976: Calais.

Thick-billed Murre
- Nov. 28, 1950: South Hero. These 1950 records were hurricane-related.
- Dec. 2, 1950: An immature in Middlesex.

Black Guillemot
- Nov. 3–30, 1955: Burlington Waterfront, Lake Champlain.
- Dec. 22, 1977: Near Oakledge Park, Lake Champlain, Burlington.
- Dec. 20, 1980: Button Bay, Lake Champlain, Ferrisburgh.
- Nov. 30, 1999: Lake Champlain, Charlotte.

Atlantic Puffin
- Dec. 10, 1960: Rutland Town.

White-winged Dove*
- Sep. 2, 2000*: Lake Champlain Bridge, Addison.

Boreal Owl
- 1891: Lunenburg.
- Prior to 1919: Newbury.
- Jul. 18, 1923: Fayston.
- Jan. 24, 1932: St. Johnsbury.
- Mar. 24, 1936: Rutland.
- Mar. 5, 1992: Enosburg Falls.
- Mar. 9-12, 1994: Bakersfield.

Acadian Flycatcher
- Jul. 14, 1904: Pownal.
- Aug. 31, 1973: A hatch-year bird banded in Shelburne.
- Sep. 9, 1981: Winhall.
- May 27–Jun. 23, 1991: Two singing males in Guilford.
- Jul. 2–31, 1992: Stone Dam, Dead Creek Wildlife Management Area, Panton.

Say's Phoebe
- Nov. 16, 1985*: Shoreham.
- Oct. 29, 1994–Apr. 28, 1995: Brandon.
- Nov. 8, 1994: Dorset.

Western Kingbird
- Sep. 22, 1989: An immature in Barnard.

Scissor-tailed Flycatcher*

- May 26, 1997*: Near the White River in Bethel.

Fork-tailed Flycatcher

- 1884: An adult in St. Johnsbury. Now residing (quietly) at the University of Vermont.
- Jun. 10–Jul. 25, 2000: An adult at Hawkins Slang, Ferrisburgh.

With this regular pattern of occurrence the next bird should be expected in the year 2116.

Cassin's Vireo

- May 21, 1997: Found among a large fallout of warblers in Red Rocks Park, South Burlington.

Steller's Jay *

- Oct. 20, 1986*: Topsham. The possibility of an escaped caged bird was considered.

Bewick's Wren

- May 27, 1975: Banded in South Woodstock.

Mountain Bluebird

- Apr. 2–8, 1989: An adult male residing in a Grand Isle orchard.

Prothonotary Warbler

- Prior to 1891: Lunenburg.
- Apr. 26, 1973: Rochester.
- Apr. 24, 1980: Burlington.
- May 20–Jun. 27, 1989: West Haven.
- May 18–21, 1998: An adult male at Long Point, Ferrisburgh.

Kentucky Warbler

- May 30, 1905: Lunenburg.
- Jun. 16, 1975: A male in Manchester.
- Jun. 30, 1984*: Wilmington.
- May 19, 1985: Cavendish.
- May 24–Jun. 5, 1988: A male in West Brattleboro.
- Jun. 13, 1990: A male in West Brattleboro.
- Sep. 14, 1990: An adult female banded in West Brattleboro.

Hooded Warbler

- Second week of May 1980: A male in Jericho.

Summer Tanager

- May 1, 1998: A male in Hartland Four Corners.
- May 11, 1999: A male in Brandon.
- May 17, 1999: A male in Albany.

Western Tanager

- Sep. 14, 1973: Winhall.

- Apr. 30, 1975: Wallingford.
- Mar. 26, 1987*: A male in Rochester.
- Nov. 19, 1988: A male in Cambridge.
- Aug. 22, 1991: A male along West Road, Panton.

Green-tailed Towhee
- Dec. 16, 1989–May 5, 1990: Near Retreat Meadows, Brattleboro.

Spotted Towhee
- Late Dec. 1989–Feb. 11, 1990: Attending feeders in Manchester Center.

Lark Sparrow*
- May 17, 1985*: At a cemetery in Rutland.
- Aug. 31, 1994*: South Londonderry.

Lark Bunting
- May 18, 1967: A female banded in Bennington.

Henslow's Sparrow
- Jun. 24, 1977: Quechee.
- Sep. 3, 1980: Herrick's Cove, Rockingham.
- Jun. 1981: Clarendon.
- Jun. 18, 1986: South Londonderry.
- Aug. 18, 1996: Herrick's Cove, Rockingham.

Endangered in Vermont. There are numerous reports prior to 1977. Once considered a regular nester, now considered extirpated in the state.

Le Conte's Sparrow*
- Oct. 10, 1988*: West Rutland Marsh.

Nelson's Sharp-tailed Sparrow or Saltmarsh Sharp-tailed Sparrow
- Oct. 8, 1916: Rutland.
- Oct. 8, 1916: Clarendon.
- Oct. 2, 1917: Rutland.
- Sep. 29, 1921: Rutland.
- Oct. 4, 1942: Newbury.
- Oct. 19: 1946: Newbury.
- Oct. 6, 1980: Winooski Delta Park, Colchester.
- Oct. 3, 1985: Winooski Delta Park, Colchester.

Harris's Sparrow
- Jan. 18–Apr. 10, 1949: At a Burlington feeder.
- Early Dec., 2000–Apr. 1, 2001: At a Putney feeder.

Smith's Longspur*
- Apr. 25, 1981*: White River Junction.

Black-headed Grosbeak
- May 18, 1978: Newfane.

Painted Bunting
- May 11 and 13, 1993*: A pair in Danby.
- May 6, 1997: An adult male in Shelburne.
- Nov. 30–Dec. 5, 1998: A female in Hartland.

Western Meadowlark*
- May 2, 1987*: Singing at Dead Creek Wildlife Management Area in Panton.

Yellow-headed Blackbird
- Mar. 28, 1981: An adult male in North Ferrisburgh with a large flock of other blackbirds.
- Jun. 4, 1982: A male in Barre.
- Jun. 9, 1990: A male in Morrisville.
- May 28, 1999: A male in Guilford.

Brewer's Blackbird
- Late Nov. 1986–Jan. 12, 1987: An adult male in South Burlington.

Bullock's Oriole
- Nov. 16–Dec. 30, 1987: An adult male in St. Johnsbury.
- May 18, 1996: West Rutland Marsh.

RESOURCES

Birdwatching has blossomed into a huge community. Numerous organizations, periodicals, and web sites can help anyone at any level enjoy and learn about the vibrant lives of birds. Conservation groups provide opportunities to give something back to the birds as well. Here are some good examples.

✒ *Vermont Organizations*

Audubon Vermont
255 Sherman Hollow Road, Huntington, VT 05462, (802)434-3068,
<www.audubon.org/chapter/vt>.

The statewide link to National Audubon includes the Green Mountain Audubon Nature Center in Huntington and chapters spread around the state: Ascutney Mountain Audubon (southeastern Vermont), Central Vermont Audubon, Green Mountain Audubon (Huntington), Northeast Kingdom Audubon, Otter Creek Audubon (Addison County), Rutland County Audubon, Southeastern Vermont Audubon, and Taconic Tri-State Audubon (southwestern Vermont). Audubon Vermont sponsors Christmas Bird Counts, performs bird research, provides environmental education, and offers various activities and volunteer opportunities. Other activities vary by chapter and include Christmas Bird Counts, outings, and meetings.

Green Mountain Club
4711 Waterbury-Stowe Road, Waterbury Center, VT 05677, (802)244-7037,
<www.greenmountainclub.org>.

The Green Mountain Club is the keeper of Vermont's "footpath through the wilderness," the Long Trail, which runs along the spine of the Green Mountains between Canada and Massachusetts. The Long Trail and its network of side trails offer some of Vermont's most remote birdwatching. The club works to preserve and protect the trail and offers its members and the general public workshops on everything from birdwatching to backpacking.

Nongame and Natural Heritage Program, Vermont Fish and Wildlife Department
103 South Main Street, Waterbury, VT 05671-0501, (802)241-3700,
<www.anr.state.vt.us/fw/fwhome/nnhp/index.html>.

This arm of the state government surveys, manages, and protects rare plants, animals (including birds), and significant natural communities in Vermont. The majority of its funding comes from donations and grants, including revenue from purchases of the state's conservation license plate and a non-game checkoff on state income tax returns (look for the loon on the form).

The Nature Conservancy of Vermont

27 State Street, Montpelier, VT 05602, (802)229-4425, <www.nature.org>.

The Vermont field office for this international conservation organization purchases and protects fragile places, mostly those with rare, threatened, or endangered species. It has protected more than 190,000 acres and manages forty preserves. Volunteer opportunities include exotic plant control, preserve stewardship (including trail work), and office work. Membership outings are also offered.

Vermont Bird Tours

113 Bartlett Road, Plainfield, VT 05667, (802)454-4640, <www.vermontbirdtours.com>.

Vermont's leading nature touring group offers guided outings for birds, butterflies, dragonflies, wildflowers, and other outdoor delights. (The founder, Bryan Pfeiffer, is co-author of this book.)

Vermont Botanical and Bird Club

959 Warren Road, Eden, VT 05652, (802)635-7794, <edenarts@vtlink.net>.

Vermont's oldest birding and botany club publishes a newsletter once a year and an occasional journal. Its annual membership meeting includes presentations and field trips.

Vermont Institute of Natural Science

27023 Church Hill Road, Woodstock, VT 05091-9642, (802)457-2779, <www.vinsweb.org>.

The Vermont Institute of Natural Science (VINS) is a leader in research and environmental education. Its Conservation Biology Department studies rare and endangered birds. The group's North Branch Nature Center in Montpelier is at (802)229-6206. The institute's many volunteer opportunities include wildlife monitoring (Common Loon, Peregrine Falcon, songbirds, amphibians), environmental education, bird care and rehabilitation, reporting bird sightings, and office work. (VINS is planning to move its headquarters from Woodstock to Quechee.)

Vermont Land Trust

8 Bailey Avenue, Montpelier, VT 05641, (802)223-5234, <www.vlt.org>.

This nonprofit organization helps landowners and communities preserve undeveloped land, including farmland and forestland, with the intent of resisting suburban sprawl and retaining Vermont's rural character.

🪶 National Organizations

American Bird Conservancy
P.O. Box 249, The Plains, VA 20198, (888)247-3624, <www.abcbirds.org>.

Dedicated above all to bird conservation, the American Bird Conservancy is active in protecting birds from habitat loss, pesticides, and local threats such as cats.

American Birding Association
P.O. Box 6599, Colorado Springs, CO 80934-6599, (800)850-2473, <www.americanbirding.org>.

The oldest American organization devoted to bird identification and bird finding. The ABA store is a resource for optics, field guides, birdsong recordings, and other birding paraphernalia.

Cornell Lab of Ornithology
159 Sapsucker Woods Road, Ithaca, NY 14850, (800)843-2473, <www.ornith.cornell.edu>.

Devoted to the study and protection of birds, Cornell's work includes compiling and reporting data from Christmas Bird Counts, feeder watches, and other "citizen science" projects.

United States Geological Survey, Patuxent Wildlife Research Center, Bird Banding Laboratory
12100 Beech Forest Road, Laurel, MD 20708-4037, (800)327-BAND (to report bands), <www.pwrc.usgs.gov/bbl>

The federal Bird Banding Laboratory keeps track of all birds banded in North America. Bird banding offers a wealth of information about birds, including distribution, migratory routes, and life span, all of which helps avian conservation efforts.

🪶 Publications

Backyard Wildlife Habitat in Vermont, by Steve Parren.

Published in 1993 and available from the Vermont Fish and Wildlife Department, this book offers practical ideas for inviting wildlife (including birds) into a Vermont backyard.

Birdwatcher's Digest
P.O. Box 110, Marietta, OH 45750, (800)879-2473, <www.birdwatchersdigest.com>.

This is a fine general-knowledge magazine, published six times a year, for experts and beginners alike. It includes features on optics, conservation, feeding, and bird appreciation.

North American Birds

c/o American Birding Association, P.O. Box 6599, Colorado Springs, CO 80934-6599, (800)850-2473, <www.americanbirding.org>.

> With articles and bird reports, this quarterly journal chronicles the distribution of birds around the continent, including outstanding records (some from Vermont), range extensions and contractions, population dynamics, and changes in migration patterns and seasonal occurrence.

Records of Vermont Birds

c/o Vermont Institute of Natural Science, 27023 Church Hill Road, Woodstock, VT 05091-9642, (802)457-2779, <www.vinsweb.org>.

> This quarterly newsletter includes a seasonal account of bird sightings from around Vermont, and an annual listing of records accepted by the Vermont Bird Records Committee.

The Atlas of Breeding Birds of Vermont, edited by Sarah B. Laughlin and Douglas P. Kibbe.

> Published by the Vermont Institute of Natural Science in 1985, this first-of-its-kind breeding bird atlas is now somewhat dated, yet it offers a thorough accounting of the distribution of Vermont's breeding birds. It is out of print.

The Nature of Vermont, by Charles W. Johnson.

> Published by University Press of New England. This classic (revised in 1998) is a comprehensive introduction to the natural and human history of Vermont.

Vermont Daily Field Card

Vermont Institute of Natural Science, 27023 Church Hill Road, Woodstock, VT 05091-9642, (802)457-2779, <www.vinsweb.org>.

> This checklist (which costs pocket change) includes the 264 most commonly encountered Vermont birds, when they are here, and whether they breed in the state.

Wetland, Woodland, Wildland—A Guide to the Natural Communities of Vermont, by Elizabeth H. Thompson and Eric R. Sorenson.

> Published in 2000 by the Vermont Department of Fish and Wildlife and The Nature Conservancy, and available from University Press of New England. This groundbreaking work offers a thorough treatment of Vermont's biophysical regions and more than eighty natural communities.

🖋 Maps

Vermont Atlas and Gazetteer
Delorme, Two Delorme Drive, P.O. Box 298, Yarmouth, ME 04096, (800)561-5104, <www.delorme.com>.

> This atlas is among the most useful tools for navigation in Vermont. Its detailed maps include public lands; road names (although some may differ from names in this book); rivers, lakes, and wetlands; detailed maps to cities and villages; even a few hiking trails.

🖋 *Internet Birding*

Better View Desired
<www.betterviewdesired.com>.

> This is a source of reliable information and analysis on optics.

Birding on the Net
<www.birdingonthe.net>.

> Rare bird alerts and listserve postings from around the country are available on this site.

Northern Prairie Wildlife Research Center
<www.npwrc.usgs.gov>.

> This comprehensive site about many things outside has a large section on birds.

Partners in Flight
<www.partnersinflight.org>.

> This international organization focuses primarily on neotropical songbird conservation and combines the efforts of government, private, professional, educational, and conservation organizations.

Vermont Bird Alert

> The listserve called "BirdEast" includes regular postings of bird alerts from across the eastern United States and Canada, including the Vermont Bird Alert. To subscribe to BirdEast, send an e-mail message whose first line is: subscribe birdeast [your-first-name] [your-last-name] (omit brackets) to <listserv@listserv.arizona.edu>. Include nothing else in the body of the message.

Virtual Birder
<www.virtualbirder.com>.

> This site is a mishmash of current birding information, including options to browse nationwide listserves and bird alerts (including Vermont).

VTBird

The University of Vermont operates a listserve for Vermont bird sightings and discussion. To subscribe, send an e-mail message whose first line is: subscribe vtbird [your-name] (omit brackets) to <listserve@list.uvm.edu>. Include nothing else in the body of the message. For more information, visit the website <list.uvm.edu>.

 *Museums*

Birds of Vermont Museum

900 Sherman Hollow Road, Huntington, VT 05462, (802)434-2167, <www.birdsofvermont.org>.

This unique museum is a tribute in wood to the value of birds. Wood carver Robert N. Spear Jr. has depicted Vermont's nesting species in their natural habitats. Surrounding the museum is a nature reserve. The museum offers guided nature walks and other programs to children and adults.

Fairbanks Museum and Planetarium

1302 Main Street, St. Johnsbury, VT 05819-2248, (802)748-2372, <www.fairbanksmuseum.com>.

Northern New England's oldest natural history museum has an impressive display of mounted birds. It offers workshops and lectures on a wide variety of topics. The museum's Northern New England Weather Center is a well-known source of weather information for Vermonters.

Montshire Museum

One Montshire Road, Norwich, VT 05055, (802)649-2200, <www.montshire.net>.

This hands-on museum (great for kids) includes self-guided displays on natural and physical sciences, ecology, and technology. Its grounds feature a network of walking trails.

INDEX

Page numbers in italics indicate maps. Page numbers in boldface indicate species accounts.

in Central Champlain Valley, 55, *56*, 57–59
in Northwestern Vermont, *36*, 37–41, 44–45
in Rutland Region, *72*, 75, 78
in Southern Champlain Valley, 61, *62*, 63, 65, 69, 71
Lake Hortonia, *72*, 74
Lake Memphremagog, *108*, 109, 111, 124, 130–132, 142, 170–172
Lake Morey, 93, *94*, 131
Lake Paran, *80*, 85, 162
Lake Runnemede, *94*, 96
Lake Willoughby, *108*, 111–112, 131
Lakewatch, 24–26, 39, 57, 69, 141
LaPlatte River Marsh, 170
    Natural Area, *46*, 54, 126
Lark, Horned, 7, 45, 64, 66–67, 71, 109, **152**, 165
Lefferts Pond, *72*, 77, 161
Leicester Junction, 71, *72*, 73
Lemon Fair River, *62*, 70–71, 129
Lewis Pond Road, *108*, 116
Little Otter Creek, 55, *56*, 59–60
Long Pond, *108*, 111
Long Swamp, *72*, 74, 146
Long Trail, *72*, 76, *80*, 83, 99, 102, *118*, 119–120, 177
Longspur
    Lapland, 7, 49, 67, 71, **165**
    Smith's, **175**
Loon, 7, 11, 25–26, 54, 57, 69, 109, 178
    Arctic, 169
    Common, xii (photo), 24, 38, 51, 53, 58, 63, 65, 69, 74, 77–78, 82, 84, 93, 97, 103–107, 111–112, **124**, 178
    Pacific, 169
    Red-throated, 17, 24, 38, 65, 69, 106, **124**

Mallard, 5, 39–40, 42, 48, 51, 58, 63, 66, 70, 73, 85, 87–88, 90–92, 96, **128**, 129
Marshfield Pond, 107
Martin, Purple, 41, 53, 89, **152**
McCuen Slang, *62*, 69–70, 132, 136, 167
McNeil Cove, *56*, 58, 129, 131
Meadowlark
    Eastern, 5, 63, 88, 105, **166**
    Western, 176
Merck Forest & Farmland Center, 79, *80*
Merganser, 63, 70
    Common, 7, 40, 48, 51, 58, 65, 78, 83, 87–88, 92, 96, 106, 109, **131**
    Hooded, 40, 43, 58, 61, 83, 87–88, 90, 92, 95–96, 104 (photo), 104, 106, 109, **131**
    Red-breasted, 40, 51, 57–58, **132**

Merlin, 51, 64, 69, **134**
Minard's Pond, *86*, 88, 90
Missisquoi
    Bay, 43, 170
    National Wildlife Refuge, *36*, 42, 124–125, 130–132, 136, 140, 143, 170
Mockingbird, Northern, 85, **156**
Montpelier, *100*, 102–103, 106–107, 146, 178
Montpelier to Wells River Railroad Bed, 107 (*see also* Railroad Bed, Montpelier to Wells River)
Moorhen, Common, 41, 68, 76, 110, **136**
Moose Bog, *108*, 112–115, 135, 149, 151, 153, 167
Mt. Ascutney, 87, 93, *94*, 97
Mt. Equinox, *80*, 81–82
Mt. Independence State Historic Site, *72*, 75
Mt. Mansfield, 99, *100*, 101–102, 155, 160
Mt. Philo, 22, 23 (photo), 23–24, 55, 58–60
    State Park, *56*, 58, *118*
Mt. Pisgah, *108*, 111–112
Mud Creek Wildlife Management Area, *36*, 41, 125–126, 135–136, 154
Murre
    Common, **173**
    Thick-billed, **173**
Mystery Trail, 93, *94*, 95

Nature Conservancy, The, 54, 78, 107, 178, 180
Newark Pond, 112
Newport, *108*, 109–111, 124, 131–132, 136, 138, 167, 170–172
    State Airport, *108*, 110, 138
Nighthawk, Common, 90, 95, **146**
Night-Heron
    Black-crowned, 54, 64, 68 (photo), **126**
    Yellow-crowned, 53, **170**
North Branch Nature Center, *100*, 102–103, 178
North Hartland Dam, *94*, 96
North Springfield Lake, *86*, 88
Nortontown Road, *62*, 71
Nuthatch, 95, 161
    Red-breasted, 4–5, 13, 74, 101, 106, 120, **153**
    White-breasted, 5, 13, 18, 120, **153**

Oldsquaw (*see* Long-tailed Duck)
Optics
    choosing, 10, 179, 181 (*see also* binoculars, spotting scopes)
Oriole
    Baltimore, 5, 41, 70, 105, 110, **167**
    Bullock's, **176**

ABOUT THE AUTHORS

Ted Murin is a native Vermonter and tireless birdwatcher who has spent years investigating and documenting the distribution and seasonal status of birds in Vermont. Whether climbing mountains, paddling rivers, or withstanding a gale on the shores of Lake Champlain, he is most content in pursuit of a greater understanding and appreciation of nature. A systems analyst and software developer, Ted lives in South Burlington, Vermont, only a mile from Lake Champlain.

Bryan Pfeiffer is a naturalist, writer, photographer, and founder of a nature touring company, Vermont Bird Tours. He loves guiding people to wildlife and wild places. Bryan's articles and essays on nature have appeared in the *New York Times*, *Northern Woodlands*, *Vermont Life*, and other publications. He hosts an award-winning radio show, "For The Birds," and is the on-camera naturalist for weekly nature features on a Vermont television station. Bryan lives in an old farmhouse near Bartlett Hill in Plainfield, Vermont, where he wanders the woods and fields enjoying everything from birds to butterflies, frogs to ferns.